MW01613634

Basic Mathematics and Algebra for Success in Our Daily Lives

A Simple Approach for Arithmetic and Algebra

Mila Cselenszky ◆ Edward L. Green ◆ Jerry Kornbluth

THOMSON

™

CUSTOM PUBLISHING

Custom Consultant: Jason Fremder
Editor: Paula Begley-Jenkins
Director of Product Creation: Becky Schwartz
Manufacturing Supervisor: Donna M. Brown
Pre-Media Services Supervisor: Christina Smith
Graphic Designer: Krista Pierson
Rights and Permissions Specialist: Kalina Ingham Hintz
Project Coordinator: Jennifer Flinchpaugh
Marketing Manager: Sara L. Hinckley

COPYRIGHT © 2004 by the Thomson Custom Publishing. Custom Publishing is a division of Thomson Learning Inc. Thomson Learning™ is a trademark used herein under license.

Printed in the United States of America.

Thomson Custom Publishing
5191 Natorp Blvd.
Mason, Ohio 45040
USA

For information about our products, contact us:
1-800-355-9983
http://www.thomsoncustom.com

International Headquarters
Thomson Learning
International Division
290 Harbor Drive, 2nd Floor
Stamford, CT 06902-7477
USA

UK/Europe/Middle East/South Africa
Thomson Learning
Berkshire House
168-173 High Holborn
London WCIV 7AA

Asia
Thomson Learning
60 Albert Street, #15-01
Albert Complex
Singapore 189969

Canada
Nelson Thomson Learning
1120 Birchmount Road
Toronto, Ontario MIK 5G4
Canada
United Kingdom

Visit us at www.thomsoncustom.com and learn more about this book and other titles published by Thomson Learning Custom Publishing.

ALL RIGHTS RESERVED. No part of this work covered by the copyright hereon may be reproduced or used in any form or by any means—graphic, electronic, or mechanical, including photocopying, recording, taping, Web distribution, or information storage and retrieval systems—without the written permission of the publisher.

0-759-33876-0

The Adaptable Courseware Program consists of products and additions to existing Custom Publishing products that are produced from camera-ready copy. Peer review, class testing, and accuracy are primarily the responsibility of the author(s).

For permission to use material from this text or product, submit a request online at http://www.thomsonrights.com
Any additional questions about permissions can be submitted by email to thomsonrights@thomson.com

PREFACE

The book was written to help college students pass College Assessment Examinations, as well as develop the necessary skills needed to pass college mathematics courses. The topics covered include: arithmetic, algebra and basic geometry.

Each section in this book relates to a different concept. Once a student masters a particular section, he should go on to the next section. The student must continue to review the sections mastered so he would not forget the material learned.

This book contains arithmetic examinations, algebra exams, as well as two complete Mathematical Skill Assessment tests.

Most colleges have mathematics laboratories. If a student is still having difficulty, he should go with the book to the mathematics laboratory at the college he attends in order to obtain extra help.

ACKNOWLEDGEMENTS

This book is dedicated to the encouragement and support my family has given me through the years. During my childhood my mother, Fae Sarah Wigder Green and my brother, Dr. William Green, encouraged me to pursue my education. My father, Jack Green, worked long hours to support his family. Furthermore, my aunts, Rose Saldinger, Molly Wigder, and Ida Wigder assisted me to obtain my goals. My brother-in-law, Jose Chavin, gave me technical assistance.

I am very fortunate in that my beautiful wife, Zelma, always encouraged me to pursue my career. While I was working late at night, she graduated from Brooklyn College with her Masters Degree in Spanish literature while taking excellent care of our three wonderful sons, Elliot, Phillip Steven and Seth Andrew.

Professor Edward L. Green

ACKNOWLEDGEMENTS

I would like to thank my wonderful wife Jane for all her support and understanding throughout the writing of this book. Special thanks goes to my children, Brett, Scott, Nancy and Missy. The light of my life, Austin, Cole, Hannah and Alexa, motivated me to write a book that they might use in the future.

Dr. Jerry Kornbluth

ACKNOWLEDGEMENTS

Very sincere and profound gratitude is due:

To the Lord Almighty, for giving me the wisdom and strength to coauthor this book.

And equally the same to my beloved family here at USA: my husband, Laszlo Cselenszky, my eldest daughter, Yolanda C. Bergold, my son-in-law, George Gergold Jr., my smart and cute grandson, Jonathan Reese Bergold, my youngest daughter, Marissa P. Cantos, and Jay-Jay Mia for their wholehearted and overwhelming love and support, assistance and inspiration, understanding and encouragement, to make this piece of work.

To my brothers and sisters in the Philippines who have continuously kept their hopes, confidence, and pride, that I will succeed in this undertaking:

To Ed Green and Dr Jerry Kornbluth for the collaborative effort in revising, revamping, editing, writing, and all the work needed to make this book a success:

To my mentors, colleagues, friends and students, at Interboro Institute who became the great source of joy and energy—my inspiration while pursuing this venture:

Book writing is impossible without you, and all your loyal support.

Professor Mila P. Cselenszky

CONTENTS

PART II: ALGEBRA—GEOMETRY

PART I: ARITHMETIC

Introduction

Students come to this course from a diversity of backgrounds. Many of the students haven't seen a math problem for years. Their lives have been filled with family matters and job concerns yet at one point most people realize the importance of developing an understanding of mathematics. A mathematics background allows all of us to experience a greater degree of success.

Therefore, we encourage the students to look at this course as a new beginning. After mastering the contents of this book, the students will be helped to navigate in this complex society. Hopefully, the students will not only be in charge of their personal finances, but they will also see the relationship between world economic decisions and their lives. People who understand the basic mathematical concepts are less likely to be taken advantage of by other individuals and institutions. For example, an advertisement that offers a "good deal" might actually result in the loss of a substantial amount of money. Only people who understand mathematics could figure this out before it's too late. Which savings plan is the best? What bank offers the most interest? How much money do we really need to buy a piece of real estate? Can we afford these payments on that beautiful car in the showroom? The only way to answer these questions is to develop an understanding of mathematics.

This text is designed to help students on all levels. However, it must be stressed that a serious approach to learning is a necessity. Students **must** spend enough time working on the book's exercises. Taking good notes, attending class on a regular basis, and listening carefully to the instructor's lessons will also assure **success**.

Good luck—and welcome to the world of Mathematics.

1. Arithmetic: Real Number System

The Real Number System consists of the rational numbers and irrational numbers.

Rational Number is the quotient of two integers. Therefore, a rational number can be written in the form $\frac{a}{b}$, where a and b are integers, and b is not zero. A rational number written in this way is commonly called a fraction.

Since an integer can be written as the quotient of the integer (whole number) and 1, every integer is a rational number. A number written in decimal notation is a rational number, $(0.3 = \frac{3}{10}$ or $0.37 = \frac{37}{100})$. A rational number can be written as a fraction or in decimal notation. Every rational number can be written as a terminating or repeating decimal. Some numbers such as $\sqrt{2}$ and π have decimal representatives that never terminate or repeat. These numbers are called irrational numbers.

BASIC CONCEPTS

A collection of numbers, such as 3, 4, and 5, is called a set. The notation for a set is the braces { } to list the numbers {3, 4, 5). This is called the roster method of writing sets.

Example 1: Use the roster method to write to the set of number between 0 and 10.

      Answer: {1, 2, 3, 4, 5, 6, 7, 8, 9}

Example 2: Use the roster method to write a set of all odd integers.

      Answer: {1, 3, 5, 7, 9.................}
                       The dots are used to indicate the numbers are written indefinitely.

The symbol "$\in$" means is "an element of." $2 \in B$ is read: "2 is an element of set B." Given $A = \{3, 5, 9\}$, then $3 \in A$, $5 \in A$ and $9 \in A$. An empty set or a null set is the set that contains no elements. The symbol $\varnothing$ or { } is used to represent the empty set. A finite set is a set of numbers that can be counted while an Infinite Set is a set of numbers without limit or end.

Basic symbols are used in mathematics.
They are used to complete a mathematics statement:

Addition	=	+	sum
Subtraction	=	–	difference
Multiplication	=	x	product ⁄
Division	=	÷	Quotient

Symbols are also used to compare two or more numbers:

Equal $=$

Less than $<$

Greater than $>$

Less than or equal to $\leq$

Greater than or equal to $\geq$

Does not equal $\neq$

EXAMPLES

1. Express: 12 plus 6 equals 18.
   Answer: $12 + 6 = 18$

2. Express: 4 is less than 9.
   Answer: $4 < 9$

3. Express: 9 is greater than 6.
   Answer: $9 > 6$

NOTE

Numerals: They are symbols for numbers.

Digits: They are the number symbols (numerals):
0, 1, 2, 3, 4, 5, 6, 7, 8, and 9 in our number system.

WHOLE NUMBER

It is written as a string of digits. For example, 8 is a one-digit number. 64 is a two-digit number with 6 being the first digit, and 4 being the second digit. 376 is a three-digit number with 3 being the first digit, 7 being the second digit, and 6 being the third digit.

Depending on its place in the number, a digit will take on different values. The chart below indicates the names of the place values.

Hundred Millions	Ten Millions	One Millions	Hundred Thousands	Ten Thousands	Thousands	Hundreds	Tens	Ones

Depending upon its place in a number, a digit will have a different value.

Example: Find the place value of the digit 6 in each of the following numbers:
     a)   60
     b)   625
     c)   6
     d)   6,479

Answers: a) 6 tens = 60
               b) 6 hundreds = 600
               c) 6 ones = 6
               d) 6 thousands = 6,000

ANSWER THE FOLLOWING QUESTIONS

1.   Write the correct answer using set notation:
    a) The counting numbers larger than four.
    b) The counting numbers three through eight.
    c) The first five whole numbers.
    d) The first four even numbers.

2.   Find the value of the digit "7" in the following numbers:
    a) 765
    b) 7
    c) 71
    d) 7,954

3.   Translate the following using mathematics symbols:
    a) Seven hundred fifty-four.
    b) Four thousand fifty-nine.
    c) Three hundred forty.
    d) Eight thousand six hundred.

4.   Write the following in words using the place value chart:
    a) 6,359
    b) 9,308
    c) 349
    d) 572,346

CHAPTER GLOSSARY

Difference:	The answer to subtraction.
Digit:	In our number system, a digit is any one of the first ten whole numbers: 0,1, 2, 3, 4, 5, 6, 7, 8, 9.
Finite Set:	A set in which the numbers can be counted.
Infinite Set:	A set of numbers without limit or end.
Irrational Number:	Irrational numbers are numbers that never terminate or repeat ($\sqrt{2}$ and π).

Null Set:	Set of numbers that is empty; being or amounting to zero.
Numeral:	The symbol used to represent a number.
Place value:	The value of the digit due to the position of the numeral.
Product:	The answer to multiplication.
Quotient:	The answer to division.
Rational Number:	A rational number is the quotient of two integers a/b.
Real Number System:	It is the system that consists of the rational number and irrational numbers.
Set:	A collection of objects or things.
Sum:	The answer to addition.
Whole Number:	Any of the numbers: 0, 1, 2, 3, etc.

2. Basic Skills: The Number Line

A number line can be divided equally and numbered.
It can be illustrated on a number line.

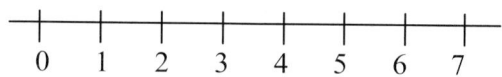

Graphs can be illustrated on a number line by putting a circle on the mark for one number.

Example: Graph the following: 0, 3, 4, 6:

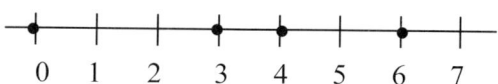

Distance can also be illustrated on a number line.

Example: Show the distance 2 on a number line.

Solution: To show the distance 2 on a number line, draw an arrow above the number line that is 2 spaces apart.

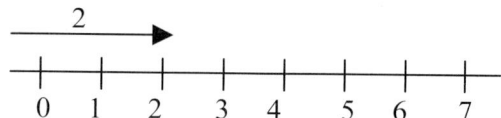

MULTIPLICATION—PRIME FACTORIZATION

To get the product, factors are multiplied. A factor is one of the numbers used to form a product. It is a number used in multiplication. A and B are factors of C, if A•B=C. For example, 3 x 4 = 12. Three and 4 are the factors, and 12 is the product. In multiplication a number can be factored and can also be expressed as the product of its factors. For example, 18 can be written as the following factors:

PRIME FACTORIZATION

To find the prime factorization of a number, it is very important that you know what prime numbers are. Prime numbers play an important role in finding the prime factorization of a number. A **prime number** is a number whose factors are only 1 and itself. Thirteen, for example, is a prime number. The only factors of 13 are 1 and 13. When a number has other factors except 1 and itself, this number is called a **composite number**. Twelve, ten, twenty-two, thirty, twenty-four and sixteen are examples of composite numbers.

These are prime numbers less than **100**:
2, 3, 5, 7, 11, 13, 17, 19, 23, 29, 31, 37, 39, 41, 43, 47, 59, 61, 67, 71, 73, 79, 83, 89, 97.

This concept can be clearly shown or illustrated by using the letter **T**. For example, we are looking for the prime factorization of 18 and 24, follow the steps below:

1. Place 18 and 24 on top of the horizontal line.
2. Start dividing the numbers using the smallest prime, which is 2 or 3.
3. Continue dividing until the quotients become one.
4. See illustrations below.

```
        18                               24
  2  9 | 18÷2=9              2  12 | 24÷2=12
  3  3 | 9÷3=3               2  6  | 12÷2=6
  3  1 | 3÷3=1               3  1  | 3÷3=1
```

The prime factorization of 18 is **2 . 3. 3**.   The prime factorization of 24 is **2 . 2 . 2 . 3**.

The **prime factorization** of a number is the **product of its prime numbers**.

Application Practice: Find the prime factorization of: 36, 38, 40, 42, 48, 50, 54, 60, 68.

You will observe that as the number grows bigger, the process of finding the prime factorization becomes more complicated. For example:

```
      106                              156
  2  | 53      106÷2=53         2  | 78     156÷2=78
  53 | 1       53÷53=53         2  | 39     78÷2=39
                               3  | 13     39÷3=13
                               13 | 1      13÷3=1
```

The prime factorization of 106 is **2 . 53**.   The prime factorization of 156 is **2 . 2 . 3 . 13**.

PROPERTIES

The **Commutative Property**: The order of addition and multiplication of two numbers does not matter. For example, $3 + 4 = 4 + 3$, and $3(4) = 4(3)$.

The Commutative Property:

If a and b represent any numbers, then:

$$a + b = b + a, \text{ and } a(b) = b(a).$$

The **Associative Property**: When there are three numbers to add or to multiply, the grouping of the number in which the operations are performed does not alter the final results. For example,

Addition: $(4 + 5) + 6 = 4 + (5 + 6)$
Multiplication: $(4 \cdot 5)6 = 4(5 \cdot 6)$

The Associative Property:

If a, b, and c represent any numbers, then:

$$(a + b) + c = a + (b + c), \text{ and } (a \cdot b)c = a(b \cdot c).$$

The order of the numbers is not altered.

The **Distributive Property**: Multiplication can be distributed over addition and over subtraction.

For example: $4 \times (5 + 6) = 4 \times 5 + 4 \times 6 = 20 + 24 = 44$

The Distributive Property:

If a, b, and c stand for any numbers, then:

$$a(b + c) = a \cdot b + b \cdot c.$$

The **Identity Properties—Inverse Law**

$6 + 0 = 6$ $18 + 0 = 18$

Adding 0 to any number does not change the value of the number. The number 0 is the identity element for addition.

Multiply 1 by any number. It does not change the value of the number.

$6 \times 1 = 6$ $18 \times 1 = 18$

Multiply 1 by any number. It does not change the value of the number. The number 1 is the identity element for multiplication.

> **Identity Properties:**
>
> Let "a" be any number:
>
> $a + 0 = a$ is the identity element in addition.
>
> $a \times 1 = a$
>
> One is the identity element in multiplication.

The **Inverse Law**: Operations that cancel each other out. For example, addition/subtraction, multiplication/division, and raising a number to a power/taking the root.

$$a + (-a) = 0 \qquad a \bullet 1/a = 1 \qquad (\sqrt{a})^2 = a$$
$$2 + (-2) = 0 \qquad 2 \bullet 1/2 = 1 \qquad (\sqrt{4})^2 = 4$$
$$3 + (-3) = 0 \qquad 3 \bullet 1/3 = 1 \qquad (\sqrt{36})^2 = 36$$

Name the property illustrated in each of the following examples. Fill in the correct answers in the space provided:

1. $7 + 3 = 3 + 7$ Answer _____

2. $9 + 0 = 9$ Answer _____

3. $6(1) = 6$ Answer _____

4. $4 \bullet 3 \bullet 5 = 3 \bullet 4 \bullet 5$ Answer _____

5. $(3 + 2) + 5 = 5 + (3 + 2)$ Answer _____

6. $3(6) = 6(3)$ Answer _____

7. $4(3 + 8) = 4 \bullet 3 + 4 \bullet 8$ Answer _____

ANSWERS

1. Commutative Property of Addition

2. Identity Element for Addition

3. Identity Element for Multiplication

4. Associative Property for Multiplication

5. Associative Property for Addition

6. Commutative Property for Multiplication

7. Distributive Property for Multiplication

DIVISION

Division is the opposite process of multiplication.

$24 \div 6$ is the same as $6 \times ? = 24$

$$divisor \overline{)dividend}^{\,quotient}$$

Rules:

If "a" stands for any number but 0, then:

$0 \div a = 0$

Division by zero is undefined.

$a \div 0 = $ undefined

When you divide by zero, you do not know the result. The quotient (answer) is undefined. However, you can find out how many times a number goes into zero (always "0" times), but you cannot divide by zero.

Examples: 1. $6 \div 0$
2. $0 \div 7$
3. $1818 \div 0$

Answers: 1. Undefined
2. 0
3. Undefined

IMPORTANT TERMS

Associative Property of Addition: In addition changing the grouping of the address does not alter the sum $a + (b + c) = (a + b) + c$ or $3 + (4 + 5) = (3 + 4) + 5$.

Associative property of multiplication: In multiplication the order in which numbers are multiplied does not alter the product. For any three numbers a, b and c, it is true that $a \cdot (b \cdot c) = (a \cdot b) \cdot c$ or $3 \cdot (4 \cdot 5) = (3 \cdot 4) \cdot 5$.

Composite Number: It is a number that can be factored into factors other than 1 and itself.

Commutative Property of Addition: Changing the order of the addends does not alter the sum. For any two numbers, a and b, it is true that $a + b = b + a$.

Commutative Property of Multiplication: Changing the order of the factors does not change the product. For example, for any two numbers, a and b, it is true that $a \cdot b = b \cdot a$.

Distributive Property (Law): The Distributive Law holds for multiplication over addition. For any three numbers a, b and c multiplication before addition a•(b+c) = (a•b)+(b•c).

Dividend: The number being divided in division.

Division: The number that divides the dividend in division. In the equation, $24 \div 6 = 4$, the divisor is 6.

Factor: It is one of the numbers used to form a product: A and B are factors of C. $A•B = C$

Identity Element in Multiplication: $a•1 = a$. 1 is the identity element in multiplication

Identity Property in Addition: Let "a" be a number $a + 0 = a$ is the identity element of addition.

Inverse Law: Operations that cancel each other out.

$a+(-a) = 0$ $a•1/a=1$ $(\sqrt{a}) = a$

Number Line: A line that extends indefinitely in both directions, if starts at zero and equally spaced units are marked off to the left as well as to the right.

Prime Factor: Any number greater than one, which has only itself and one as factors.

Quotient: The answer to division.

Undefined: Any number divided by zero is undefined.

CHAPTER GLOSSARY

Addend: A number being added in the equation $7 + 4 = 11$. The addends are 7 and 4.
Difference: The answer to subtraction.
Dividend: The number being divided in division.
Divisor: The number that divides the dividend. In $24 \div 6 = 4$, divisor is 6.
Factor: It is one of the numbers used to form a product. A and B are factors of C if $A•B = C$.
Minuend: The number from which another (the subtrahend) is to be subtracted.
Multiplicand: The number being multiplied.
Multiplier: The number by which another is to be multiplied.
Product: The answer to multiplication.
Remainder: The number left over after completing a division problem.
Subtrahend: The number to be taken from another.
Sum: The answer to addition.

3. Basic Skills: Addition, Subtraction, Multiplication, Division

A. Addition
Sum: The result of addition.
Addend: A number being added.

Example 1:   349 + 568

Solution: Arrange in columns and carry the appropriate numbers.

100's	10's	1's
3	4	9
5	6	8
9	1	7

Answer: 917

B. Subtraction
Difference: The result of subtraction.
Subtrahend: The number to be taken from another.
Minuend: The number from which another is to be subtracted.

Example 1:   415 – 289

Solution:

Step 1: Borrow from the 10's column to increase the 5 to 15.

$$
\begin{array}{r}
{\scriptstyle 0\ \ 15} \\
4\,\cancel{1}\,\cancel{5} \\
-2\,8\,9 \\
\hline
6
\end{array}
$$

Step 2 : Borrow from the 100's column 10 tens

$$
\begin{array}{r}
{\scriptstyle 3\ \ 10\ \ 15} \\
\cancel{4}\,\cancel{1}\,5 \\
-2\,8\,9 \\
\hline
1\,2\,6
\end{array}
$$

Answer: 1 2 6

C. Multiplication
Product: The result of multiplication.
Multiplication: The number to be multiplied by another.
Multiplier: The number by which another is to be multiplied.
Factor: Two or more numbers being multiplied.

Example 1:   327 x 289

Solution:

$$
\begin{array}{r}
327 \\
\times 289 \\
\hline
2943 \\
26160 \\
+\ 65400 \\
\hline
94503
\end{array}
$$

Answer: 94503

D. Division

Quotient: The result of division
Divisor: The number doing the dividing
Dividend: The number being divided
Remainder: The number left over after completing a division problem.

Example 1: $3750 \div 25$

Solution: The number 25 is the divisor and the number 3750 is the dividend.

```
        150
   25)3750
      -25↓
       125
      -125↓
        00
        -0
         0
```

Multiply 1 x 25 = 25.
Subtract and bring down the 5.
Multiply 5 x 25 = 125.
Subtract and bring down the 0.
Multiply and subtract.
Remainder is 0.

Fill in the correct answer in the space provided:

1. $33 + 129 + 7$ Answer _____

2. $169 + 17 + 405$ Answer _____

3. $39 + 79 + 129 + 6$ Answer _____

4. $1,459 + 39 + 279 + 1,524$ Answer _____

5. $67 + 9 + 135 + 6,759$ Answer _____

6. $137 + 13 + 7 + 1,377$ Answer _____

7. $6,758 + 495 + 39 + 1,006$ Answer _____

8. $7 + 77 + 777 + 7,777$ Answer _____

9. $1,234 + 7 + 164 + 29$ Answer _____

10. $79 + 125 + 61 + 3,759$ Answer _____

11. $69 + 9 + 35 + 1,234$ Answer _____

12. $129 + 145 + 39 + 7,654$ Answer _____

13. $7 + 349 + 27 + 6,198$ Answer _____

14. $7,198 + 8 + 449 + 37$ Answer _____

15. $129 + 12 + 7 + 7,777$ Answer _____

16. $666 + 66 + 6 + 6{,}666$ Answer _____

17. $3 + 449 + 27 + 5{,}159$ Answer _____

18. $23{,}495 + 6{,}498 + 16{,}543$ Answer _____

19. $39 + 1{,}270 + 6 + 77{,}777$ Answer _____

20. $6{,}161 + 5{,}116 + 516$ Answer _____

Fill in the correct answer in the space provided:

1. $749 - 37$ Answer _____

2. $648 - 589$ Answer _____

3. $4{,}007 - 3{,}999$ Answer _____

4. $6{,}789 - 3{,}456$ Answer _____

5. $609 - 598$ Answer _____

6. $3{,}461 - 2{,}999$ Answer _____

7. $705 - 631$ Answer _____

8. $2{,}001 - 1{,}892$ Answer _____

9. $4{,}000 - 239$ Answer _____

10. $3{,}749 - 2{,}001$ Answer _____

11.   Subtract 16 from 49   Answer _____

12.   Subtract 91 from 349   Answer _____

13.   Subtract 239 from 341   Answer _____

14.   Subtract 1,999 from 8,001 Answer _____

15.   Subtract 160 from 910   Answer _____

16.   What number must be added
       to 19 to obtain 74?   Answer _____

17.   What number must be added
       to 124 to obtain 671?   Answer _____

18.   671 – 309   Answer _____

19.   7,349 – 6991   Answer _____

20.   129 – 98   Answer _____

Fill in the correct answer in the space provided:

1.   6 x 39   Answer _____

2.   12 x 7   Answer _____

3.   39 x 74   Answer _____

4.   67 x 19   Answer _____

5.   100 x 200   Answer _____

6.   300 x 1,200   Answer _____

7.   307 x 609   Answer _____

8.   1,001 x 100   Answer _____

9.   2,002 x 200   Answer _____

10.   375 x 29   Answer _____

11.   400 x 400   Answer _____

12.   2,000 x 2,000   Answer _____

13.   37 x 129   Answer _____

14.   674 x 85   Answer _____

15.   6,000 x 3,000   Answer _____

16.   7,000 x 4,000   Answer _____

17.   379 x 27   Answer _____

18.   4,567 x 38   Answer _____

19.   201 x 403   Answer _____

20.   708 x 506   Answer _____

Fill in the correct answer in the space provided:

1. $64 \div 2$ Answer _____

2. $375 \div 5$ Answer _____

3. $375 \div 25$ Answer _____

4. 8 into 24   Answer _____

5. 12 into 144   Answer _____

6. 16 divided by 4   Answer _____

7. 27 divided by 9   Answer _____

8. $546 \div 13$ Answer _____

9. $3,090 \div 30$ Answer _____

10. $5,562 \div 206$ Answer _____

11. $4,949 \div 49$ Answer _____

12. $7,007 \div 7$ Answer _____

13. 12 into 360   Answer _____

14. 12 into 300   Answer _____

15. $12 \div 0$ Answer _____

16. $0 \div 12$ Answer _____

17. $165 \div 0$ Answer _____

18. $0 \div 165$ Answer _____

19. $1,616 \div 16$ Answer _____

20. $3,006 \div 6$ Answer _____

Fill in the correct answers in the space provided:

1. 3,049 + 27 + 6,750 — Answer _____

2. 34,598 + 670 + 3,409 — Answer _____

3. 375 + 6,750 + 9 — Answer _____

4. 709 − 698 — Answer _____

5. 3,001 − 2,999 — Answer _____

6. 3,450 − 2,789 — Answer _____

7. 329 x 102 — Answer _____

8. 675 x 39 — Answer _____

9. 349 x 210 — Answer _____

10. 1,212 ÷ 12 — Answer _____

11. 2,457 ÷ 63 — Answer _____

12. 595 − 35 — Answer _____

13. 207 x 104 — Answer _____

14. 309 − 254 — Answer _____

15. 275 + 5,750 + 8 — Answer _____

16. 2,424 ÷ 24 — Answer _____

17. 304 x 12 — Answer _____

18. 607 − 508 — Answer _____

19. 207 x 21 — Answer _____

20. 305 + 67 + 3,508 — Answer _____

21. 209 x 15 — Answer _____

22. 309 − 81 — Answer _____

23. 425 − 369 — Answer _____

24. 3,075 + 67,591 + 397 — Answer _____

25.   398 − 279   Answer _____

4. Words Written as Numerals

INTEGER

An integer is a whole number which may be positive or negative, not a fraction.

1,000,000's	100,000's	10,000's	1,000's	100's	10's	1's
↓	↓	↓	↓	↓	↓	↓
Millions	Hundred Thousands	Ten Thousands	Thousands	Hundreds	Tens	Ones

Example 1: Write "Seven million twenty-four thousand sixty-eight" in numerals.

Solution:

1,000,000's	100,000's	10,000's	1,000's	100's	10's	1's
↓	↓	↓	↓	↓	↓	↓
7	0	2	4	0	6	8

Answer: 7,024,068

Fill in the letter of the correct answer in the space provided:

1.   Fifty-four thousand three hundred is written:
      (a) 54,030   (b) 540,300   (c) 54,300
      (d) 54,000,300   (e) 54,003   Answer _____

2.   Three million and twelve is written:
      (a) 30,000,012   (b) 3,000,120   (c) 30,012
      (d) 300,000,012   (e) 3,000,012   Answer _____

3.   Ten million one hundred sixty-three is written:
      (a) 10,000,163   (b) 1,000,163   (c) 100,163
      (d) 100,000,163   (e) 100,000,063   Answer _____

4.   Twenty-three thousand nine is written:
      (a) 2,309   (b) 23,009   (c) 230, 090
      (d) 230,000   (e) 23,000,009   Answer _____

5.   Seventy-two million thirty nine is written:
      (a) 720,039   (b) 7,200,039   (c) 72,039
      (d) 72,000,039   (e) 720,039   Answer _____

6.   Three hundred thousand two hundred ten is written:

    (a) 300,210   (b) 30,210   (c) 3,000,210
    (d) 3,002,100   (e) 30,000,210   Answer _____

7.   Six thousand seventy-five is written:
    (a) 67,500   (b) 6,075   (c) 675
    (d) 675,000   (e) 6,750   Answer _____

8.   Twenty nine thousand three is written:
    (a) 2,903   (b) 29,030   (c) 290,003
    (d) 2,930   (e) 29,003   Answer _____

9.   Five million and sixty five is written:
    (a) 500,065   (b) 5,000,065   (c) 50,000,065
    (d) 5,000,650   (e) 565,000   Answer _____

CHAPTER GLOSSARY
Integer: A whole number—not a fraction.

5. Adding and Subtracting Units

Example 1:

    4 hours 54 minutes
    +2 hours 12 minutes

    Solution:

      6 hours 66 minutes
    +1 hour −60 minutes
      7 hours   6 minutes

> Change minutes to hours
> 66 minutes = 60 minutes + 6 minutes
>   = 1 hour 6 minutes

    Answer: 7 hours 6 minutes

Example 2: Subtract 6 pounds 11 ounces from 11 pounds 3 ounces.

    Solution:
    Borrow 1 pound = 16 ounces.

          10   19
       11̶ pounds 3̶ ounces
      −6 pounds 11 ounces
        4 pounds   8 ounces
   Answer: 4 pounds 8 ounces

The following information is provided to help you answer the questions in this section:

1 hour	=	60 minutes
1 minute	=	60 seconds
1 pound	=	16 ounces
1 yard	=	3 feet
1 foot	=	12 inches

Fill in the correct answers in the space provided:

1. 6 hours 17 minutes
    +2 hours 49 minutes

    Answer_____

2. 12 feet 9 inches
    +6 feet 7 inches

    Answer_____

3. 4 hours 9 minutes
    –2 hours 12 minutes

    Answer_____

4. 3 feet 7 inches
    –2 feet 12 inches

    Answer_____

5. 6 hours 7 minutes
    –4 hours 12 minutes

    Answer_____

6. 4 feet 2 inches
    –2 feet 7 inches

    Answer_____

7. A movie started at 7:35 P.M. and ended at 10:15 P.M. How long did the movie last?

    Answer_____

8. A flight left Kennedy at 7:42 P.M. and arrived in Los Angeles at 11:29 p.m. How long did it last?

    Answer_____

9. A meeting began at 9:42 A.M. and ended At 10:19 A.M. How long did the meeting last?

    Answer: _____

10. A class begins at 8:40 A.M. and ends at 9:45 A.M. How long did the class last?   Answer: _____

6. Average Problems

To find the average, add all the numbers and then divide by the amount of numbers added.

AVERAGE

The quotient is found by dividing the sum of a group of numbers by the number of addends.

Example 1: Find the average of 30, 0 and 60.

Solution: STEP 1: Add the three numbers.

$$
\begin{array}{r}
30 \\
0 \\
\underline{60} \\
90
\end{array}
$$

STEP 2: Divide by 3.
$$\frac{90}{3} = 30$$

Answer: 30

Write the answer in the space provided:

1. Find the average of 70, 40 and 0.   Answer_____

2. Find the average of 80, 60 and 40.   Answer_____

3. Jose scored a 90, 80, and 70 on his mathematics tests. What is his average?   Answer_____

4. A sales sells 12 suits on Monday, 14 suits on Tuesday, and 16 suits on Wednesday. What is the average number of suits sold for the three days?   Answer_____

5. Find the average of 12, 39 and 9.   Answer_____

6. Lana scored 70 and 80 on her social studies tests. What grade must she receive on the third test to have an 80 average?   Answer_____

7. Zelma scored 90 and 80 on her mathematics tests. What must her grade be on the next test to have a 90 average?   Answer_____

8. John gained 72 pounds in 6 months. What
   is his average weight gain per month?   Answer_____

9. Find the average of 30, 40 and 50.   Answer_____

10. A salesman sells 3 dresses on Monday,
    12 dresses on Tuesday, and 15 dresses
    on Wednesday. What is the average number
    of dresses sold for the three days?   Answer_____

CHAPTER GLOSSARY
Average: The quotient is found by dividing the sum of a group of numbers by the
         number of addends.

7. Order of Operations

RULES FOR ORDER OF OPERATIONS

1. Perform indicated operations inside the parenthesis.
2. Evaluate the roots and the powers.
3. Multiply and divide from left to right.
4. If necessary, add or subtract.

Squaring a Number: A number multiplied by itself.
Power or Exponent: It is the number of times a base is used as a factor.
Base: The number that serves as a starting point.

For Example: $2^3 = 2 \cdot 2 \cdot 2 = 8$
$3^5 = 3 \cdot 3 \cdot 3 \cdot 3 \cdot 3 = 243$

Example 1:   3(4+5)
              3(9)
              27 | Perform operations within parentheses: |

       Answer: 27

Example 2: $4 + 3(5 + 6)^2$
              $4 + 3(11)^2$
              $4 + 3(121)$ | Perform operations within parentheses: Powers Multiplication Addition |
              $4 + 363$
              367

       Answer: 367

Example 3:

$$4 + (8 - 5)3 - 8 \div (4 - 2)$$
$$4 + (3)3 - 8 \div 2$$
$$4 + 9 - 4$$
$$9$$

Answer: 9

Perform operations within parentheses:
Multiplication
Addition
Subtraction

Evaluate each of the expressions. Fill in the correct answer in the space provided:

1. $3 \times 9 - 7$ Answer _____

2. $12 + 7(2)$ Answer _____

3. $3 + 4(5)^2$ Answer _____

4. $34 - 3(10\text{-}2)$ Answer _____

5. $6 + 4 \times 9 - 2$ Answer _____

6. $15 - 6 \div 2$ Answer _____

7. $6 \times 8 \div (2 + 1)$ Answer _____

8. $36 \div 12 \div 3$ Answer _____

9. $14 \div 2 \times 7$ Answer _____

10. $3(7)^2$ Answer _____

11. $3(6 + 8)^2$ Answer _____

12. $3 + (6 + 8)^2$ Answer _____

13. $2(7) + 3(6)$ Answer _____

14. $2 + 3(4 + 1)^2$ Answer _____

15. $6 \div 2 \times 3$ Answer _____

CHAPTER GLOSSARY

Base: The number that serves as a starting point.

Exponent: ⎫
                 ⎬ It is the number of times a base is used as a factor.
Power: ⎭

8. Rounding Numbers

Many times an exact answer is not necessary. To know it is approximately 200 miles from New York to Washington D.C. is a good enough estimate. To estimate a number is to round it off to a certain place.

Place Values

Hundred Millions	Ten Millions	One Million	Hundred Thousands	Ten Thousands	Thousands	Hundreds	Tens	Ones

---

Rules for Rounding:

If the digit to the right of the rounded digit is less than five, leave the digit alone and substitute zeros for the digits to the right.

If the digit to the right of the rounded digit is greater than five, increase the rounded digit by one and substitute zeros for the digits to the right.

Example 1:   Round 415 to the nearest hundred.

Solution: The digit 4 is in the hundreds place. The digit to the right of 4 is 1. If it is less than 5, the numeral 415 becomes 400. The zeros must be used to keep the proper place value.

Answer: 400

Example 2:   Round 6,872 to the nearest thousand.

Solution: The digit 6 is in the thousands place. The digit to the right of 6 is 8. If it is 5 or greater, the number 6,872 becomes 7,000. The zeros must be used to keep the proper place value.

Answer: 7,000

Example 3:   Round 2,756 to the nearest hundred.

Solution: The digit 7 is in hundreds place. The digit to the right of 7 is 5. If it is 5 or greater, the numeral 2,756 becomes 2,800. The zeros must be used to keep the proper place value.

Answer: 2,800

Round the number to the indicated place.
Write the correct answer in the space provided:

1.	176	tens	Answer _____
2.	4,365	tens	Answer _____
3.	6,359	hundreds	Answer _____
4.	4,312	hundreds	Answer _____
5.	18,181	thousands	Answer _____
6.	203,678	thousands	Answer _____
7.	394,251	hundred thousands	Answer _____
8.	4,659,341	millions	Answer _____
9.	8,394,192	ten thousands	Answer _____
10.	679	hundreds	Answer _____

CHAPTER GLOSSARY

Digit: In the number system a digit is any one of the first ten whole numbers:
0, 1, 2, 3, 5, 6, 7, 8, 9.

Place value: The value of the digit due to the position in the numeral.

Rounding Numbers: It is to estimate an answer by rounding it off to a certain place. If the digit to the right of the rounded digit is less than five, leave the digit alone and substitute zeros for the digits to the right. If the digit to the right of the rounded digit is greater than five, increase the rounded digit by one and substitute zeros for the digits to the right.

9. Decimal System

Our system of numbers is called the decimal system. The prefix "deci" is defined as ten. The decimal system uses ten symbols: 0, 1, 2, 3, 4, 5, 6, 7, 8, and 9.

PLACE VALUE

The numbers to the left of the decimal are whole numbers. Separating the whole number is a decimal point. The new place values to the right of the decimal point are called tenths, hundredths, thousandths, etc.

Place value chart

Hundreds	Tens	Ones	Tenths	Hundredths	Thousandths	Ten Thousandths

Decimal Point

10. Reading Decimals

The number 2.435 contains the following:

      2 in the units place
      4 in the tenths place
      3 in the hundredths place
      5 in the thousandths place.

The number is read as "two and four hundred and thirty five thousandths."

Rule—Reading Decimals:

The decimal point is read as "and."
The decimals are read as whole numbers followed by the name of the furthest right place.

Example: Read each of the following:
        a) 0.749   b) 70.0789   c) 900.8

Answer: a) Seven hundred forty-nine thousandths
           b) Seventy and seven hundred eighty-nine ten thousandths
           c) Nine hundred and eight-tenths

          *Remember to read decimal points as "and."

Example: Using mathematical symbols, write the number six thousand and four hundred sixty-eight ten thousandths.

Solution: 6,000.0468
           The empty places must be filled in by zeros.
Answer: 6,000.0468

Fill in the correct answer in the space provided:

1. In which place is the digit 6?

   a) 6.057   Answer _____

   b) 54.069   Answer _____

   c) 137.621   Answer _____

   d) 2.7596   Answer _____

   e) 18.615   Answer _____

   f) 60.0593   Answer _____

2. Write out the number as you would read it.

   a) 43.54   Answer _____

   b) 68.9   Answer _____

   c) 12.325   Answer _____

   d) 16.0295   Answer _____

   e) 100.2   Answer _____

   f) 300.25   Answer _____

3. Write in decimal notation:

   a) Seven and three thousandths   Answer _____

   b) Thirty-two and twelve hundredths   Answer _____

   c) Two hundred and seven hundredths   Answer _____

   d) One hundred fifty-nine ten thousandths   Answer _____

   e) Three thousand and six tenths   Answer _____

   f) Twenty-seven ten thousandths   Answer _____

CHAPTER GLOSSARY

Decimal: A numeral that uses place value digits and a decimal point to write numbers that show tenths, hundredths, thousandths and so on.

Decimal Point: A period used to separate whole numbers from decimals.

Decimal System: Our system of numbers is called the decimal system.

Tenths: Being one of ten equal parts (one tenth = 1/10 = .1).

Hundredths: Being one of a hundred equal parts (one hundredth = 1/100 .01).

Place Value: The value of the digit due to the position of the number.

Thousandths: Being one of a thousand equal parts (one thousandth = 1/1000 = .001).

11. Comparing Size of Decimals

Decimal: A numeral that uses place value digits and a decimal point to write numbers that shows tenths, hundredths, thousandths, etc.

Tenth: Being one of ten equal parts (one tenth = 1/10 or .1).

Hundredth: Being one of a hundred equal parts (one hundredth = 1/100 = .01).

Thousandth: Being one of a thousand equal parts (one thousandth = 1/1000 = .001).

PLACE VALUE

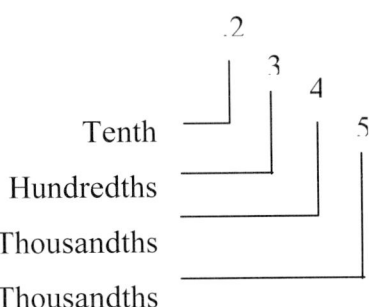

TO COMPARE THE SIZE OF DECIMALS

1.   First compare the integral parts.
2.   If they are the same, compare the first number after the decimal points (tenths digits).
3.   If the tenths digits are the same, then compare the second number after the decimal point (the hundredths digits).
4.   Continue the process until the correct answer is found.

Example 1: Which is the smallest number?
  a) 3.04   b) .042   c) 031   d) .03

Solution: In b, c and d, the integral part is 0. Thus, (a) is eliminated. Now, look at the tenths digit in (b), (c) and (d). The tenths digit is zero for all of them. Look at the hundredths digit. The smallest is (c) and (d) for the hundredths digit. Finally, look at the thousandths digit for (c) and (d). Since (d) has no number in the thousandths digit, it is 0. Thus, the smallest is (d).

Answer: (d)

Example 2: Which is the largest number?

a) .038   b) .067   c) .793   d) .749

Solution: Look at the tenths digit. The largest is (c) and (d). Now look at the hundredths digit. The largest is (c).

Answer: (c)

A. Which number is the *smallest*? Write the letter of the correct answer in the space provided:

1. a) .31   b) .34   c) .36   d) .39   e) .30   Answer _____

2. a) .62   b) .6   c) .65   d) .69   e) .605   Answer _____

3. a) .456   b) .451   c) .452   d) .457   e) .458   Answer _____

4. a) 2.75   b) 2.89   c) 2.761   d) 2.758   e) 2.77   Answer _____

5. a) .08   b) .008   c) .0008   d) .8   e) .00008   Answer _____

6. a) 6.75   b) 6.175   c) 6.075   d) 6.275   e) 6.891   Answer _____

B. Which the number is the *largest*? Write the letter of the correct answer in the space provided.

1. a) .84   b) .89   c) .82   d) .87   e) .86   Answer _____

2. a) .31   b) .34   c) .3   d) .39   e) .37   Answer _____

3. a) 6.1   b) 6.07   c) 6.21   d) 6.04   e) 6.39   Answer _____

4. a) 3.7   b) 3.07   c) 3.75   d) 3.72   e) 3.79   Answer _____

5. a) 5.09   b) .059   c) 5.90   d) 5.009   e) 5.097   Answer _____

6. a) .88   b) .0881   c) .0808   d) .0888   e) .0880   Answer _____

12. Rounding Decimals

- Leave the digit alone, if the digit to the right of the rounded digit is less than 5.
- Increase the rounded digit by one, if the digit to the right of the rounded digit is 5 or more.
- Discard the digits to the right of the rounded digit.

ROUNDING OFF TO NEAREST HUNDREDTH OR THOUSANDTH

1. To round to the nearest *hundredth*, the answer must be expressed to two decimal digits (two numbers after the decimal point). Look at the third decimal digit (third number after the decimal point) If the third digit is 5 or more, the second decimal digit must be made 1 digit larger (Example: .576 = .58 or .574 = .57).

2. To round to the nearest thousandth, the answer must be expressed to three decimal digits (three numbers after the decimal point). Look at the fourth decimal digit (fourth number after the decimal point). If the fourth digit is 5 or more, the third digit must be made 1 digit larger (Example: .5892 = .589, .5876 = .588).

Example 1 : Convert $\dfrac{3}{19}$ to a decimal rounded to the nearest hundredth.

Solution: Divide numerator by denominator and add three 0's.

$$
\begin{array}{r}
.157 \\
19\overline{)3.000} \\
-19\downarrow \\
\hline
110 \\
-95\downarrow \\
\hline
150 \\
-133 \\
\hline
17
\end{array}
$$

Answer is to be expressed as hundredths (two digits to the right of the decimal point). Since the third digit to the right of the decimal is 5 or greater than 5, then increase the second decimal from 5 to 6.

Answer: .16

Example 2: Convert $\dfrac{2}{19}$ to a decimal rounded to the nearest thousandth.

Solution: Divide numerator by the denominator and add four 0's.

$$
\begin{array}{r}
.2222 \\
9\,)\,2.0000 \\
-18\downarrow \\
\hline
20 \\
-18\downarrow \\
\hline
20 \\
-18\downarrow \\
\hline
20 \\
-18 \\
\hline
0
\end{array}
$$

Answer is to be expressed as thousandths (three digits to the right of the decimal point). Since the fourth digit to the right of the decimal is not 5, nor greater than 5, the third digit remains 2.

Answer: .222

A. Change each fraction to a decimal rounded to the nearest *hundredth*. Fill in the correct answer in the space provided:

1. $\dfrac{3}{8}$ Answer _____   5. $\dfrac{2}{7}$ Answer _____

2. $\dfrac{2}{9}$ Answer _____   6. $\dfrac{3}{17}$ Answer _____

3. $\dfrac{6}{7}$ Answer _____   7. $\dfrac{8}{9}$ Answer _____

4. $\dfrac{4}{19}$ Answer _____   8. $\dfrac{5}{6}$ Answer _____

B. Change each fraction to a decimal rounded to the nearest *thousandth*. Fill in the correct answer in the space provided:

1. $\dfrac{3}{11}$ Answer _____   5. $\dfrac{8}{17}$ Answer _____

2. $\dfrac{10}{13}$ Answer _____   6. $\dfrac{11}{19}$ Answer _____

3. $\dfrac{2}{7}$ Answer _____   7. $\dfrac{4}{7}$ Answer _____

4. $\dfrac{3}{8}$ Answer _____   8. $\dfrac{7}{9}$ Answer _____

13. Addition and Subtraction of Decimals

1.	Line up decimal digits.
2.	Add or subtract in appropriate columns.
3.	Carry down the decimal point.

Example 1: Add 12.75 + 19.02 + 6.71

     Solution: 12.75
                           19.02
                      + 6.71
     Answer: 38.48

Example 2: Subtract 39.2 – 6.97

     STEP 1: Line up decimal points.
Convert 39.2 to 39.20 and then proceed to subtract.

                    39.20
                   –6.97
                    32.23
     Answer: 32.23

Fill in the correct answer in the space provided:

A. Addition

1. .271 + 2.71 + 27   Answer _____

2. 6.89 + 35.02 + .086   Answer _____

3. 16.02 + 1.62 + .162   Answer _____

4. 3.7 + 6.09 + .075   Answer _____

5. 6.9 + 12.7 + 3.85   Answer _____

6. 7.5 + .75 + .075   Answer _____

7. .089 + 89 + 8.9   Answer _____

8. 6.75 + 7.2 + 13.89   Answer _____

9. 7.2 + .72 + 72   Answer _____

10. 6.89 + 68.9 + .075 + 3.8   Answer _____

B. Subtraction

1. 37.2 – 12.1   Answer _____

2. 16.89 – 7.54   Answer _____

3. 3 – .078   Answer _____

4. 16.2 – 3.45   Answer _____

5. 6.78 – 2.89   Answer _____

6. 72 – .72   Answer _____

7. 17.2 – 15.9   Answer _____

8. 6 – .089   Answer _____

9. 424.75 – 189.53   Answer _____

10. 678.2 – 129.87   Answer _____

14. Multiplication of Decimals

1. Multiply as an ordinary problem and obtain the product.
2. Determine where the decimal point belongs by counting the total number of decimal digits after the decimal point in both numbers.
3. Place the decimal point in the product by counting from right to left. If there are not enough digits, then add the appropriate number of zeros.

Example 1: Multiply .58 x 7.4
Solution:

```
        .58        2 Decimal Digits
      x 7.4        +1 Decimal Digit
        232
     + 4060
Answer:  4.292     3 Decimal Digits
```

Example 2: Find the cost of 12 pints of cole slaw at $1.39 per pint.
Solution: Each point of cole slaw costs $1.39. To find the total cost, you multiply the number of pints by the cost of each pint.

```
       $1.39       2 Decimal Digits
       x  12       +0 Decimal Digits
        278
     +  1390
Answer:   $16.68   2 Decimal Digits
```

A. Write the answer in the space provided:

1. .4 x .5   Answer _____

2. .39 x .6   Answer _____

3. 12 x .08   Answer _____

4. 17 x .001   Answer _____

5. 1.62 x .05   Answer _____

6. 507 x 4.16   Answer _____

7. .16 x .02   Answer _____

8. 3.2 x 4.5   Answer _____

9. .07 x 18   Answer _____

10. 12 x .0004 Answer _____

11. 16.2 x 5.1 Answer _____

12. 7.89 x 653 Answer _____

B. Write the answer in the space provided:

1. How much does three quarts of orange juice cost at $.98 a quart?

Answer _____

2. Ice cream cones cost $1.10 each. What is the cost of two dozen ice cream cones?

Answer _____

3. Pears sell for $.79 a pound. What is the cost of five
   pounds of pears?   Answer _____

4. Jannie earns $ 7.35 per hour where she works.
   How much does she earn for twenty-eight hours of work? Answer _____

5. Coffee sells for $3.75 a pound. What is the cost of
   twelve pounds of coffee?   Answer _____

15. Division of Decimals

1. The number after the division sign is called the divisor. The other number is
   called the dividend. The answer to a division problem is called the quotient.

2. Move the decimal point as many places as necessary to make the divisor an
   integer.

3. Move the decimal point in the dividend the same number of places. If there are
   not enough places, the appropriate number of zeros must be added.

4. Proceed to divide. Write the decimal point in the correct place in the quotient.

Example 1: $12.5 \div .05$

Solution:
$$\frac{\text{Quotient}}{\text{Divisor })\text{Dividend}}$$

```
    .05 )12.5
         250
     5 )1250
        -10
          25
         -25
          00
          -0
           0
```

| Move decimal point in divisor two places to the right. Then, move decimal point in dividend two places to the right and add a 0. Then, proceed to divide. |

Answer: 250

Example 2: Pencils cost $.12 each. How many can be purchased for $24.00?

Solution:
```
    .12 ) 24.00

          200
    12 ) 2400
```

| Move decimal in divisor and in the dividend two places to the right and proceed to divide. |

Answer: 200

A. Fill in the correct answer in the space provided:

1. $36 \div .6$ Answer _____

2. $72 \div .03$ Answer _____

3. $140 \div .7$ Answer _____

4. $.49 \div 7$ Answer _____

5. $12.5 \div 2.5$ Answer _____

6. $720 \div .06$ Answer _____

7. $.84 \div 6$ Answer _____

8. $14.4 \div 1.2$ Answer _____

9. $7.5 \div .15$ Answer _____

10. $12.12 \div 12$ Answer _____

11. $160 \div 8$ Answer _____

12. $.42 \div 7$ Answer _____

B. Write the answer in the space provided:

1. Pens cost $.75 each. How many pens can be purchased for $ 30.00?   Answer _____

2. Apples cost $.25 each. How many can be purchased for $6.00?   Answer _____

3. Nuts sell for $3.60 a pound. How many pounds can be purchased for $72.00?   Answer _____

4. Zelma pays $23.20 for a tank of gasoline. If gasoline sells for $ 1.45 a gallon, how many gallons does she buy?   Answer _____

16. Percentage, Base and Rate

Before we proceed solving problems that relate to percentage, base, and rate, it's very important that you know the meanings, differences, and relationships of these three variables. A lot of students used percentage interchangeably with percent indicating confusion in interpreting and understanding these two variables. Likewise the formula for finding percentage is sometimes used to calculate base. Understand clearly the definitions of each variable and you'll find these concepts very interesting.

Percentage means a **portion** of a whole. That "whole" can be anything. It could be a whole team, whole amount, or total number of anything. If that "whole" you are talking about is money, the portion, refers to money also. If that total number refers to students, the portion refers to students also. Percentage must always be in the same terms as the whole amount, total number, or the base. In solving problems involving *Percentage, Base*, and *Rate*, it is **essentially important that you properly identify which number in the problem represents those variables.** Once the variables are correctly identified, it's simple and easy to follow the formula that corresponds to the problem. Some definitions below will help you identify these variables in a problem.

> **Percentage** refers to the **portion** of the total number or amount.
> Percentage is calculated by multiplying the rate by the base. **P = R x B**
>
> That **total** number of people, cars, houses, buildings, students, workers, shops, or a whole amount (100%) is the **base.** The base is usually introduced by the preposition "**of**". If the problem is looking for the base, the answer is usually a huge number, or a large amount. The base is computed by dividing the percentage by the rate. **B = P ÷ R**.
>
> Identifying the **rate** is not difficult at all. You can easily recognize the rate in a percent problem, because this is the number represented by a **percent sign (%).** **To solve for Rate, you divide the percentage by the base**. R = P ÷ B

Let's say a leather jacket costing $250 is given a discount of 50%; you would grab this opportunity to save a lot of money. What does this mean to you? You are looking for a great savings here. But the question is, (and most college students don't know) how much will you save? Simple! What is 50% of $250? You can easily figure this out. 50% has the same value as ½. So, 50% or ½ of $250 is $125. But, in most instances, it is not this simple. You can solve this problem in two different ways, mathematically (division of decimals), and algebraically (using proportion).

The *definitions* above will help you remember and identify the variable and choose the appropriate number in the problem that suits the variable.

What is 50% of $250?

Identify the numbers given in the problem. Rate is 50%; Base is $250.

Therefore, the *portion* or the *percentage* is missing.

HOW TO SOLVE PERCENTAGE PROBLEMS:

1. Identify the given data and the unknown (usually one) in the problem.
2. Apply the appropriate formula. (P = R x B)
3. Plug in the values to the letters in the formula, and solve the equation.

Following the formula in finding Percentage, *P = B x R,* where P= 250 x 0.50
The question here is **what portion** is 50% of $250? In using this formula, it's very important that, you **always** change the *Rate (50%)* to *decimals (0.5)* before multiplying it with the *Base* ($250)

Therefore, P = $250 x 0.5   **P = $125**

Your savings is $125. You save one half of the price. Do you wonder why a lot of people wait for a sale to come before they shop? Big Savings is the answer!

Approaching this question algebraically, using proportion, is this way:
Translate 50% to fraction, reduced to lowest terms, = a variable (**P**) written over the total amount or the base, $250. Use cross multiplication. Check the solution below:

$$\frac{50}{100} = \frac{1}{2} \quad then, \quad \frac{1}{2} = \frac{P}{\$250}$$

$$2P = \$250$$
$$P = \frac{\$250}{2}$$
$$\mathbf{P = 125}$$

Comparatively speaking, the first solution seems easier and less complicated than the second solution. What do you think?

Try the following problems:

1. What is 8% of 95?
2. 15% of $145 is what?
3. What is 25% of 815?
4. Solve 5% of 65.
5. Compute 18% of $264.
6. Calculate 0.05% of 828.
7. Calculate 90% of 355.
8. Find 85% of $3,450.
9. What is 55% of $1300?
10. 3% of 450 is what?
11. What is 2% of 157?
12. 12% of 240 is what?
13. 1% of 1 is what?
14. What is 8.25% of $225?
15. Estimate 4.5% of $75.
16. Solve 2.5% of 400.

In the examples above, you will notice that the problems are asked differently. It doesn't really matter; they mean the same thing. What is essential, is you identify correctly the **given data** and the **unknown**, or what the problem is asking you, to find. Then, use the appropriate formula.

SOLVING FOR THE BASE:

Now, what if the portion or the percentage is present, and the rate (%) is also given in the problem, and you are asked to look for the **total amount** or **the whole, or the total number**; the problem has to be approached differently. Since we have already defined and distinguished the percentage, base, and rate, at the beginning of this lesson, the rest will be easy. Follow the following steps or procedures in solving for the base or total amount.

HOW TO SOLVE FOR THE BASE:

1. **Identify the given data and the unknown (usually one) in the problem.**
2. **Apply the appropriate formula. $B = P \div R$.** (Since you are dividing the percentage by the rate (%), don't forget to change the (%) to decimals, and remember to follow the rules in decimal division).
3. **Substitute the values for the letters in the formula and solve the problem.**

Example 1: **50% of what amount is $125?** This problem is derived from the first example (finding percentage). Remember? The value of **P** is $125. This time, we are using that amount ($125), to find the base.

Following the steps enumerated above, the two given data are: Rate (50%) and Percentage ($125). Remember, you are looking for the total amount, 50% of which is $125. Therefore, you simply divide the portion or percentage by the rate, and your quotient equals the base.

Solution: Given data: Rate: 50%, Percentage: $125, Unknown: Base
Formula: $B = P \div R$

Therefore: $B = \$125 \div 0.5$
$B = \$250$

Example 2: 360 is 12% of what number?

Solution: Given data: Rate: 12%, Percentage: 360
Unknown: Base
Formula: $B = P \div R$
Therefore: $B = 360 \div 0.12$ $B = 3,000$

Like percentage, base can also be solved algebraically using proportion. Again, convert the percent to fraction, reduced to lowest terms. This time we are looking for the total number, not the portion. Therefore the solution looks like this:

First, express 12% as a fraction, which is $\frac{12}{10}$ or 0.12 (in decimals)

$$\frac{12}{100} \times \frac{360}{B} \qquad \frac{2}{25} \times \frac{360}{B}$$

$(\dfrac{3}{25}$ is the reduced fraction of $\dfrac{12}{100}$, both terms were divided by **4**)

$$\dfrac{3B}{3} = \dfrac{9,000}{3} \qquad B = 3,000$$

If the given **Rate** is in a **fraction** form, the fraction has to be changed to **decimals first,** and then follow the steps listed above. Example: ¾ % of what number is 15? **¾ % = 0.0075**

Example 3: ¼ % of what number is 8?

Solution: 1.   Change ¼% to decimals. (0.0025)
2.   Use the formula: B = P ÷ R.
(Percentage is 8; rate is ¼ % or 0.0025)
3.   Therefore: B = 8 – 0.0025.
B = 3,200

Try the following *Base* Problems:

1. 15% of what number is 45?

2. 9% of what number is 180?

3. 10% of what amount is $100?

4. 2% of what amount is $50?

5. 300 is 6% of what number?

6. 150 is 45% of what number?

7. 7% of what amount is $14?

8. 1.5% of what number is 3?

9. ¼ % of what number is $12?

10. ½ % of what amount is $38?

SOLVING RATE (PERCENT) PROBLEMS:

May be most of you haven't realized the significance of this concept in our daily lives. Regardless of what work you do, or the occupation you have, the place you live, the food you eat, the car you drive, and the clothes you wear, ***Percent*** problems always confront you. In business, profits and losses are usually expressed in percent. It is imperative that every student in Math knows how to compute and solve percent problems.

Like percentage and base, ***Rate*** follows a formula. When both percentage and base are given, and the rate is unknown, divide the portion by the total amount or number. Thus:

$$\text{Rate} = \dfrac{\text{Percentage}}{\text{Base}} \qquad \text{or} \qquad \mathbf{R = \dfrac{P}{B}}$$

Example 1:   What % of 100 is 50?

    Solution: Identify the given data: Base is 100; Percentage is 50.
                      The unknown variable is Rate.
                      Plug the values found in the problem to the formula.
                      Therefore: $R = \dfrac{50}{100}$

                $R = 0.5$ or 50%

Example 2:   **What % of 30 is 6?**
        $R = \dfrac{6}{30}$ $R = 0.2$ or 20%

Solve the following *Rate* problems:

1. What percent of 40 is 20?

2. What percent of 8 is 5?

3. What percent of 20 is 15?

4. What % of 30 is 12?

5. What % of 40 is 5?

6. What % of 90 is 45?

7. What % of 100 is 25?

8. What % of 60 is 20?

9. What % of 15 is 5?

10. What % of 25 is 4?

WORKBOOK:

1. Find 15% of 95.

2. What is 18% of $1500?

3. What number is 0.5% of 300?

4. What percent of 300 is 60?

5. 25% of $145 is what?

6. What is 90% of 1000?

7. 12% of what number is 240?

8. 8.25% of $1.00 is what?

9. 14% of what amount is $420?

10. What percent of 250 is 50?

11. 30% of what number is 12?

12. Calculate 35% of $299.

13. 7% of what number is 210?

14. What % of 300 is 120?

15. Compute 4.5% of $185.

17. Multiplication and Division by Powers of 10

Examples:

$$6 \times 10^0 = 6 \times 1 \qquad = \quad 6$$
$$6 \times 10^1 = 6 \times 10 \qquad = \quad 60$$
$$6 \times 10^2 = 6 \times 100 \quad = \quad 600$$
$$6 \times 10^3 = 6 \times 1000 = \quad 6{,}000$$

Multiplication and division are opposite processes.

$$6{,}000 \div 10^0 = 6{,}000 \div 1 \qquad = \qquad 6{,}000$$
$$6{,}000 \div 10^1 = 6{,}000 \div 10 \qquad = \qquad 600$$
$$6{,}000 \div 10^2 = 6{,}000 \div 100 \qquad = \qquad 60$$
$$6{,}000 \div 10^3 = 6{,}000 \div 1000 \qquad = \qquad 6$$

Rule: Multiplication and Division by Powers of 10

Multiply by 10, move decimal point one place to the right.
Multiply by 100, move decimal point two places to the right.
Multiply by 1000, move decimal point three places to the right.

In general, move the decimal point to the right the same number of places as the exponent.

Divide by 10, move the decimal point one place to the left.
Divide by 100, move the decimal point two places to the left.
Divide by 1000, move decimal point three places to the left.

In general, move the decimal point to the left the same number of places as the exponent.

Multiply or divide in your head. Write the correct answer in the space provided:

1. 0.049 x 10   Answer _____
2. 0.395 x 100   Answer _____
3. 8,951 ÷ 1000   Answer _____
4. 386 ÷ 100   Answer _____
5. 0.0395 x 100   Answer _____
6. 0.06 x 1,000   Answer _____
7. 19.8 ÷ 100   Answer _____
8. 379 ÷ 10,000   Answer _____
9. .062 x 100   Answer _____
10. .3 x 1,000   Answer _____
11. 12.2 ÷ 1,000   Answer _____
12. 7.9 ÷ 100   Answer _____

18. Conversions, Decimals, Fractions and Percents

To change a fraction to a decimal, divide the denominator into the numerator. Add a decimal point and at least two zeros. The fraction bar is a division sign.

Example 1: Convert 3/8 to a decimal.

Solution: Divide the numerator, 3, by the denominator, 8. Add the necessary number of 0's to the right of the decimal point.

$$\frac{N}{D} = D\overline{)N} = 8\overline{)3.000}$$

$$\begin{array}{r} .375 \\ 8\overline{)3.000} \\ \underline{-24} \\ 60 \\ \underline{-56} \\ 40 \\ \underline{-40} \\ 0 \end{array}$$

Answer: .375

A.   Change each fraction to a decimal.
Fill in the correct answer in the space provided:

1. $\dfrac{6}{25}$ Answer _____

2. $\dfrac{11}{17}$ Answer _____

3. $\dfrac{9}{200}$ Answer _____

4. $\dfrac{3}{100}$ Answer _____

5. $\dfrac{6}{2}$ Answer _____

6. $\dfrac{7}{20}$ Answer _____

7. $\dfrac{9}{25}$ Answer _____

8. $\dfrac{7}{4}$ Answer _____

TO CONVERT A DECIMAL TO A FRACTION

Decimals can be converted to fractions by reading the decimal number properly. For example, 0.03 is 3 hundredths or 3/100.

Example 1: Change .08 to a fraction in lowest terms.

Solution: $.08 = \dfrac{8}{100}$

Answer: $\dfrac{2}{25}$

> Divide both the numerator and the denominator by 4.

DECIMAL TO FRACTION

Rewrite the decimal as a fraction and reduce answer to lowest terms.

B.   **Change each decimal to a fraction and reduce answer to lower terms. Fill in the correct answer in the space provided:**

1.   .35   Answer _____   6.   0.045   Answer _____

2.   .02   Answer _____   7.   .08   Answer _____

3.   .025   Answer _____   8.   6.4   Answer _____

4.   1.2   Answer _____   9.   0.089   Answer _____

5.   4.35   Answer _____   10.   .725   Answer _____

PERCENT TO FRACTION

1. Cross out the percent symbol.
2. Create a fraction by using 100 as the denominator.
3. Reduce answer to lowest terms.

TO CONVERT A PERCENT TO A FRACTION

Example 1: Express 65% as a fraction. Reduce answer to lowest terms.

Solution: $65\% = \dfrac{65}{100} - \dfrac{13}{20}$

Divide both the numerator and the denominator by 5.

Answer: $\dfrac{13}{20}$

C.   **Change each percent to a fraction. Reduce answer to lowest terms. Fill in the correct answer in the space provided:**

1.   35%   Answer _____   6.   70%   Answer _____

2.   8%   Answer _____   7.   79%   Answer _____

3.   19%   Answer _____   8.   245%   Answer _____

4.   24%   Answer _____   9.   36%   Answer _____

5.   150%   Answer _____   10.   4%   Answer _____

CONVERT A PERCENT TO A DECIMAL

1.	Place decimal point to the left of the percent symbol, if none is present.
2.	Cross out the percent symbol.
3.	Move the decimal point two digits to the left.

Example 1: Convert 137% to a decimal

Solution: 137% = 1.37
Answer: 1.37

> Decimal points is moved two places to the left and the percent sign is eliminated.

D.   Change each percent to a decimal. Fill in the correct answer in the space provided:

1.	39%	Answer _____	6.	54%	Answer _____
2.	7%	Answer _____	7.	429%	Answer _____
3.	125%	Answer _____	8.	.7%	Answer _____
4.	.8%	Answer _____	9.	4%	Answer _____
5.	6%	Answer _____	10.	16%	Answer _____

19. Verbal Problems in Cost and Profit

Example 1: Candy cost $.40 a bar. How many bars can be purchased for $24?

Solution: Divide the total cost $24 by the cost per bar $.40

$$\$24 \div \$.40 \quad = \quad .40\overline{)24}$$

$$\begin{array}{r} 60 \\ 40\overline{)2400} \end{array}$$

> Move decimal in the divisor two places to the right. Add a decimal and two 0's in the dividend and move it two places to the right.

Answer: 60 bars

Example 2: 18 oranges cost $.15 each. What is the total cost?

Solution: Multiply the cost of one orange $.15 by the number of oranges to find the total cost.

$ .15	2 Decimal Digits
x 18	0 Decimal Digits
120	
15	
$2.70	2 Decimal Digits

Answer: $2.70

PROFIT = TOTAL SALE – COST

1.   What is the total cost of 35 pencils at 15¢ each?   Answer _____

2.   Find the total cost of 3 pounds of apples at 39¢
     per pound and 5 pounds of pears at 59¢ per pound.   Answer _____

3.   A piano teacher charges $15.00 for the first lesson
     and $12.00 for each additional lesson. What is the
     cost of 9 lessons?   Answer _____

4.   The Johnson Moving Company charges $35.00 for
     the first hour of work and $27.00 for each additional
     hour. What is the cost of a moving job that takes six hours?   Answer _____

5.   A drama group sells 325 tickets to a play written by
     Cervantes. Each ticket sells for $5.00. The group spends
     $475.00 to rent the auditorium and $147.00 in
     additional expenses. What is the profit?   Answer _____

6.   A department store buys 75 coats for $3,000.00. All
     the coats are sold at $89.00 each. What is the profit?   Answer _____

7.   Pedro's Superette buys 15 dozen rolls at 79¢ dozen.
     Only 11 dozen of the rolls are sold at $ 1.39 per
     dozen. What is the profit?   Answer _____

8.   Martin Luther King High School sells 635 tickets to
     a baseball game at $7.00 per ticket. It cost $1,700.00
     to rent the stadium. Other expenses amount to $ 925.00.
     What is the profit?   Answer _____

9.   Elliot spent $9.35 in the Superertte. How much change
     did he receive from $20.00 bill?   Answer _____

10. Philip bought two candy bars at 65¢ each. How much
     change did he receive from a $5.00 bill?   Answer _____

20. Percent Problems

1. Change the percent to a decimal.
2. What is 12% of 72? (Change the percent to a decimal and proceed to
   multiply; 72 x .12 = 8.64).
3. If 30% of a number is 60, find the number. (Change the percent to a
   decimal and proceed to divide; 60 ÷ .30 = 200).

Example 1: What is 30% of 45?

Solution: Change 30% to a decimal.
30% = .30 = .3
and then proceed to multiply.
.3 x 45 = 13.5
Answer: 13.5

Example 2: If 40% of a number is 80, find the number.

Solutions: METHOD 1: Change percent to a decimal and proceed to divide.
80 ÷ .40 = 200
Answer: 200.

METHOD 2: Algebraic solution:
Let n = the unknown number
40% = .40 = .4
80 = .4 x n

| Divide both sides .4. |

Answer: 200

Example 3: 30% of 300 is what number?

Solution: Change percent to a decimal and proceed to multiply .30 x 300 = 90
Answer: 90

Example 4: What percent of 50 is 20?

Solution: 20 ÷ 50 = .40 = 40%   **or**
20/50 x 100/1 = 2000/50 = 40%
Answer: 40%   (To change a fraction to a percent multiply by $\frac{100}{1}$.)

Example 5: On a mathematics examination Seth had 21 questions correct and 4 questions incorrect. What percent did Seth have correct?

Solution: 1. Determine the number of questions on the examination.
21 + 4 = 25 questions
2. Determine the value of each question.
100 ÷ 25 = 4%
3. Multiply the number of correct questions by the percent value for each question.
21 (.04) = .84 = 84%
Answer: 84%

Example 6: If a mortgage company requires a 20% down payment, what is the down payment on a $230,000 house?

Solution: Change percent to a decimal and multiply $230,000 x .20 = $46,000
Answer: $46,000.

A.   Fill in the letter of the correct answer in the space provided:

1.   What is 12% of 30?
     (a) 36   (b) 250   (c) 3.6   (d) 360   (e) 25   Answer _____

2.   What is 35% of 70?
     a) 24.5   b) 245   c) 200   d) 20   e) 2.45   Answer _____

3.   If 30% of a number is 60, what is the number?
     a) 18   b) 20   c) 1.8   d) 2   e) 200   Answer _____

4.   If 25% of a number is 240, find the number.
     a) 9.6   b) 60   c) 6   d) 960   e) 96   Answer _____

5.   What is 75% of 60?
     a) 45   b) 80   c) 8   d) 4.5   e) 800   Answer _____

6.   If 70% of a number is 140, find the number.
     a) 98   b) 20   c) 9.8   d) 200   e) 980   Answer _____

7.   What is 15% of 30?
     a) 4.5   b) 20   c) 45   d) 2.0   e) 450   Answer _____

8.   What is 30% of 70?
     a) 200   b) 21   c) 37   d) 69   e) 210   Answer _____

9.   40% of what number is 200?
     a) 240   b) 24   c) 80   d) 260   e) 500   Answer _____

10.   What percent of 80 is 20?
      a) 25%   250%   c) 40%   d) 400%   e) 20%   Answer _____

11.   On a chemistry examination Jose had 39 questions correct and 11 questions incorrect. What percent did Jose have incorrect?
      a) 78%   b) 22%   c) 44%   d) 69%   e) 33%   Answer _____

12.   If a mortgage company requires a 30% down payment, what is the down payment on a $120,000 house?
      a) $36,000   b) $3,600   c) $40,000   d) $4,000
      e) $36   Answer _____

13.   30% of what number is 18?
      a) 60   b) 600   c) 5.4   d) 54   e) .6   Answer _____

14.   What percent of 60 is 15?
      a) 25%   b) 2.5%   c) 4%   d) 20%   e) 40%   Answer _____

15. On a mathematics examination Zelma had 19 questions correct and 1 question incorrect. What percent did Zelma get correct?
   a) 95%   b) 5%   c) 90%   d) 85%   e) 80%   Answer _____

16. If a mortgage company requires a 20% down payment, what is the down payment of $160,000 house?
   a) $8,000   b) $800   c) $4,000   d) $3,200   e) $32,000   Answer _____

CHAPTER GLOSSARY

Mortgage: A bank loan used to buy a house or some property.

Percent: Hundredths written with a % sign and no decimal point: .38 = 38%.

21. Verbal Problems in Sales Tax and Percent Increase

> 1. Change the percent to a decimal.
> 2. Multiply the original amount by the percent in terms of a decimal.
> 3. Add on sales tax or increase to the original amount.

Example 1: Philip earns $85,000. He receives an 8% increase in salary. What is his new salary?

Solution: STEP 1: Change 8% to a decimal.
                      8% = .08

              STEP 2: Multiply salary of $85,000 x .08 to find the increase in salary.
                      $85,000 x .08 = $6,800

              STEP 3: Original Salary + Increase = New Salary
                      $85,00 + $6,800 = $91,800.

Answer: $91,800

Example 2: A coat sells for $125.00. There is a 4% sales tax. What is the total price?

Solution: STEP 1: Change 4% to a decimal.
                      4% = .04

              STEP 2: Multiply cost of coat at $125.00 x .04.
                      $125.00 x .04 = $5.00

              STEP 3: Cost + Sales Tax = Total Cost
                      $125.00 x $5.00 = $130.00

Answer: $130.00

Fill in the correct answer in the space provided:

1.   A coat sells for $90.00. There is an 8% sales tax.
      What is the total price?   Answer _____

2.   Seth Earns $29,000 a year. He receives a 6% increase in salary.
      What is the new salary?   Answer _____

3.   Eddie buys Zelma a gold bracelet for $475.00.
      If there is an 8% sales tax, what is the sales tax?   Answer _____

4.   Bill's original paycheck was $375.00. It was increased by 12%.
      How much was the increase?   Answer _____

5.   The population of New York City increased by 4% last year.
      If the original population was 8,000,000, what is its new population?
                                                          Answer _____

6.   Box seat tickets to Mets games was increased by 12%.
      Last season the tickets sold for $15.00 each.
      What do they sell for this season?   Answer _____

7.   A shirt sells for $19.50 plus a 7% sales tax. What is the total price?
                                                          Answer _____

CHAPTER GLOSSARY
Sales Tax: The amount of tax added to the selling price.

22. Verbal Problems in Discount and Percent Decrease

1.	Change the percent to a decimal and then multiply.
2.	Subtract the discount or the decrease.

SALE PRICE = ORIGINAL PRICE – DISCOUNT

Example 1: In order to keep his job, Seth took a 4% decrease in salary.
            His original salary was $95,000. What is his new salary?

Solution: STEP 1: Change 4% to a decimal
                        4% = .04
             STEP 2: Multiply the salary $95,000 by the percentage
                      decrease in salary of 4%.
                      $95,000 x 0.04 = $3,800
             STEP 3: New salary = Original Salary – Decrease
                      New salary = $95,000 - $3,800
                      New salary = $91,200
Answer: $91,200

Example 2: A coat sold for $125.00. The discount is 20%. What is the final price?

Solution: STEP 1: Change 20% to a decimal.
20% = .02 = .2

STEP 2 Multiply the cost of the coat of $125.00 by the percentage discount of 20%.
$125.00 x .2 = $25.00 Discount

STEP 3: Final Price = Original Price – Discount
Final Price = $ 125.00 - $25.00
Final Price = $100

Answer: $100.00

Fill in the correct answer in the space provided:

1. Elliot's weekly salary is $425.00. It is reduced by 9%. What is his new weekly salary?   Answer _____

2. There is a 20% decrease on all luggage. Zelma bought an attaché case that originally sold for $89.00. What is the sale price?   Answer _____

3. New York City has 8,000,000 people. It loses 7% of its population. What is the new population?   Answer _____

4. Philip earns $25,000 a year. He has 12% of his salary deducted for taxes. What is his yearly take-home pay?   Answer _____

5. A dress that sold for $37.95 is reduced by 8%. What is the sale price?   Answer _____

6. Seth buys a sweater that originally sells for $25.00. It is reduced by 35%. What is the sale price?   Answer _____

7. Milk sells for $2.40 a gallon. The price is reduced by 30%. What is the sale price?   Answer _____

8. The population of a city is reduced by 40%. If the original population was 3,300,000, what is its new population?   Answer _____

CHAPTER GLOSSARY
Discount: Amount of reduction from the original price.

23. Verbal Problems in Area, Perimeter and Cost

FORMULAS

1.	Area of Rectangle – length x width (square units).
2.	The perimeter of a closed figure is the sum of the lengths of all its sides.

PERIMETER OF RECTANGLE = 2 LENGTHS + 2 WIDTHS

Area: It is the number of square units needed to cover the surface to be measured.
Perimeter: The perimeter of a closed figure, such as a rectangle, is the sum of all the sides.

Example 1: Find the area of a rectangle whose length is 18 inches and whose width is 6 inches.

      Solution: STEP 1: Write the formula
                           Area = length x width
                           $A = lw$
               STEP 2: Substitute and evaluate
                           $A = 18 \times 6$
                           $A \times 108 \text{ in}^2$ (square inches)
      Answer: 108 inches^2

Example 2: What is the cost to carpet a room 15 yards by 8 yards at $12 per square yard?

      Solution: STEP 1: Find the area
                           $A = l \times w$
                           $A = 15 \times 8$
                           $A = 120$ square yards
               STEP 2: Multiply the number of square yards (120) by the cost per square yard ($12.00).
                           $120 \times \$12.00 = \$1,440.00$
      Answer: $1,440.00

Example 3: Find the perimeter of a rectangle whose length is 12 feet and whose width is 8 feet.

      Solution: STEP 1: Write the formula
                           Perimeter = 2 length + 2 width
                           $P = 2l + 2w$

               STEP 2: Substitute and evaluate
                           $P = 2(12) + 2(8)$
                           $P = 24 + 16$
                           $P = 40$ feet
      Answer: 40 feet

Example 4: Find the cost to fence in a garden that is 30 feet long and 20 feet wide
at a cost of $6.00 per foot for fencing.

Solution: STEP 1: Write the formula
$$P = 2l + 2w$$
STEP 2 Substitute and evaluate
$$P = 2(30) + 2(20)$$
$$P = 60 + 40$$
$$P = 100 \text{ feet}$$
STEP 3: Multiply the perimeter 100 ft. by the cost per foot at $6.00.
$$100 \times \$6.00 = \$600.00$$
Answer: $600.00

Fill in the correct answer in the space provided:

1. Find the area of a room that is 8 yards by 5 yards.   Answer _____

2. Find the area of a tablecloth that is 65 inches long
and 30 inches wide.   Answer _____

3. How much does it cost to carpet a room 9 yards by
8 yards at $7.00 per square yard?   Answer _____

4. Carpeting costs $9.00 per square yard. How much
does it cost to carpet a room 7 yards by 5 yards?   Answer _____

5. Find the perimeter of a rectangle whose length is
9 feet and whose width is 6 feet.   Answer _____

6. How much fencing is needed to fence in a swimming
pool 35 feet long and 20 feet wide?   Answer _____

7. Fencing costs $6.00 per yard. How much doest it cost
to fence in a rectangular yard that is 40 yards by
30 yards?   Answer _____

8. How much does it cost to fence in a rectangular garden
18 feet by 9 feet at $7.00 per foot of fencing?   Answer _____

9. Carpeting costs $12.00 per square yard. How much
does it cost to carpet a room 9 yards by 8 yards?   Answer _____

10. Find the perimeter of a triangle whose sides are 3,
4, and 5 inches.   Answer _____

CHAPTER GLOSSARY

Area: The number of square units needed to cover the surface to be measured. In a rectangle it is the length times the width.

Length: The longest sides of a rectangle. The measurement of distance from one end to the other—the longest side.

Perimeter: The distance around a plane figure. It is the sum of the lengths.

Rectangle: A four sided figure with opposite sides equal.

Square: A four sided figure with all four sides equal.

Width: The shortest sides of a rectangle. The measurement of the shortest sides from one end to the other.

24. Fractions

A fraction consists of the following three parts:

- **Numerator**: Is the top number of a fraction.
- **Denominator**: Is the bottom number of a fraction.
- **Fraction Bar**: Is a slash that separates the numerator from the denominator.

In the fraction $\frac{4}{5}$, the 4 is the numerator and the 5 is the denominator. The denominator tells how many parts the whole is divided into, and the numerator tells how many of these parts. The number 7 can be written as a fraction ($\frac{7}{1}$).

A fraction can be considered a division problem not complete.

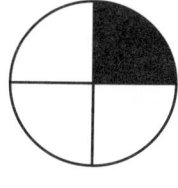   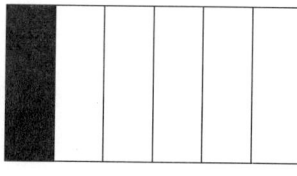   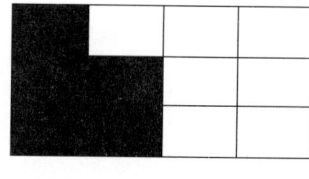

    A.   B.   C.

A.   What fractional part of the circle is shaded?

B.   What fractional part of the figure B is not shaded?

C.   What fractional part of figure C is shaded?

ANSWERS

A. $\frac{1}{4}$ B. $\frac{5}{6}$ C. $\frac{5}{12}$

25. Understanding Fractions

What is a fraction?

The word "fraction" indicates only a part of a whole, that part is something that is taken away or broken off, from a whole. Again, the whole can be anything. It could be a whole class, a whole cake, a whole group of demonstrators, or employees, etc. For example: Here is a bar of chocolate and I would like to eat $\frac{1}{2}$ of it. I am dividing the chocolate bar into 4 parts. If I intend to give $\frac{1}{2}$ of the same bar of chocolate to my daughter, that means I have to break the bar into 4 parts, and keep one half of it, which is $\frac{2}{4}$. $\frac{2}{4}$ is the same as $\frac{1}{2}$.

How a fraction is written, indicates or shows relationships between numbers. If I say that $\frac{2}{3}$ of the class is late today, that means that only $\frac{1}{3}$ of the class is punctual. In the business world it is quite common to use fraction to indicate a part of a whole; the same way, percent and decimals are used. Earlier in the chapter, we discussed the relationships between fractions and percents, and fractions with decimals.

Very clearly, a fraction also indicates division. The fraction $\frac{1}{4}$ can be interpreted as 1 divided by 4, which is 0.25, or $\frac{2}{4}$ means 2 divided by 4, which is 0.5

Understanding the parts of a fraction will help every student greatly. In the fraction $\frac{3}{8}$, the number on top of the division line is called the **numerator.** The numerator is the number of parts being considered, which is divided by the **denominator**, or the number of parts contained in the whole thing. The denominator divides the numerator. In other words, 3 becomes the dividend, and 4 becomes the divisor. Thus, in $\frac{3}{4}$, 3 is divided by 4, which is 0.75.

TYPES OF FRACTIONS

Fractions are of different types. When the numerator of a fraction is smaller than the denominator, that is called a **proper** fraction. A proper fraction has a value less than one. However, when the numerator of a fraction is larger than the denominator, the fraction is called **improper.** The value of an improper fraction is either one or greater than one.

Examples of proper fractions: $\frac{1}{3}, \frac{3}{5}, \frac{4}{7}, \frac{3}{8}, \frac{6}{15}, \frac{1}{10}, \frac{3}{7}$

Interpret the following:

Three out of five balls are blue, is written as $\frac{3}{5}$.

Seven out of nine children are girls, is written as $\frac{7}{9}$.

Eleven out of 19 buildings are commercial. The fraction is $\frac{11}{19}$.

The fractions $\frac{3}{2}$ and $\frac{5}{5}$ are improper fractions. The **value** of an improper fraction is either **one** or **more than one. In an improper fraction, the numerator is either equal or more than the denominator.**

The following are examples of improper fractions:

$$\frac{5}{2}, \frac{7}{4}, \frac{8}{3}, \frac{4}{1}, \frac{7}{5}, \frac{8}{5}, \frac{14}{12}, \frac{2}{1}, \frac{5}{4}$$

Interpret the following:

Eight over six. The fraction is $\frac{8}{6}$.

Fifteen over ten. The fraction is $\frac{15}{10}$.

Nine over four. The fraction is $\frac{9}{4}$.

What about if zero is either the numerator or a denominator of a fraction? If you have five equal parts and you wanted to take none of them? Representing that using division, the fraction would appear $\frac{0}{5}$ or $0 \div 5 = 0$.

> **Any fraction with a zero numerator equals zero; thus zero divided by any number equals zero.**

What happens if zero becomes the denominator of five? Does it make sense to take five out of zero? Any number with zero as the denominator as in 5/0, is called **undefined.**

CHANGING AN IMPROPER FRACTION TO A WHOLE OR A MIXED NUMBER

What is a mixed number? As the word itself suggests, a mixed number is a combination of a whole number and a fraction. Since an improper fraction has a value of one or more than one, when the numerator is divided by the denominator, the answer will be a mixed number.

For example: $\dfrac{7}{2} = 3\dfrac{1}{2}$

$\dfrac{8}{5}$ or $8 \div 5 = 1\dfrac{3}{8}$ $\dfrac{3}{3} = 1$

$\dfrac{12}{5}$ or $12 \div 5 = 2\dfrac{2}{5}$ $12 \div 3 = 4$

$\dfrac{8}{7}$ or $8 \div 7 = 1\dfrac{1}{7}$ $\dfrac{15}{4} = 15 \div 4 = 3\dfrac{3}{4}$

HOW TO CHANGE AN IMPROPER TO A MIXED NUMBER

RULES to remember:

---

1. Divide the numerator of the improper fraction by the denominator.
2. If the quotient (answer in division) is an exact number, that means that, the improper fraction is changed to a whole number.
3. If the quotient is not even, the whole number becomes the whole number part of the mixed number, the remainder becomes the numerator of the fraction, and the divisor, as the denominator. (If you examine the examples above, you'll understand these rules very clearly.)

Illustration: $\dfrac{21}{8} = 21 \div 8 = 2\dfrac{5}{8}$

2 is the whole number of the mixed number ($2\dfrac{5}{8}$)

5 is the remainder of the division process. 21 cannot be divided exactly by 6.

Therefore, 5 becomes the numerator of the fraction $\dfrac{5}{8}$.

8 is the divisor, and therefore, will be the denominator of the fraction.

CHANGING MIXED NUMBERS TO IMPROPER FRACTIONS

Mixed numbers and improper fractions have the same value. Changing a mixed number to an improper fraction follows the steps listed below:

1. Multiply the whole number by the denominator of the fraction;
    Example: $4\dfrac{2}{3}$

    4 is the whole number. Multiply it by 3(denominator) The product is 12.
2. The product (answer in multiplication) is then added to the numerator of the fraction.
    12 + **2**(numerator) = 14
3. Use the same denominator **3**(in the mixed number) for the denominator of the improper fraction
    Thus: the answer is: $\dfrac{14}{3}$

Try the following exercises:

Change to improper fractions: **Change to a mixed number:**

1. $4\frac{1}{2} =$ _____   1. $\frac{9}{5} =$ _____

2. $3\frac{2}{3} =$ _____   2. $\frac{11}{4} =$ _____

3. $4\frac{2}{4} =$ _____   3. $\frac{13}{4} =$ _____

4. $3\frac{4}{5} =$ _____   4. $\frac{15}{7} =$ _____

5. $5\frac{2}{3} =$ _____   5. $\frac{14}{4} =$ _____

6. $1\frac{3}{4} =$ _____   6. $\frac{18}{9} =$ _____

7. $7\frac{1}{2} =$ _____   7. $\frac{12}{3} =$ _____

8. $9\frac{2}{3} =$ _____   8. $\frac{19}{8} =$ _____

9. $5\frac{2}{4} =$ _____   9. $\frac{22}{14} =$ _____

10. $4\frac{2}{6} =$ _____   10. $\frac{32}{17} =$ _____

11. $6\frac{2}{5} =$ _____   11. $\frac{31}{20} =$ _____

12. $7\frac{1}{4} =$ _____   12. $\frac{24}{19} =$ _____

13. $12\frac{3}{5} =$ _____   13. $\frac{17}{5} =$ _____

REDUCING TO LOWEST TERMS

As a general rule, all fractional units must be reduced to lowest terms. A fraction is said to be in its **lowest terms** when the numerator and the denominator cannot be exactly divided by the same number **except one.**

Rules to observe and follow in reducing fraction to lowest terms:

1. Check the numerator and the denominator of a given fraction.

    Examples: $\dfrac{3}{6}$ $\dfrac{10}{12}$

2. Find out a number that the numerator and the denominator can be both evenly divided by. If you know the factors of a number, that will be very helpful.

    In $\dfrac{3}{6}$, both the numerator and the denominator can be divided by 3.

    Right? $3 \div 3 = 1$ and $6 \div 3 = 2$.

    Therefore, the reduced fraction of $\dfrac{3}{6}$ is $\dfrac{1}{2}$.

    In $\dfrac{10}{12}$, both the numerator and the denominator can be divided by 2.

    Correct? $10 \div 2 = 5$ and $12 \div 2 = 6$. The lowest terms of $\dfrac{10}{12}$ is $\dfrac{5}{6}$.

3. Sometimes the whole number you choose to have the numerator and the denominator to be divided is not the largest number to divide them both. Thus, the fraction is not yet reduced to its lowest terms. If this happens, always check the fraction, and apply Rule #2, until you get the reduced or prime fraction. Remember, a reduced fraction can only be divided by one.

4. The quickest way to reduce fractions to lowest terms is to divide the numerator and the denominator by the GCD (greatest common denominator).

Reduce the following fractions to lowest terms:

1. $\dfrac{2}{4}$ = _____   2. $\dfrac{3}{4}$ = _____

3. $\dfrac{3}{9}$ = _____   4. $\dfrac{4}{8}$ = _____

5. $\dfrac{10}{12}$ = _____   6. $\dfrac{3}{12}$ = _____

7. $\dfrac{12}{15}$ = _____   8. $\dfrac{9}{15}$ = _____

9. $\dfrac{11}{22} = $ _____

10. $\dfrac{12}{24} = $ _____

11. $\dfrac{13}{24} = $ _____

12. $\dfrac{8}{9} = $ _____

13. $\dfrac{21}{28} = $ _____

14. $\dfrac{6}{18} = $ _____

15. $\dfrac{3}{15} = $ _____

16. $\dfrac{7}{14} = $ _____

17. $\dfrac{5}{20} = $ _____

18. $\dfrac{9}{30} = $ _____

19. $\dfrac{4}{28} = $ _____

20. $\dfrac{12}{60} = $ _____

EQUIVALENT FRACTIONS

To find the equivalent fractions of those fractions in its simplest form, simply multiply both numerator and denominator by the same number. For example: **2/3** is in its reduced form. If we multiply this fraction by **2** (both the numerator and the denominator), the **equivalent fraction**, will be **4/6**. Equivalent fraction means, two or three fractions that have the same value. One of these fractions is in its reduced form and the two could be in their higher form.

Examples: $\dfrac{3}{4}$ is equivalent to $\dfrac{9}{12}$. What number did you multiply both the numerator and the denominator? The number is 3.

Similarly, if you choose to multiply $\dfrac{3}{4}$ by 5, the equivalent fraction is $\dfrac{15}{20}$, or if you use 2 to multiply the numerator 3 and the denominator 4, the equivalent fraction is $\dfrac{6}{8}$.

Therefore, $\dfrac{6}{8}$, $\dfrac{9}{12}$, and $\dfrac{15}{20}$ are equivalent fractions of $\dfrac{3}{4}$.

Write an equivalent fraction with the given denominator:

1. $\dfrac{2}{3} = \dfrac{}{12}$

2. $\dfrac{4}{6} = \dfrac{}{18}$

3. $\dfrac{5}{6} = \dfrac{}{30}$

4. $\dfrac{6}{10} = \dfrac{}{20}$

5. $\dfrac{1}{6} = \dfrac{}{18}$

6. $\dfrac{8}{9} = \dfrac{}{27}$

7. $\dfrac{3}{7} = \dfrac{}{35}$

8. $\dfrac{10}{22} = \dfrac{}{66}$

FINDING THE LEAST COMMON DENOMINATOR (LCD)

In adding and subtracting fractions when the denominators are not the same, the first thing to do is to find an LCD, which means least common denominator. The LCD is the smallest number which can be divided exactly by all the denominators given or by each original denominator. For example: Add $\dfrac{2}{3} + \dfrac{3}{9} =$ what? To approach this problem, inspect the denominators given which are 3 and 9. Is the least common denominator found in one of those given denominators? The answer is, yes. The LCD is 9. You can divide 9 by 3 evenly, and you can divide 9 by itself too, which is one.

WAYS OF FINDING THE LEAST COMMON DENOMINATOR (LCD)

1. The easiest and the most common is by **inspection.** The above example ($\dfrac{2}{3} + \dfrac{3}{9}$) uses this method. The given denominators are 3 and 9. Obviously, the LCD is 9.
2. The second method is by **multiplication.** After inspecting all the denominators given, and neither could be an LCD, try multiplication. For example: $\dfrac{3}{7} + \dfrac{2}{4} =$ The given denominators are 7 and 4. Neither one of them could be an LCD. Therefore, you can multiply 7 and 4, which is equal to 28. If there are more than two addends, with different denominators, use the third method.
3. The third method is by **simplification.** This is the longest, but the safest method to find an LCD when there are more fraction addends given with different denominators. It also involves more fundamental processes.

Find the sum of: $\dfrac{5}{6} + \dfrac{3}{18} + \dfrac{3}{10}$

To simplify in finding the LCD, do the following:

1. Write the denominators in a row and divide each one by smallest prime number that any of the numbers can be exactly divided by. In other words, find the least common multiple (LCM). Least common multiple means the smallest of the common multiples in a set of number.

> Hint: If majority of the numbers are even numbers, try 2.
> If most of the numbers are odd numbers, use 3.

```
2 | 6    18    10
3 | 3    9     5
    1    3     5
```

2. Write the quotients below the division line as the process continues. If the number cannot be divided by the divisor being used, just bring down the number.

```
2 | 6    18    10
3 | 3    9     5
    1    3     5
```

3. Continue this process until you have a row of prime numbers and 1s.

```
2 | 6    18    10
3 | 3    9     5
3 | 1    3     5
5 | 1    1     5
    1    1     1
```

4. Multiply together all the prime numbers you used to divide the denominators and the final quotients. The product represents the LCD of the fraction.

In this example the LCD is: $2 \cdot 3 \cdot 3 \cdot 5 = 90$

Try out exercises: Finding the LCD

1. $\dfrac{2}{3}, \dfrac{4}{5}$ = _____

2. $\dfrac{1}{4}, \dfrac{3}{5}, \dfrac{1}{10}$ = _____

3. $\dfrac{3}{5}, \dfrac{2}{6}, \dfrac{11}{12}$ = _____

4. $\dfrac{8}{12}, \dfrac{2}{10}, \dfrac{1}{5}$ = _____

9. $\dfrac{1}{3}, \dfrac{2}{4}, \dfrac{3}{36}$ = _____

10. $\dfrac{15}{30}, \dfrac{5}{10}, \dfrac{2}{5}$ = _____

11. $\dfrac{3}{4}, \dfrac{1}{5}$ = _____

12. $\dfrac{7}{8}, \dfrac{2}{3}$ = _____

5. $\dfrac{5}{6}, \dfrac{2}{4}, \dfrac{3}{12} =$ _____

13. $\dfrac{3}{16}, \dfrac{5}{8} =$ _____

6. $\dfrac{6}{7}, \dfrac{2}{3}, \dfrac{2}{2} , =$ _____

14. $\dfrac{13}{36}, \dfrac{8}{9} =$ _____

7. $\dfrac{2}{6}, \dfrac{1}{3}, \dfrac{2}{4} =$ _____

15. $\dfrac{5}{7}, \dfrac{2}{6}, \dfrac{6}{42} =$ _____

8. $\dfrac{3}{4}, \dfrac{1}{25}, \dfrac{2}{8} =$ _____

26. Adding and Subtracting Fractions with Unlike Denominators

How to Add Fractions with Unlike Denominators:

The following steps will benefit students who have difficulty in adding fractions with different or unlike denominators: When adding fractions whose denominators are unlike, follow the steps below.

Step 1. Find the least common denominator. (LCD) A least common denominator is that number wherein the denominators given divide into that number evenly.(allows no remainder).

Example: Add: $\dfrac{4}{5} + \dfrac{2}{4}$

The denominators of the fractions are 5 and 4. They are not the same. Therefore, you have to find an LCD. The LCD is 20. Why? Because 20 is the smallest number where 5 and 4 will divide into exactly.

Step 2. Once the LCD is obtained, multiply the numerators by (4 and 5), numbers, when used to multiply the given denominators will give the right product as the obtained LCD.

Example continued: $\dfrac{4}{5} \text{x} \dfrac{4}{4} = \dfrac{16}{20}$, $\dfrac{2}{4} \text{x} \dfrac{5}{5} = \dfrac{10}{20}$

Step 3.   Now, that the denominators are the same, you can add the numerators 16 and 10, whose sum is 26, and keep the same denominator.

The answer is $\dfrac{26}{20}$

Step 4.   When your sum is an improper fraction, (the numerator is larger than the denominator) like 26/20, change it to a mixed number, (divide the numerator by the denominator, and the remainder becomes the numerator of the fraction).

Therefore, $\dfrac{26}{20}$ is equal to $1\dfrac{6}{20}$.

Step 5. Reduce the fractional unit to lowest terms if it is not yet a prime fraction. (Find the largest number that can divide into both of them exactly) 6/20 is not a prime fraction yet. To reduce 6/20 to lowest terms, divide 6 and 20 by 2. Two is the largest number that can go to both of them evenly.

Therefore, the final answer is $1\frac{3}{10}$.

Adding Mixed Numbers with Unlike Denominators:

A mixed number or a mixed fraction contains a whole number and a fractional unit. Adding mixed numbers with unlike denominators basically follows the same steps discussed before; the only difference is that, the sum of the whole numbers is added to the sum of the fractional units.

> **TIP:** Don't change the mixed number to an improper fraction especially if the numbers are big. Although you will get the same answer at the end, it will kill a lot of your time. Time is of the essence. The simpler the approach, the better and less confusing it becomes.

Deal with the fractional units first. Once you get the answer from the fractional units, add that sum to the sum of your whole numbers. Simple!

Example: $5\frac{3}{7}+4\frac{5}{8}$

Step 1. The denominators are different, so find the LCD. The process involved in finding the LCD here, is by multiplication. $7 \times 8 = 56$.

Step 2. Set up the addends as in example no. 1. Multiply 3 by 8 and 5 by 7. The equivalent fractions are $\frac{24}{56}$ and $\frac{35}{56}$.

$$5\frac{3}{7}\times\frac{8}{8}=\frac{24}{56}$$
$$4\frac{5}{8}\times\frac{7}{7}=\frac{35}{56}$$

Step 3. Add 24 and 35 because their denominators are already similar. The sum of the numerators is 59 over 56. $\frac{59}{56}$

Step 4. Change 59/56 to a mixed number. Divide 56 into 59. The quotient is $1\frac{3}{56}$.

Is $1\frac{3}{56}$, a reduced fraction already? Yes, because there is no other number that can divide both of them except one and itself.

Step 5. Add the whole numbers (5 + 4) in the problem. The sum is 9. Add 9 to $1\frac{3}{56}$, which is equal to $10\frac{3}{56}$.

Try the following examples: After doing 10 to 20 examples, you will be able to master the procedure.

TIP: One more effective way of adding fractions or mixed numbers when the fractional units are in large numbers and with different denominators, is to reduce them to lowest terms right away. This way, you get rid of big numbers. It's easier to deal with smaller numbers. Remember, when you reduce the fractional units to lowest terms, their values remain the same.

Add the following fractions/mixed numbers:

1. $\dfrac{3}{10} + \dfrac{2}{5} = $ _____

2. $\dfrac{4}{7} + \dfrac{1}{2} = $ _____

3. $\dfrac{5}{6} + \dfrac{3}{4} = $ _____

4. $\dfrac{2}{4} + \dfrac{3}{7} = $ _____

5. $\dfrac{6}{11} + \dfrac{4}{5} = $ _____

6. $\dfrac{10}{20} + \dfrac{2}{5} = $ _____

7. $2\dfrac{1}{3} + 4\dfrac{3}{4} = $ _____

8. $6\dfrac{2}{5} + 4\dfrac{3}{7} = $ _____

9. $10\dfrac{1}{4} + 3\dfrac{5}{8} = $ _____

10. $4\dfrac{6}{9} + 2\dfrac{1}{3} = $ _____

11. $4\dfrac{2}{5} + 6\dfrac{3}{8} = $ _____

12. $\dfrac{9}{18} + \dfrac{10}{36} = $ _____

13. $5\dfrac{3}{4} + 4\dfrac{1}{2} = $ _____

14. $8\dfrac{12}{15} + \dfrac{3}{8} = $ _____

15. $\dfrac{7}{14} + 4\dfrac{2}{7} = $ _____

16. $\dfrac{5}{12} + 2\dfrac{1}{5} = $ _____

17. $4 + 13\dfrac{4}{9} = $ _____

18. $5\dfrac{9}{18} + \dfrac{10}{36} = $ _____

19. $1\dfrac{3}{6} + \dfrac{15}{36} = $ _____

20. $\dfrac{7}{8} + 2\dfrac{4}{9} = $ _____

How to Subtract Fractions with Unlike Denominators:

Like addition of fractions, numerators cannot be subtracted when the denominators are not the same. Look for an LCD also. Subtraction of fractions can vary in difficulty. There are simple problems that don't deal with borrowing. However, in case borrowing is involved and the denominators are different the steps below should be observed.

Example: $5\dfrac{4}{5} - 2\dfrac{6}{7} =$

     Step 1. Look for an LCD. 5 x 7 = 35. The LCD is 35

     Step 2. Set up the problem. The minuend is 5 ^{4}/5 and the subtrahend is 2 ^{6}/7. Find the numbers that when you multiply the existing denominators will give you the LCD. Use the same numbers to multiply the given numerators 4 and 6.

Solution:
$$5\dfrac{4}{5} \times \dfrac{7}{7} = \dfrac{28}{35}$$
$$2\dfrac{6}{7} \times \dfrac{5}{5} = \dfrac{30}{35}$$

     Step 3. $\dfrac{30}{35}$ is larger than $\dfrac{28}{35}$. Therefore, borrow one from the whole number 5. Five becomes four. The "one" that is borrowed from 5, is changed to an improper fraction $\dfrac{35}{35}$. Why $\dfrac{35}{35}$? Whatever denominator is used (in this case is 35), use the same number as its numerator.

Solution:

$$
\begin{array}{l}
\overset{4}{\cancel{5}}\,4 \times 7 = 28 \\
\quad\;\, 5 \times 7 = 35 \\
-\;\,2\,6 \times 5 = 30 \\
\quad\;\,\underline{7 \times 5 = 35}
\end{array}
$$

One becomes:
$$\dfrac{35}{35} = 1$$

     Step 4. Then, add $\dfrac{35}{35}$ to $\dfrac{28}{35}$. The sum is $\dfrac{63}{35}$. Now, $\dfrac{30}{35}$ can be subtracted from $\dfrac{63}{35}$.

$$
\begin{array}{l}
\overset{4}{\cancel{5}}\,4 \times 7 = 28 \\
\quad\;\, 5 \times 7 = 35 \\
-\;\,2\,6 \times 5 = 30 \\
\quad\;\,\underline{7 \times 5 = 35}
\end{array}
\qquad
\begin{array}{l}
+\,\dfrac{35}{35} = \dfrac{63}{35} \\[2mm]
-\,\dfrac{30}{35} \\[2mm]
\end{array}
$$

4 – 2 = 2 $\dfrac{33}{35}$ (already a reduced fraction)
(add 2 to 33/35)

The difference of the whole numbers is 2. Add 2 to $\dfrac{33}{35}$, so the final answer is $2\dfrac{33}{35}$.

TIP: Always change improper fractions to mixed numbers and reduce the fractional part to lowest terms.

Try these exercises: Follow the steps above strictly.

1. $8\dfrac{1}{2} - 5\dfrac{3}{4} =$ _____

2. $3\dfrac{1}{4} - \dfrac{7}{8} =$ _____

3. $1\dfrac{4}{5} - \dfrac{6}{7} =$ _____

4. $6\dfrac{3}{4} - 1\dfrac{4}{5} =$ _____

5. $3\dfrac{2}{3} + 2\dfrac{3}{4} =$ _____

6. $4\dfrac{1}{2} - 2\dfrac{2}{3} =$ _____

7. $10\dfrac{8}{9} - 5\dfrac{10}{11} =$ _____

8. $2\dfrac{9}{12} - \dfrac{12}{15} =$ _____

9. $5\dfrac{7}{8} + 3\dfrac{9}{10} =$ _____

10. $4\dfrac{2}{30} + 2\dfrac{4}{15} =$ _____

Subtracting a Mixed Number from a Whole Number:

When a mixed number is taken away from a whole number, do the following steps:

Example: $12 - 3\dfrac{4}{10} =$

Step 1. Set up the problem vertically. Borrow one from the whole number of the minuend (12 now becomes 11), and convert it to an improper fraction. The fraction is 10/10 which is = to one.

$$
\begin{array}{r}
11\ \dfrac{10}{ }\\
\cancel{12}\ 10\\
-\quad 3\ \dfrac{4}{10}\\
\hline
8\ \dfrac{6}{10}
\end{array}
$$

Step 2. Subtract $^{4}/10$ from $^{10}/10$. The difference is $^{6}/10$

$$
\begin{array}{r}
11\ \dfrac{10}{ }\\
\cancel{12}\ 10\\
-\quad 3\ \dfrac{4}{10}\\
\hline
8\ \dfrac{6}{10}
\end{array}
$$

Step 3. Change the fractional unit (6/10) to lowest terms. Divide both parts of the fraction by 2. The reduced fraction is $^3/_5$. The final answer is $8\,^3/_5$.

$$
\begin{array}{r}
11\ \underline{10} \\
\cancel{12}\ 10 \\
-\ \ 3\ \ \underline{4} \\
\underline{\hspace{2em}10} \\
8\dfrac{6}{10}=8\dfrac{3}{5}
\end{array}
$$

TIP: The improper fraction equivalent to one that is borrowed from the whole number is always based on the existing denominator. Use the same number as the numerator. For instance, the given denominator is 15, the fraction will be $\dfrac{15}{15}$ which is = to one.

Try these examples:

1. $5 - 3\dfrac{3}{8} =$ _____

2. $12 - 2\dfrac{7}{9} =$ _____

3. $8 - 2\dfrac{11}{14} =$ _____

4. $7 - 1\dfrac{2}{3} =$ _____

5. $9 - \dfrac{7}{8} =$ _____

6. $32 - 14\dfrac{3}{5} =$ _____

7. $15 - \dfrac{9}{10} =$ _____

8. $20 - 3\dfrac{2}{6} =$ _____

9. $25 - \dfrac{23}{25} =$ _____

10. $16 - \dfrac{4}{7} =$ _____

Subtracting a Whole Number from a Mixed Number

This type of subtraction of fraction is the simplest to do. Just bring down the fractional unit and find the difference of the whole numbers.

Example:
$$
\begin{array}{r}
20\dfrac{5}{7} \\
-\ \ 7\ \ \ \\
\hline
13\dfrac{5}{7}
\end{array}
$$

TIP: Don't forget to reduce the fractional units to lowest terms.

Perform the following indicated operations:

1. $9\dfrac{4}{10} - 5 =$ _____

2. $8\dfrac{2}{6} - 4 =$ _____

3. $17\dfrac{10}{35} - 14 =$ _____

4. $31\dfrac{4}{12} - 5 =$ _____

5. $23\dfrac{7}{21} - 4 =$ _____

6. $21\dfrac{3}{4} - 7 =$ _____

7. $6\dfrac{19}{38} - 6 =$ _____

8. $15\dfrac{8}{24} - 12 =$ _____

9. $18\dfrac{4}{16} - 6 =$ _____

10. $17\dfrac{9}{18} - 13 =$ _____

27. Improper Fractions and Proper Fraction

Improper Fraction: A fraction in which the numerator is equal to or greater than the denominator. All improper fractions can be changed to a mixed number. A mixed number consists of an integer and a proper fraction. An example is $3\,^1/_7$. To change an improper fraction to a mixed number, divide the denominator into the numerator and then reduce the fractional part of the answer to lowest terms.

Proper Fraction: A fraction in which the numerator is smaller than the denominator.

Example 1: Change the improper fraction $\dfrac{7}{2}$ to a mixed number.

Solution:
$7 \div 2 = 3$ with a remainder

of $1 = 3\dfrac{1}{2}$

Answer: 3½.

> **Rule:**
> To change an improper fraction to a mixed number, divide the denominator into the numerator. The quotient is the whole number part of the answer and the remainder is the numerator. Look at the fraction part of the mixed number to see if it can be further reduced.

Example 2: Change the improper fraction 19/12 to a mixed number.

Solution: $19 \div 12 = 1$ with a remainder of $7 = 1\dfrac{7}{12}$

Answer: $1\dfrac{7}{12}$.

> **Rule:**
> To change a mixed number to an improper fraction, multiply the whole number by the denominator and add on the numerator. This becomes the new numerator. Keep the original denominator.

Example 3: Change $3\dfrac{4}{7}$ to an improper fraction.

Solution: 3 wholes is 3 x 7 = 21 sevenths.

Add the twenty-one sevenths ($\dfrac{21}{7}$) to the four sevenths ($\dfrac{4}{7}$) = $\dfrac{25}{7}$

CHAPTER GLOSSARY

Improper Fraction: A fraction in which the numerator is equal or greater than the denominator, an example is $\frac{4}{3}$.

Mixed Number: A mixed number consists of an integer and a proper fraction. An example is $4\frac{7}{9}$.

Proper Fraction: A fraction in which the numerator is smaller than the denominator an example is $\frac{3}{4}$.

A.   Change the proper fraction to a mixed number. Fill in the correct answer in the space provided:

1. $\frac{7}{4}$ Answer _____

2. $\frac{23}{7}$ Answer _____

3. $\frac{13}{5}$ Answer _____

4. $\frac{17}{3}$ Answer _____

5. $\frac{9}{2}$ Answer _____

6. $\frac{17}{4}$ Answer _____

7. $\frac{25}{7}$ Answer _____

8. $\frac{16}{5}$ Answer _____

9. $\frac{7}{2}$ Answer _____

10. $\frac{29}{3}$ Answer _____

B. **Change the mixed number to a proper fraction. Fill in the correct answer in the space provided:**

1. $2\frac{3}{7}$ Answer _____

2. $4\frac{1}{9}$ Answer _____

3. $6\frac{1}{5}$ Answer _____

4. $5\frac{9}{14}$ Answer _____

5. $10\frac{7}{9}$ Answer _____

6. $6\frac{2}{7}$ Answer _____

7. $3\frac{2}{9}$ Answer _____

8. $12\frac{4}{5}$ Answer _____

9. $7\frac{4}{5}$ Answer _____

10. $6\frac{2}{3}$ Answer _____

28. Equivalent Fractions

Cut a pizza into two equal pieces. Each piece is half the pizza. If the pizza was cut into four equal pieces, half the pie would be two pieces (2/4). Similarly, cut the pizza into six equal pieces, half the pie would be three pieces.

Equivalent fractions are fractions that can be expressed in numerous different ways 1/2 , 2/4, and 3/6.

 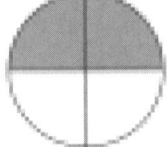 

What is an equivalent fraction to 2/7 with a denominator of 49? Divide each of the seven pieces of a pizza into 7 equal parts. Two of the original pieces give 14 smaller parts. Thus, 2/7 = 14/49.

OBSERVE THE FOLLOWING

A. $\dfrac{1}{4} = \dfrac{1}{4} \times \dfrac{2}{2} = \dfrac{2}{8}$ 　　　　 B. $\dfrac{1}{2} = \dfrac{1}{2} \times \dfrac{3}{3} = \dfrac{3}{6}$

C. $\dfrac{1}{6} = \dfrac{1}{6} \times \dfrac{4}{4} = \dfrac{4}{24}$ 　　　 D. $\dfrac{2}{9} = \dfrac{2}{9} \times \dfrac{6}{6} = \dfrac{12}{54}$

In the preceding examples, to obtain equivalent fractions, the denominator and the numerator are each multiplied by the same number.

IDENTITY PROPERTY FOR MULTIPLICATION

a x 1 = a

One is the identity element for multiplication.

To obtain equivalent fractions with a smaller numerator, use prime factorization.

A. $\dfrac{4}{8} = \dfrac{2 \cdot 2}{2 \cdot 2 \cdot 2.} = \dfrac{1}{2}$

B. $\dfrac{6}{18} = \dfrac{3 \cdot 2}{2 \cdot 2 \cdot 2} = \dfrac{3}{4}$

C. $\dfrac{6}{18} = \dfrac{2 \cdot 3}{2 \cdot 3 \cdot 3} = \dfrac{1}{3}$

D. $\dfrac{20}{24} = \dfrac{5 \cdot 2 \cdot 2}{2 \cdot 2 \cdot 2 \cdot 3} = \dfrac{5}{6}$

A.   Write the equivalent fractions in the space provided:

1.　$\dfrac{3}{7} = \dfrac{}{49}$ 　　　　　Answer _____

2.　$\dfrac{7}{9} = \dfrac{}{63}$ 　　　　　Answer _____

3.　$\dfrac{3}{5} = \dfrac{24}{}$ 　　　　　Answer _____

4.　$\dfrac{5}{6} = \dfrac{35}{}$ 　　　　　Answer _____

5.　$\dfrac{3}{8} = \dfrac{}{48}$ 　　　　　Answer _____

6. $\dfrac{3}{5} = \dfrac{}{150}$ Answer _____

7. $\dfrac{5}{12} = \dfrac{}{60}$ Answer _____

8. $\dfrac{4}{9} = \dfrac{36}{}$ Answer _____

9. $\dfrac{2}{5} = \dfrac{10}{}$ Answer _____

10. $\dfrac{2}{9} = \dfrac{}{27}$ Answer _____

CHAPTER GLOSSARY

Equivalent Fractions: Fractions that can be expressed in several different ways $\dfrac{1}{3}, \dfrac{3}{9}, \dfrac{4}{12}$.

29. Common Factors—Prime Factorization

It is not always easy to find any number that divides evenly into the numerator and into the denominator. A common factor is a number that divides evenly into two or more numbers. The following rules apply for numbers divisible by 2, 3, and 5.

Numbers divisible by 2: All even numbers.

Numbers divisible by 3: The sum of the digits is divisible by 3.

For example, (27: 2 + 7 = 9), which is divisible by 3.
Another example is (246: 2 + 4 + 6 = 12), which is divisible by 3.

Numbers divisible by 5: Any number that ends in 0 or 5 (20, 25, 45, 50).

Prime Factorization: is a type of factoring in which each factor is a prime. The number 18 can be factored as follows:

18 = 18 x 1
18 = 9 x 2 x 1
18 = 3 x 3 x 2 x 1
18 = 3 x 3 x 2 (prime factors)

FUNDAMENTAL THEOREM OF ARITHMETIC

Every composite number can be factored into prime factors. The factors must be arranged in the order of size.

THE GREATEST COMMON FACTOR

It is the largest factor that divides evenly into two or more numbers.

Example 1: Find the greatest common factor for 60 and 72.

> Solution: $60 = 2 \times 2 \times 3 \times 5$
> $72 = 2 \times 2 \times 2 \times 3 \times 3$
> The greatest common factors are the factors the two numbers have in common.

> Answer: GCF (60 and 72) = $2 \times 2 \times 3$

Example 2: Find the greatest common factor for 18 and 32.

> Solution: $18 = 2 \times 3 \times 3$
> $32 = 2 \times 2 \times 2 \times 2 \times 2$

> Answer: GCF (18 and 32) = 2

EXERCISE: Factor each of the following into prime factors.
Write the correct answer in the space provided:

1. 14   Answer _____

2. 48   Answer _____

3. 18   Answer _____

4. 144   Answer _____

5. 360   Answer _____

6. 81   Answer _____

7. 56   Answer _____

8. 64   Answer _____

EXERCISE: Find the greatest common factor. Write the correct answer in the space provided:

1. 9, 15   Answer _____

2. 18, 42   Answer _____

3. 27, 45   Answer _____

4. 56, 84   Answer _____

5. 80, 160   Answer _____

6. 75, 125   Answer _____

7. 144, 256   Answer _____

8. 88, 144   Answer _____

CHAPTER GLOSSARY

Common Factor: A common factor is a number that divides evenly into two or more numbers.

Composite Number: A number that can be divided by another number other than itself and one.

Fundamental Theorem of Arithmetic: Every composite number (a number that can be divided by another number other than itself and one) can be factored into prime factors.

Greatest Common Factor: The largest number that is a factor of two or more given numbers. The GCF of 9 and 12 is 3.

Prime Factorization: Prime factorization is a type of factoring in which each factor is a prime, such as 2•2•3•5 = 60.

Prime Number: Any number greater than one, which has only itself and one as factors.

30. Reducing Fractions

Fraction: It is a part of a whole. The denominator cannot equal zero.

Numerator: The top number in a fraction that tells how many equal parts of the whole are being considered.

Denominator: The bottom number of a fraction which tells the number of equal parts in a fraction. It cannot be zero.

Improper Fraction: A fraction in which the numerator is equal to or greater than the denominator.

Proper Fraction: A fraction in which the numerator is less than the denominator.

To reduce fractions to lowest teams, find an equivalent fraction with the smallest numerator and denominator.

The reduce a proper fraction to lowest terms, find the largest number that divides evenly into the numerator and into the denominator.

Example 1: Reduce $\dfrac{18}{24}$ to lowest terms.

Solution: $\dfrac{18}{24}$ Answer: $\dfrac{3}{4}$

| Divide numerator and denominator by six = $\dfrac{3}{4}$. |

To reduce an improper fraction (numerator larger than the denominator) to lowest terms, divide the denominator into the numerator and then see if the fraction part of your answer can be further reduced.

Example 2: $\dfrac{20}{6}$

Solution: $3\dfrac{2}{6}$. Reduce fraction part of your answer = $3\dfrac{1}{3}$.

Answer: $3\dfrac{1}{3}$

| Divide the denominator into the numerator = $3\,{}^2/_6$. |

Fill in the correct answer in the space provided. Reduce to lowest terms.

1. $\dfrac{3}{9}$ Answer _____

2. $\dfrac{5}{4}$ Answer _____

3. $\dfrac{24}{32}$ Answer _____

4. $\dfrac{32}{24}$ Answer _____

5. $\dfrac{18}{4}$ Answer _____

6. $\dfrac{4}{18}$ Answer _____

7. $\dfrac{24}{36}$ Answer _____

8. $\dfrac{36}{24}$ Answer _____

9. $\dfrac{17}{4}$ Answer _____

10. $\dfrac{14}{4}$ Answer _____

11. $\dfrac{18}{27}$ Answer _____

12. $\dfrac{6}{28}$ Answer _____

31. Multiplication of Fractions

> 1. Change improper fractions to proper fractions.
> 2. Cancel by reducing the numerators and denominators by the same factor.
> 3. Multiply the numerators and the denominators.
> 4. Reduce answer to lowest terms.

FACTORS

Two or more numbers when multiplied give you a product.

Example 1: $\dfrac{2}{5} \times \dfrac{1}{7}$

        Solution: Numerator and denominator have no common factors. Multiply numerators and denominators. Reduce answer to lowest terms.

$$\dfrac{2}{5} \times \dfrac{1}{7} =$$

        Answer: $\dfrac{2}{35}$

Example 2: $\dfrac{7}{10} \times \dfrac{5}{14}$

        Solution: Divide 7 and 14 by 7. Divide 5 and 10 by 5.

$$\dfrac{\cancel{7}^{1}}{\cancel{10}_{2}} \times \dfrac{\cancel{5}^{1}}{\cancel{14}_{2}} = \dfrac{1 \times 1}{2 \times 2} = \dfrac{1}{4}$$

Example 3: $3\dfrac{2}{5} \times 3\dfrac{1}{3}$

        Solution: $3\dfrac{2}{5} = 3 + \dfrac{2}{5} = \dfrac{15}{5} + \dfrac{2}{5} = \dfrac{17}{5}$

                       $3\dfrac{1}{3} = 3 + \dfrac{1}{3} = \dfrac{9}{3} + \dfrac{1}{3} = \dfrac{10}{3}$

                       $3\dfrac{2}{5} \times 3\dfrac{1}{3}$

> 1. Reduce within the problem one numerator with one denominator.
> 2. Multiply numerators and denominators.
> 3. Reduce answer to lowest terms. Divide denominator into the numerator (improper fraction). Look at the fraction and see if your answer can be further reduced.

        Solution: 1. $17/\cancel{5}_{1} \times \cancel{10}^{2}/3$

                    2. $34/3$

                    3. $11\ ^{1}/_{3}$

Fill the correct answer in the space provided. Reduce the answers to lowest terms:

1. $\dfrac{2}{7} \times \dfrac{1}{6}$ Answer _____

2. $\dfrac{3}{4} \times \dfrac{1}{9}$ Answer _____

3. $6 \times \dfrac{1}{7}$ Answer _____

4. $\dfrac{2}{3} \times 9$ Answer _____

5. $\dfrac{1}{3} \times 6$ Answer _____

6. $3\dfrac{2}{5} \times 3\dfrac{4}{7}$ Answer _____

7. $2\dfrac{1}{4} \times 1\dfrac{5}{9}$ Answer _____

8. $\dfrac{2}{3} \times \dfrac{1}{5} \times \dfrac{9}{14}$ Answer _____

9. $\dfrac{3}{4} \times \dfrac{8}{9}$ Answer _____

10. $\dfrac{2}{7} \times \dfrac{1}{6}$ Answer _____

11. $2 \times \dfrac{1}{8}$ Answer _____

12. $\dfrac{3}{5} \times 25$ Answer _____

13. $3\,^1/_2 \times 4$ Answer _____

14. $4\,^1/_5 \times 2\,^7/_9$ Answer _____

15. $2\dfrac{1}{7} \times \dfrac{7}{15}$ Answer _____

16. $\dfrac{2}{9} \times \dfrac{5}{6} \times \dfrac{18}{25}$ Answer _____

32. Division of Fractions

1. Change improper fractions to proper fractions.
2. Invert (turn upside down) the fraction after the division sign.
3. Change the division sign to multiplication.
4. Follow the rules for multiplication. Cancel and then multiply numerators and denominators.
5. Reduce answer to lowest terms.

Invert: Turn a fraction upside down.
Reciprocal: It occurs when the numerator and the denominator of a fraction are interchanged.

Example 1: $\dfrac{2}{5} \div \dfrac{7}{9}$

Divide fractions: Invert the fraction after the division sign, called the divisor, and then follow rules for multiplication.

Solution: $\dfrac{2}{5} \div \dfrac{7}{9} = \dfrac{2}{5} \times \dfrac{7}{9}$

Answer: $\dfrac{18}{35}$

Example 2: $\dfrac{7}{24} \div \dfrac{14}{23}$

Solution: $\dfrac{7}{24} \div \dfrac{14}{23} = \dfrac{\cancel{7}^{1}}{24} \times \dfrac{23}{\cancel{14}_{2}}$

Answer: $\dfrac{23}{48}$

Example 3: $6 \div 3\,{}^{1}/_{7}$

Solution: $6 \div 3\,{}^{1}/_{7}$

Improper Fraction: To reduce, divide the denominator into the numerator and see if the fraction part of your answer can be further reduced.

$\dfrac{6}{1} \div \dfrac{22}{7}$

$\dfrac{\cancel{6}^{3}}{1} \times \dfrac{7}{\cancel{22}_{11}}$

$\dfrac{21}{11} \Rightarrow 1\dfrac{10}{11}$

Answer: $1\dfrac{10}{11}$

Fill in the correct answer in the space provided. Reduce answers to lowest terms:

1. $\dfrac{2}{5} \div \dfrac{4}{5}$ Answer _____

2. $\dfrac{3}{4} \div \dfrac{6}{7}$ Answer _____

3. $6 \div \dfrac{1}{8}$ Answer _____

4. $\dfrac{2}{7} \div 4$ Answer _____

5. $\dfrac{2}{3} \div \dfrac{5}{9}$ Answer _____

6. $1\dfrac{2}{3} \div 5$ Answer _____

7. $2\dfrac{1}{4} \div 3\dfrac{3}{8}$ Answer _____

8. $4\dfrac{2}{5} \div 1\dfrac{1}{10}$ Answer _____

9. $\dfrac{2}{9} \div \dfrac{2}{27}$ Answer _____

10. $\dfrac{2}{9} \div \dfrac{1}{9}$ Answer _____

11. $3 \div \dfrac{1}{7}$ Answer _____

12. $\dfrac{4}{9} \div 8$ Answer _____

13. $\dfrac{2}{9} \div \dfrac{1}{6}$ Answer _____

14. $3\dfrac{2}{5} \div 1\dfrac{1}{10}$ Answer _____

15. $2\dfrac{3}{8} \div \dfrac{9}{16}$ Answer _____

16. $2\dfrac{1}{5} \div 3\dfrac{3}{10}$ Answer _____

CHAPTER GLOSSARY

Invert: It is the reciprocal of a fraction (a fraction turned upside down).

Reciprocal: Reciprocity occurs when the numerator and the denominator of a fraction are interchanged—two numbers whose product is 1.

The reciprocal of $\dfrac{2}{3}$ is $\dfrac{3}{2}$. The product of $\dfrac{2}{3} \cdot \dfrac{3}{2} = 1$.

33. Addition of Fractions

> **Rule:** If a, b, and c stand for any number and $c \neq 0$, then
> $$\frac{a}{c} + \frac{b}{c} = \frac{a+b}{c}$$

Suppose the denominators are different. Equivalent fractions must be found.

1. Fractions must have a common denominator.
2. Find the lowest common denominators (if denominators are different) and re-evaluate the numerators to find equivalent fractions.
3. Add numerators and re-write the common denominator. Also add the integral parts of the fractions if necessary.
4. Reduce answer to lowest terms.

Least Common Multiple (LCM): The least multiple excluding 0 of two or more numbers. For example, the (LCM) of 6 and 10 is 30.

> Multiples of 6 are 6, 12, 18, 24, $\boxed{30}$, 36, 42.
> Multiples of 10 are 10, 20, $\boxed{30}$, 40, 50, 60, 70.
> The least common multiple is 30.

Example 1: $\dfrac{3}{7} + \dfrac{2}{7} = \dfrac{5}{7}$

> Solution: Both fractions have the same denominator. Add the numerators.
>
> Answer: $\dfrac{5}{7}$ (Answer is already in lowest terms.)

Example 2: $\dfrac{3}{5} + \dfrac{2}{7}$

> Solution: Find the (LCD) for 5 and 7.
>
> STEP 1: Multiples of 5 are 5, 10, 15, 20, 25, 30, $\boxed{35}$
> Multiples of 7 are 7, 14, 21, 28, $\boxed{35}$, 42, 49
> The (LCM) for both fractions = 35.
> STEP 2: Reevaluate the numerator by dividing the original denominator into the new denominator and multiply the numerator by the result of the division.
>
> $$\frac{3}{5} + \frac{2}{7} = \frac{7 \times 3}{35} + \frac{5 \times 2}{35} = \frac{21}{35} + \frac{10}{35}$$

Answer: $\dfrac{31}{35}$

> Answer is in lowest terms.

Example 3: $3 \frac{2}{7} + 4 \frac{5}{7}$

Solution: $3 \frac{2}{7} + 4 \frac{5}{7} = 7 \frac{7}{7}$

$= 7 + 1 = 8$

> Add the integers and then the fraction part of the example. Reduce answer to lowest terms.

Fill in the correct answer in the space provided. Reduce answer to lowest terms:

1. $\frac{2}{7} + \frac{1}{6}$ Answer _____

2. $\frac{3}{4} + \frac{1}{8}$ Answer _____

3. $7 + \frac{1}{9}$ Answer _____

4. $\frac{2}{3} + \frac{3}{4}$ Answer _____

5. $3 \frac{6}{7} + 1 \frac{1}{7}$ Answer _____

6. $2 \frac{1}{4} + 3 \frac{5}{8}$ Answer _____

7. $\frac{6}{7} + \frac{1}{5}$ Answer _____

8. $\frac{2}{9} + \frac{1}{5}$ Answer _____

9. $\frac{5}{6} + \frac{1}{12}$ Answer _____

10. $8 + \frac{1}{4}$ Answer _____

11. $\frac{2}{7} + \frac{4}{9}$ Answer _____

12. $4 \frac{1}{5} + 3 \frac{4}{5}$ Answer _____

13. $2 \frac{3}{5} + 1 \frac{5}{8}$ Answer _____

14. $6 \frac{1}{4} + 2 \frac{3}{7}$ Answer _____

CHAPTER GLOSSARY

Integer: A whole number; not a fraction.

Least Common Multiple (LCM): The least multiple excluding 0, of two or more numbers. The LCM of 6 and 10 is 30.

34. Subtraction of Fractions

1. Fractions must have a common denominator.
2. Find the lowest common denominator (if denominators are different) and reevaluate the numerators to find equivalent fractions.
3. If the first fraction is smaller than the second fraction, borrow "1" from the integral part in the form of a fraction.
4. Subtract numerators and rewrite the denominator. Also, subtract the integral parts of a fraction if necessary.
5. Reduce answer to lowest terms.

Least Common Multiple (LCM): The least common multiple excluding 0 of two or more numbers. For example, the (LCM) of 6 and 10 is 30.

Multiples of 6 are 6, 12, 18, 24, $\boxed{30}$, 36, 42
Multiples of 10 are 10, 20, $\boxed{30}$, 40, 50, 60, 70
The least common multiple is 30.

Example 1: $\dfrac{6}{7} - \dfrac{2}{7} = \dfrac{4}{7}$

Solution: Both fractions have the same denominators.
Subtract the numerators.

Answer: $\dfrac{4}{7}$

Example 2: $\dfrac{3}{7} - \dfrac{1}{6}$

Solution:

STEP 1: Find the (LCD) for 7 and 6
7, 14, 21, 28, 35, $\boxed{42}$, 49
6, 12, 18, 24, 30, 36, $\boxed{42}$
The (LCM) for both fractions = 42.

STEP 2: Re-evaluate the numerator by dividing the original denominator into the new denominator and multiply the numerator by the result of the division.

$$\dfrac{3}{7} - \dfrac{1}{6}$$

$$\dfrac{6 \times 3}{42} \times \dfrac{7 \times 1}{42} = \dfrac{18}{42} - \dfrac{7}{42} = \dfrac{11}{42}$$

Answer: $\dfrac{11}{42}$

Answer is in lowest terms.

Example 3: $6\dfrac{1}{2} - 3\dfrac{3}{4}$

STEP 1: Find the (LCD) = 4

$6\,{}^1/_2 = 6\,{}^2/_4$ $5\,{}^2/_4 + {}^4/_4 = 5\,{}^6/_4$
$3\,{}^3/_4 = -3\,{}^3/_4$ $-3\,{}^3/_4$
                                                   $2\,{}^3/_4$

Answer: $2\dfrac{3}{4}$

Answer is in lowest terms.

Since the top fraction is smaller than the bottom fraction, borrow 1 from the 6 in terms of the fraction 4/4.

Fill in the correct answer in the space provided. Reduce the answer to lowest terms:

1. $\dfrac{3}{8} - \dfrac{1}{8}$ Answer _____   9. $\dfrac{3}{4} - \dfrac{1}{4}$ Answer _____

2. $\dfrac{3}{4} - \dfrac{1}{8}$ Answer _____   10. $\dfrac{2}{7} - \dfrac{2}{6}$ Answer _____

3. $3\dfrac{2}{7} - 1\dfrac{1}{6}$ Answer _____   11. $5\dfrac{2}{9} - 3\dfrac{4}{9}$ Answer _____

4. $5\dfrac{4}{9} - 2\dfrac{1}{4}$ Answer _____   12. $6\dfrac{1}{8} - 3\dfrac{2}{7}$ Answer _____

5. $6 - \dfrac{7}{8}$ Answer _____   13. $9 - \dfrac{2}{3}$ Answer _____

6. $\dfrac{5}{9} - \dfrac{1}{3}$ Answer _____   14. $\dfrac{4}{5} - \dfrac{1}{3}$ Answer _____

7. $3 - \dfrac{1}{5}$ Answer _____   15. $5\dfrac{1}{4} - 3\dfrac{2}{7}$ Answer _____

8. $\dfrac{2}{5} - \dfrac{1}{4}$ Answer _____   16. $6\dfrac{1}{8} - 4\dfrac{5}{7}$ Answer _____

35. Comparing Size of Fractions

1. Find the equivalent fraction if denominators are different.
2. Compare the numerators. The fraction with the largest numerator is the largest. The fraction with the smallest numerator is the smallest.
3. Sometimes it is easier to cross multiply and to eliminate one of the fractions. Continue this process until the largest or smallest fraction is found.

Example 1: Which of the fraction is the smallest?

a) $\dfrac{2}{15}$ b) $\dfrac{7}{15}$ c) $\dfrac{11}{15}$ d) $\dfrac{13}{15}$ e) $\dfrac{1}{15}$

Solution: Each fraction has a denominator of 15. The smallest fraction is the one with the smallest numerator.

Answer: $\dfrac{1}{15}$ Choice (e)

Example 2: Which is smaller $\dfrac{2}{7}$ or $\dfrac{1}{6}$?

Solution: Write equivalent fractions. Use a denominator of 42.

$$\frac{2}{7} = \frac{6 \times 2}{6 \times 7} = \frac{12}{42}$$

> Fractions with the same denominator—the smallest fraction—smallest numerator.

$$\frac{1}{6} = \frac{7 \times 1}{7 \times 6} = \frac{7}{42}$$

Notice: You can also obtain the answer by "cross multiplication."

$$\overset{12}{}\qquad\overset{7}{}$$

$$\frac{2}{7} \times \frac{1}{6}$$

Answer: $\dfrac{1}{6}$

Example 3: Which fraction is the smallest?

a) $\dfrac{2}{7}$ b) $\dfrac{1}{8}$ c) $\dfrac{4}{9}$ d) $\dfrac{3}{16}$

Solution: Use the process of elimination by cross multiplication:

STEP 1:

$$\overset{16}{\underset{7}{\frac{2}{7}}} \qquad \overset{7}{\underset{8}{\frac{1}{8}}}$$

Cross multiply smallest: $\dfrac{1}{8}$

STEP 2:

$$\overset{9}{\underset{8}{\frac{1}{8}}} \qquad \overset{32}{\underset{9}{\frac{4}{9}}}$$

Keep the smallest and bring down the next fraction. Cross multiply.

STEP 3:

$$\overset{16}{\underset{8}{\frac{1}{8}}} \qquad \overset{24}{\underset{16}{\frac{3}{16}}}$$

Keep the smallest and bring down the next fraction. Cross multiply.

Answer: $\dfrac{1}{8}$

COMPARING FRACTIONS (LARGEST)

Example 4: Which of the fractions is the largest?

a) $\dfrac{5}{18}$ b) $\dfrac{7}{18}$ c) $\dfrac{11}{18}$ d) $\dfrac{1}{18}$ e) $\dfrac{17}{18}$

Solution: Each fraction has a denominator of 18. The largest fraction is the one with the largest numerator.

Answer: $\dfrac{17}{18}$ Choice e)

Example 5: Which is larger $\dfrac{4}{9}$ or $\dfrac{1}{18}$?

Solution: Write equivalent fractions. Use a denominator of 72.

$$\frac{4}{9} = \frac{8 \times 4}{8 \times 9} = \frac{32}{72}$$

Fractions with the same denominator—the largest fraction—the largest numerator.

$$\frac{1}{8} = \frac{9 \times 1}{9 \times 8} = \frac{9}{72}$$

Notice: You can also obtain answer by "cross multiplication."

Answer: $\dfrac{4}{9}$

Example 6: Which fraction is the largest?

a) $\dfrac{4}{9}$ b) $\dfrac{2}{11}$ c) $\dfrac{4}{11}$ d) $\dfrac{2}{7}$

Solution: Use the process of elimination by cross multiplication.

STEP 1:

$$\overset{68}{\dfrac{4}{9}} \qquad \overset{18}{\dfrac{2}{17}}$$

Cross multiply largest $\dfrac{4}{9}$.

STEP 2:

$$\overset{44}{\dfrac{4}{9}} \qquad \overset{36}{\dfrac{4}{11}}$$

Keep the largest and bring down the next fraction. Cross multiply.

STEP 3:

$$\overset{28}{\dfrac{4}{9}} \qquad \overset{18}{\dfrac{2}{7}}$$

Keep the largest and bring down the next fraction. Cross multiply.

Answer: $\dfrac{4}{9}$

A. In each exercise, which fraction is the smallest? Write the letter of the correct answer in the space provided:

1. a) $\dfrac{2}{7}$ b) $\dfrac{1}{6}$ c) $\dfrac{3}{13}$ d) $\dfrac{2}{9}$ e) $\dfrac{2}{13}$ Answer _____

2. a) $\dfrac{1}{10}$ b) $\dfrac{2}{5}$ c) $\dfrac{2}{19}$ d) $\dfrac{3}{5}$ e) $\dfrac{6}{7}$ Answer _____

3. a) $\dfrac{1}{5}$ b) $\dfrac{3}{7}$ c) $\dfrac{2}{15}$ d) $\dfrac{1}{6}$ e) $\dfrac{2}{9}$ Answer _____

4. a) $\dfrac{2}{7}$ b) $\dfrac{1}{8}$ c) $\dfrac{3}{17}$ d) $\dfrac{1}{9}$ e) $\dfrac{2}{15}$ Answer _____

5. a) $\dfrac{3}{8}$ b) $\dfrac{2}{7}$ c) $\dfrac{1}{5}$ d) $\dfrac{2}{11}$ e) $\dfrac{1}{8}$ Answer _____

B. In each exercise, which fraction is the largest? Write the letter of the correct answer in the space provided:

1. a) $\frac{2}{9}$ b) $\frac{3}{7}$ c) $\frac{3}{5}$ d) $\frac{2}{7}$ e) $\frac{1}{4}$ Answer _____

2. a) $\frac{1}{5}$ b) $\frac{2}{7}$ c) $\frac{3}{15}$ d) $\frac{2}{17}$ e) $\frac{1}{3}$ Answer _____

3. a) $\frac{4}{7}$ b) $\frac{2}{5}$ c) $\frac{3}{17}$ d) $\frac{7}{15}$ e) $\frac{2}{9}$ Answer _____

4. a) $\frac{1}{5}$ b) $\frac{2}{7}$ c) $\frac{3}{8}$ d) $\frac{1}{6}$ e) $\frac{2}{5}$ Answer _____

5. a) $\frac{4}{9}$ b) $\frac{3}{8}$ c) $\frac{1}{8}$ d) $\frac{1}{9}$ e) $\frac{2}{7}$ Answer _____

6. a) $\frac{3}{9}$ b) $\frac{2}{7}$ c) $\frac{3}{5}$ d) $\frac{2}{5}$ e) $\frac{1}{7}$ Answer _____

7. a) $\frac{1}{2}$ b) $\frac{3}{4}$ c) $\frac{2}{7}$ d) $\frac{1}{8}$ e) $\frac{2}{9}$ Answer _____

8. a) $\frac{3}{7}$ b) $\frac{2}{5}$ c) $\frac{3}{17}$ d) $\frac{4}{19}$ e) $\frac{1}{5}$ Answer _____

9. a) $\frac{1}{2}$ b) $\frac{2}{7}$ c) $\frac{3}{19}$ d) $\frac{7}{20}$ e) $\frac{4}{5}$ Answer _____

36. Solving Verbal Problems Using Fractions

Solving verbal problems involves the use of critical thinking. Read the problem: Slowly and carefully break it up into small segments. Interpret each segment as follows: given, prove, and method used.

Example 1: If 1 pound of beef costs \$5.25, what is the cost of $2\frac{2}{3}$ pounds of beef?

GIVEN: PROVE:

1 pound cost \$ 5.25   Cost of 2 $^2/_3$ pounds

METHOD: Multiplication
SOLUTION: $5\,^1/_4$ x $2\,^2/_3$

$$\frac{\overset{7}{\cancel{21}}}{\underset{1}{\cancel{4}}} \times \frac{\overset{2}{\cancel{8}}}{\underset{1}{\cancel{3}}}$$

Answer: $\dfrac{14}{1} = \$14$

Example 2: Seth spent $\dfrac{2}{7}$ of the day working and $\dfrac{1}{6}$ of the day playing chess. What part of the day was left over for Seth to do what he wants?

GIVEN: PROVE:

1. $\dfrac{2}{7}$ day working   Part of day left over

2. $\dfrac{1}{6}$ day playing chess

METHOD   1. Addition 2. Subtraction
SOLUTION:

1. Addition:

$$\frac{2}{7} + \frac{1}{6}$$

$$\frac{2 \times 6}{42} + \frac{1 \times 7}{42}$$

$$\frac{12}{42} + \frac{7}{42} = \frac{19}{42}$$

2. Subtraction:

$$1 - \frac{19}{42}$$

$$\frac{42}{42} - \frac{19}{42}$$

Answer: $\dfrac{23}{42}$

EXERCISE: Solve each of the following verbal problems: Fill in the correct answer in the space provided:

1. Zelma purchased $7\frac{3}{4}$ yards of linen to make a dress.

   She used $3\frac{2}{3}$ yards. How much linen is not used?   Answer _____

2. Phil bought a suit for $300. He put $\frac{1}{3}$ down as a deposit.

   How much does he owe?   Answer _____

3. Phil has a full tank of gasoline. He used $\frac{2}{3}$ of the tank

   driving to see his brother Elliot and to see his other brother
   Seth. How much gasoline did he use?   Answer _____

4. $\frac{2}{3}$ of what number is 90?   Answer _____

5. Find $\frac{2}{3}$ of $\frac{1}{6}$.   Answer _____

6. Zelma and Eddie purchased a house for $609,000. They

   are required to put a $\frac{1}{3}$ down payment in order to obtain

   a mortgage. How much is the mortgage?   Answer _____

7. On her butcher bill Zelma saw an item for $17 for $4\frac{1}{4}$

   pounds of steak. What was the cost per pound?   Answer _____

8. Elliot spent $\frac{1}{3}$ of the day sleeping, $\frac{1}{6}$ of the day in

   school and $\frac{1}{4}$ of the day commuting. What part of the

   day was left over for Elliot to do as he wishes?   Answer _____

9. Elliot and his brothers decided to drive from New York City

   to Miami. They kept track of the traveling time: Monday $9\frac{3}{4}$

   hours, Tuesday $8\frac{2}{3}$ hours, and Wednesday $8\frac{1}{2}$ hours.

   How many hours did they travel?   Answer _____

10. Steel is composed of $\frac{2}{3}$ iron. How much iron is in 12 tons

    of steel?   Answer _____

37. Measurements—Exponential Notation

METRIC SYSTEM:

The metric system of measurements is based on multiples of 10. It first surfaced in France around 1640. However, it was not accepted until after the French Revolution in 1791. The United States uses the English System of Measurement. However, the Trade Act of 1988 forced the federal government to adopt the metric system. The Metric System has become the International System of Measurement.

POWERS OF 10

Exponential notation is a short form of multiplication.

1. For example, $10^4 = 10 \times 10 \times 10 \times 10 = 10,000$.
    100,000   10,000   1,000   100   10   1

2. Instead of writing numbers out, we could use exponential notation.
    10^5 10^4 10^3 10^2 10^1 10^0

3. Look at the pattern for exponents in place value.
    $5 \rightarrow 4 \rightarrow 3 \rightarrow 2 \rightarrow 1 \rightarrow ?$

4. If this pattern is accurate the next exponent is 0. Thus, the next exponent is 0.
    $10^0 = 1$.

5. Moving from left to right among place values indicates each time we divide by 10.
    $10^5 \div 10 = 10^4$ and $10^4 \div 10 = 10^3$. The exponent decreases by 1 each time one divides by 10.

6. Thus, $10^1 \div 10 = 10^{1-1} = 10^0 = 1$.
    Not only $10^0 = 1$, but also any number raised to the zero power $= 1$.
    For example, $6^2 \div 6^2 = 36 \div 36 = 1$; or $6^2 \div 6^2 = 6^{2-2} = 6^0$.

DEFINITION

Any non-zero number raised to the zero power is equal to 1. 0^0 is not defined.

1. Place values with negative exponents are located to the right of the units place.
    0.1   0.01   0.001
    Tenth   Hundredth   Thousandth

2. Written in exponential notation, we have:
    10^{-1} 10^{-2} 10^{-3}

3. In conclusion:
    $10^{-1} = 0.1$ $10^{-2} = 0.01$ $10^{-3} = 0.001$

4.   Also, it follows:
$10^{-1} = 0.1 = 1/10$
$10^{-2} = 0.01 = 1/100$
$10^{-3} = 0.001 = 1/1000$

Example 1: Write 10^{-6} in fractional and decimal form.

  Solution: $10^{-6} = 1/10^6 = 0.000001$.

Example 2: Write 0.000001 in fractional and exponential form.

  Solution: $0.000001 = 1/1,000,000 = 1/10^6 = 10^{-6}$.

EXERCISE: Write the correct answer in the space provided:

1. Write as a fraction and as a decimal.
  a) 10^{-6} Answer _____
  b) 10^{-4} Answer _____
  c) 10^{-5} Answer _____
  d) 10^{-2} Answer _____
  e) 10^{-3} Answer _____

2. Write in exponential notation and as a decimal.
  a) 1/10,000   Answer _____
  b) 1/100,000   Answer _____
  c) 1/1,000   Answer _____
  d) 1/1,000,000   Answer _____

3. Write in exponential notation and as a fraction.
  a) 0.00001   Answer _____
  b) 0.001   Answer _____
  c) 0.0000001   Answer _____
  d) 0.000001   Answer _____

38. Multiplication and Division by Powers of 10

If a decimal is multiplied by 10, the decimal point is moved one place to the right. When multiplying a decimal by 100, move the decimal point two places to the right, and so on.

Example 1: Multiply 0.0475×10^4.

  Solution: Move decimal point four places to the right.
      $0.0475 \times 10^4 = 475$.

Example 2: Multiply 75×10^{-6}.

  Solution: Move decimal point six places to the left.
      $75 \times 10^{-6} = 0.000075$.

Example 3: Divide $639 \div 10^3$.

    Solution: Move decimal point three places to the left.
                    $639 \div 10^3 = 0.639$

Example 4: Divide $0.6 \div 10^{-3}$

    Solution: Move decimal point three places to the right.
                    $0.6 \div 10^{-3} = 600$.

Rule:

Multiply:	**Move decimal point**
10^1	1 place → right
10^2	2 places → right
10^3	3 places → right
10^{-1}	1 place → left
10^{-2}	2 places → left
10^{-3}	3 places → left

Divide	**Move decimal point**
10^1	1 place → left
10^2	2 places → left
10^3	3 places → left
10^{-1}	1 place → right
10^{-2}	2 places → right
10^{-3}	3 places → right

EXERCISE: Multiply. Write the correct answer in the space provided:

1) 2.654×10^3 Answer _____

2) 12.7×10^2 Answer _____

3) 34.75×10^3 Answer _____

4) 16.75×10 Answer _____

5) 430×10^{-2} Answer _____

6) 6.75×10^{-3} Answer _____

7) 3.956×10^{-4} Answer _____

8) 6.75×10^{-6} Answer _____

EXERCISE: Divide: Write the correct answer in the space provided:

1) $650 \div 10^2$ Answer _____

2) $17.3 \div 10^4$ Answer _____

3) $0.0069 \div 10$ Answer _____

4) $0.079 \div 10^3$ Answer _____

5) $0.073 \div 10^{-1}$ Answer _____

6) $18 \div 10^{-3}$ Answer _____

7) $369 \div 10^{-2}$ Answer _____

8) $4,598 \div 10^{-6}$ Answer _____

CHAPTER GLOSSARY

English System: In this system the units used to measure lengths are the inch, foot, yard, and mile. These units are different to work with because the relations between them involve many different numbers. To measure weight, the units used are ounces and pounds. To measure volume, the units used are pints, quarts, and gallons.

Exponent: Exponent names the number of times a factor is being used. It tells the number of times a base is used as a factor. For example, $2^3 = 2 \times 2 \times 2 = 8$.

Exponential Notation: It is a short form of multiplication.

Measurement: Comparing an object with some unit of measure.

Metric System: The Metric System is a system of measurements based upon multiples of 10.

Power: The number of times a base is used as a factor.
For example, $3^4 = 3 \times 3 \times 3 \times 3 = 81$.

39. Scientific Notation and Standard Notation

Scientists use very large or very small numbers. A number written in scientific notation always has one non-zero whole number digit. 2.7×10^2 is the number 270 written in scientific notation. 0.27×10^3 cannot be considered scientific notation, as 0.27 is not a number between 1 and 10. Standard notation is the traditional way to write numbers. Examples are 3,479 and 2,003. It does not use the power of 10.

DEFINITION

Scientific notation is written as a product of a number between 1 and 10 and a power of 10.

Example 1: Write 3×10^3 in standard notation.

Solution: $3 \times 10^3 = 3,000$ (move decimal point 3 places to the right).

Example 2: Write 6.7×10^{-2} in standard notation.

Solution: $6.7 \times 10^{-2} = 0.067$ (move decimal point 2 places to the left).

Example 3: Write 357.6 in scientific notation.

Solution: The decimal belongs after the 3. Divide by 100.
$(100 = 10^2)$
$357.6 = 3.576 \times 10^2$.

Example 4: Write 0.0046 in scientific notation.

Solution: $0.0046 = 4.6 \times 10^{-3}$.
(The exponent is positive if you move the decimal point to the left and the exponent is negative if you move the decimal point to the right.)

EXERCISE: Fill in the correct answer in the space provided:

1. Write your answer in standard notation.
   a) 2.43×10^5 Answer _____
   b) 15.7×10^2 Answer _____
   c) 7.9×10^3 Answer _____
   d) 6.789×10^4 Answer _____
   e) 5.7×10^{-5} Answer _____
   f) 2.9×10^{-3} Answer _____
   g) 5.92×10^{-11} Answer _____
   h) 6.7×10^{-14} Answer: _____

2. Write your answer in scientific notation.
   a) 3,570   Answer _____
   b) 679   Answer _____
   c) 18   Answer _____
   d) 0.0081   Answer _____
   e) 0.071   Answer _____
   f) 2,345,678   Answer _____
   g) 0.0000003   Answer _____
   h) 0.00000018   Answer _____

CHAPTER GLOSSARY

Scientific Notation: Scientific Notation is written as a product of a number between 1 and 10 and a power of 10. For example, 2.3×10^7.

Standard Notation: A number written in the usual way and not as a power of 10. For example, 3,125 and 4,321.

40. The Metric System

Metric measurements are constantly used in our daily lives. Foods, drinks, and medicines are measured in units of the metric system. Our neighbors in Mexico and Canada use this system. The metric system of measurements is easy to learn. It is based upon the decimal system. To change from one measure to another, you multiply or divide by the power of 10.

$$1 \text{ meter} = 10 \text{ decimeters} = 100 \text{ centimeters} = 1000 \text{ millimeters}$$

When we measure an object, we compare its size (length, weight, volume) to a standard measure. The standard for length is the meter. The unit of weight is the kilogram (mass). A liter is used to measure volume.

METRIC PREFIXES

kilo (k)	=	thousand	10^3
hecto (h)	=	hundred	10^2
deka (d)	=	ten	10
deci (d)	=	tenth	10^{-1}
centi (c)	=	hundredth	10^{-2}
milli (m)	=	thousandth	10^{-3}

RELATIONSHIP OF LENGTH MEASURES

1 kilometer (km)	=	1,000m
1 hectometer (hm)	=	100m
1 decameter (dam)	=	10m
1 meter	=	1m
1 decimeter (dm)	=	0.1m
1 centimeter	=	0.01m
1 millimeter	=	0.001m

To convert between units, multiply or divide by powers of 10:

- To convert from a larger unit to a smaller unit, multiply.
- To convert from a smaller unit to a larger unit, divide.

Example 1: Convert 4.7 km to meters.

　　　Solution:　Multiply by 1,000 (move decimal point three places to the right).
　　　　　　　　km x 1000 = 4700 m.

Example 2: Convert 12 dm to meters.

　　　Solution:　Divide by 10 or multiply by 0.1
　　　　　　　　(move decimal point one place to the left).

WEIGHT (MASS) AND VOLUME UNITS HAVE THE SAME PREFIXES

WEIGHT (MASS)			VOLUME		
1 kilogram (kg)	=	1000g	1 kiloleter (kL)	=	1,000L
1 hectogram (hg)	=	100g	1 hectoliter (hL)	=	100L
1 decagram (dag)	=	10g	1 decaliter (daL)	=	10L
1 gram (g)	=	1g	1 liter (L)	=	1L
1 decigram (dg)	=	0.1g	1 deciliter (dL)	=	0.1L
1 centigram (cg)	=	0.01g	1 centiliter (cL)	=	0.1L
1 milligram (mg)	=	0.001g	1 milliliter (mL)	=	0.001L

Example 1: Convert 4.7hL to L.

Solution: 1 hL = 100L.
            Thus, 4.7 hL x 100 = 470L.

Example 2: Convert 0.03L to mL.

Solution: 1 mL = 0.001L.
            Thus 0.03 ÷ 0.001 = 30 mL.

Rule: Changing Units In The Metric System

- To convert to a smaller unit, multiply.
- To convert to a larger unit, divide.

EXERCISE 1: Convert each metric unit to the smaller unit. Fill in the correct answer in the space provided:

a) 6m   = _____ cm   e) 0.5g   = _____ cg
b) 4g   = _____ cg   f) 0.06L   = _____ cL
c) 12.1L   = _____ cL   g) 0.0030m = _____ mm
d) 25m   = _____ cm   h) 0.63g   = _____ mg

EXERCISE 2: Convert each metric unit to the larger unit. Fill in the correct answer in the space provided:

a) 300mm   = _____ m
b) 200mg   = _____ g
c) 5,400ml = _____ L
d) 240hg   = _____ g
e) 400m   = _____ g
f) 4,800ml = _____ L
g) 4,000mg = _____ g

CHAPTER GLOSSARY

Centi: A prefix that means hundredth used in the metric system.
Deci: A prefix that means tenth used in the metric system.
Deka: A prefix that means ten used in the metric system.
Distance: The amount of separation in space or time. The distance from New York to Washington, D.C.
Gram: A unit of weight used in the metric system.
Hecto::   A prefix that means hundred used in the metric system.
Length: The longest sides. The measure of distance from one end to the other.
Liter: A unit of volume used in the metric system.
Meter: A unit of distance used in the metric system.
Milli: A prefix that means thousandth used in the metric system.
Volume: The number of cubic units that fill the inside of a space figure.
Weight: Amount by which something weighs.
Width: The shortest side. The measure of distance from one end to the other.

41. The English System of Measurement Conversions Within the English System

LENGTH	WEIGHT	VOLUME
1 mile = 5280 feet	1 pound = 16 ounces	1 gallon = 4 quarts
1 yard = 3 feet		1 quart = 2 pints
1 foot = 12 inches		1 pint = 2 cups
		16 fluid ounces = 1 pint
		1 cup = 8 fluid ounces

Example: What part of a quart is 2 cups?

Solution: 2 cups = 1 pint
2 pints = 1 quart
1 quart = 4 cups
2 cups = 2/4 quart = 1/2 quart

EXERCISE: Answer the questions written below. Fill in the correct answer in the space provided:

1) How many feet are there in 1/3 of a mile?   Answer _____

2) 2/3 of a mile is equivalent to how many feet?   Answer _____

3) How many inches are there in three three miles?   Answer _____

4) How many cups of water are needed to fill
   16 one-gallon containers?   Answer _____

5) Zelma drank 8 cups of water. How many
   quarts of water did she drink?   Answer _____

6) How many one-gallon containers are needed
   to hold 34 cups of orange juice?   Answer _____

7) Each third grade student eats 4 ounces of cereal
   for breakfast. There are 35 students in Mr.Chavin's
   class. How many 1 pound boxes of cereal are needed
   to feed the class on Monday (assume no students are
   absent)   Answer _____

8) How many pounds are there in 40 ounces of juice? Answer _____

CHAPTER GLOSSARY

Cup: A United States customary unit for capacity (2 cups = 1 pint).
Foot: A United States customary unit for distance (1 foot = 12 inches).
Gallon: A United States customary unit for capacity (64 fluid ounces = 1 gallon).
Inch: A United State customary unit for distance (12 inches = 1 foot).
Mile: A United States customary unit for distance (1 mile = 1,760
            yards = 5,280 feet).
Ounce: A United States customary unit for weight. (16 ounces = 1 pound)
Pint: A United States customary unit for capacity (1 pint = 2 cups).
Pound: A United States customary unit for weight (1 pound = 16 ounces).
Ton: A United States customary unit for weight (1 ton = 2,000 pounds).
Quart: A United States customary unit of capacity (1 quart = 2 pints).
Yard: A United States customary unit for measuring length (1 yard = 3 feet).

42. Conversions Between the Customary System and Metric System

Use the following table to convert from one system to the other:

Converting Between the Customary and the Metric Systems:		
LENGTH	**WEIGHT**	**VOLUME**
1 in = 2.54 cm	1 lb = 454 g	1 qt = 0.946 L
1 km = 0.6 mi	1 kg = 2.2 lb*	1 L = 1.06 qt.
1 mi = 1.6 km	1 oz = 28 g	
	*(lb = pounds)	

Example: How many centimeters are there in 7 inches?

Solution: 1 in = 2.54 cm.
$7 \times 2.54 = 17.78$ cm.

Example: How many inches are there in 35 cm.?

Solution: 1 in. = 2.54 cm.
35 cm. $\div$ 2.54 cm. = 13.779 in. = 13.8 in. (rounded).

EXERCISE: Answer all of the following questions: Fill in the correct answer in the space provided:

1. Convert 4 tons to kilograms (1 ton = 2,000 lb).   Answer _____

2. Eddie is 5 feet 11 inches tall.
    What is his height in centimeters?   Answer _____

3. Convert 60 inches to centimeters.   Answer _____

4. Convert 5.08 centimeters to inches.   Answer _____

5. Zelma drinks 3 quarts of orange juice each week.
    How many liters of orange juice does she drink?   Answer _____

6. Bill drinks 4 liters of milk each week. How many
    quarts of milk does he drink?   Answer _____

7. Philip has a $\frac{3}{8}$ inch wrench. What would this
    be in centimeters?   Answer _____

8. Elliot weighs 90 kg. How many pounds does he weigh?   Answer _____

9. Seth wears jeans with a 36-inch waist and a 34-inch length.
    What are these measurements in centimeters?   Answer _____

10. The Junior Olympics has a 7-mile relay race.
    (1 mi = 5,280 ft). How many feet does this represent?   Answer _____

CHAPTER GLOSSARY

Conversion: To change from one measurement system to the other (Metric System
                     to the English System).

English System: In this system the units used to measure lengths are the inch, foot,
                     yard, and mile. These units are different to work with because the
                     relations between them involve many different numbers. To meager
                     weight the units used are ounces and pounds. To measure volume the
                     units used are pints, quarts, and gallons.

Metric System: A system based upon the number 10. It is also called the decimal
                     system.

43. Arithmetic Examination and Answers

ARITHMETIC EXAM #1

A. **Write the letter of the correct answer in the space provided:**

1. Find the average of 30, 40, 0, and 50.

   a) 40   b) 120   c) 30
   d) 20   e) 60   Answer _____

2. Write three million thirty thousand fifty-six.

   a) 330,056   b) 3,030,056   c) 30,056
   d) 3,030,560   e) 30,030,056   Answer _____

3. 649 – 56 equals:

   a) 593   b) 705   c) 583
   d) 603   e) 503   Answer _____

4. 11 hours 40 minutes

   –6 hours 56 minutes

   a) 5 hours 16 minutes   b) 3 hours 2 minutes
   c) 4 hours 12 minutes   d) 4 hours 44 minutes
   e) 3 hours 12 minutes   Answer _____

5. $\dfrac{3}{7} + \dfrac{1}{6}$

   a) $\dfrac{4}{13}$ b) $\dfrac{11}{21}$ c) $\dfrac{2}{21}$ d) $\dfrac{3}{42}$ e) $\dfrac{25}{24}$ Answer _____

6. $1212 \div 12$

   a) 11   b) 101   c) 202
   d) 22   e) 102   Answer _____

7. $3\dfrac{1}{6} - 1\dfrac{5}{6}$

   a) $1\dfrac{1}{3}$ b) $1\dfrac{1}{2}$ c) $2\dfrac{1}{3}$

   d) $2\dfrac{1}{2}$ e) $1\dfrac{2}{3}$ Answer _____

8. $3.08 + 30.8 + 1.2$ equals:

    a) 35.8   b) 3.58   c) 35.08

    d) 3.508   e) 350.8   Answer _____

9. $\dfrac{2}{3} \div \dfrac{1}{4}$

    a) $\dfrac{1}{6}$ b) $\dfrac{3}{8}$ c) $\dfrac{5}{8}$

    d) $\dfrac{2}{3}$ e) $2\dfrac{2}{3}$ Answer _____

10. Which of the fractions is the smallest?

    a) $\dfrac{2}{7}$ b) $\dfrac{1}{6}$ c) $\dfrac{4}{9}$

    d) $\dfrac{4}{7}$ e) $\dfrac{2}{9}$ Answer _____

11. A theater club sells 312 tickets to a play at $6.00 each. The club rents a theater for $450.00 and it has $325.00 in other expenses. How much profit does the club make?

    a) $1,547   b) $1,422   c) $997

    d) $1,457   e) $1,097   Answer _____

12. $39.1 - 12.76$ equals:

    a) 26.34   b) 16.34   c) 6.34

    d) 36.34   e) 26.46   Answer _____

13. What is 30% of 40?

    a) 120   b) 75   c) 60

    d) 130   e) 12   Answer _____

14. $3(-2)^2 + 4(-7)$.

    a) 16   b) 40   c) -40

    d) -16 e) 160   Answer _____

15. If 60% of a number is 30, find the number.

   a) 18   b) 180   c) 50

   d) 5   e) 72   Answer _____

16. Change $\dfrac{6}{7}$ to a decimal rounded to the nearest hundredth.

   a) .86   b) .85   c) .857

   d) .83   e) .81   Answer _____

17. A $20 shirt is reduced by 30%. What is the sale price?

   a) $6   b) $14   c) $12

   d) $8   e) $15   Answer _____

18. Which number is the smallest?

   a) .035   b) .305   c) 3.05

   d) .036   e) .0305   Answer _____

19. Find the cost to carpet a room 8 yards by 5 yards at $6 per square yard.

   a) $48   b) $240   c) $120

   d) $156   e) $96   Answer _____

20. 3.4 ÷ .2 equals:

   a) 17   b) .17   c) 1.7

   d) .017   e) 170   Answer _____

ANSWERS:

ARITHMETIC EXAM #1

1.	c	11.	e
2.	b	12.	a
3.	a	13.	e
4.	d	14.	d
5.	e	15.	c
6.	b	16.	a
7.	a	17.	b
8.	c	18.	e
9.	e	19.	b
10.	b	20.	a

ARITHMETIC EXAM #2

B.   Write the letter of the correct answer in the space provided:

1. Write two million thirty-seven.
    a) 20,000,037   b) 2,000,037
    c) 2,000,307   d) 200,037
    e) 200,307   Answer _____

2. 701 – 49 equals:
    a) 652   b) 750
    c) 662   d) 752
    e) 692   Answer _____

3. 2/7 + 1/4
    a) 3/11   b) 2/7
    c) 2/14   d) 15/28
    e) 6/7   Answer _____

4. 9 hours 12 minutes
    <u>–4 hours 16 minutes</u>

    a) 5 hours 56 minutes   b) 4 hours 34 minutes
    c) 4 hours 56 minutes   d) 5 hours 34 minutes
    e) 3 hours 12 minutes   Answer _____

5. 8.47 – .59 equals:
    a) 8.88   b) 78.8
    c) 64.7   d) 6.08
    e) 7.88   Answer _____

6. Find the average of 30, 40 and 80.
    a) 150   b) 50
    c) 30   d) 35
    e) 55   Answer _____

7. 1 2/3 ÷ 6
    a) 10   b) 5/18
    c) 3 3/5   d) 2/9
    e) 4/9   Answer _____

8. 3.7 + .37 + 37 equals:
    a) 4.44   b) 4.107
    c) 40.07   d) 4.007
    e) 41.07   Answer _____

9. What is 12% of 72?
    a) 8.64   b) 7.92
    c) 86.4   d) 79.2
    e) 7.64   Answer _____

10. $6(-1)^2 + 3(-6)$
   a) -24 b) -12
   c) 24   d) 12
   e) -18 Answer _____

11. If 30% of a number is 30, find the number.
   a) 9   b) 10
   c) .9   d) 100
   e) 90   Answer _____

12. Which number is the smallest?
   a) .04   b) .41
   c) .047   d) .004
   e) .0045   Answer _____

13. $2 \div .2$ equals:
   a) 1   b) 10
   c) .1   d) 100
   e) .01   Answer _____

14. Change $\dfrac{3}{7}$ to a decimal rounded to the nearest hundredth.

   a) .42   b) .428
   c) .43   d) .41
   e) .429   Answer _____

15. Express 65% as a fraction.
   a) $\dfrac{13}{20}$ b) $\dfrac{13}{100}$

   c) $1\dfrac{7}{20}$ d) $\dfrac{13}{200}$

   e) $3\dfrac{7}{20}$ Answer _____

16. 20% of the students of City College register for biology. If 200 students register for biology, how many students are enrolled at City College?
   a) 40   b) 400
   c) 10,000   d) 100
   e) 1,000   Answer _____

17. If pens sells for $.15 each, how many can be purchased for $45?
   a) 300   b) 62
   c) 3,000   d) 620
   e) 30   Answer _____

18. 3.2 x .001 equals:
    a) .3200   b) .032
    c) .0032   d) .32
    e) .00032   Answer _____

19. $3\frac{5}{8} - 1\frac{1}{4}$

    a) $2\frac{1}{2}$ b) $3\frac{3}{8}$

    c) $4\frac{7}{8}$ d) $2\frac{3}{8}$

    e) $4\frac{1}{2}$ Answer _____

20. 12 ÷ 1.2 equals:
    a) 100   b) 1000
    c) .1   d) .01
    e) 10   Answer _____

ANSWERS:

ARITHMETIC EXAM #2

1.	b	11.	d
2.	a	12.	d
3.	d	13.	b
4.	c	14.	c
5.	e	15.	a
6.	b	16.	e
7.	b	17.	a
8.	e	18.	c
9.	a	19.	d
10.	b	20.	e

PART II ALGEBRA--GEOMETRY

44. Introduction

Algebra is a course that cannot be learned by observation or by kicking your chair back and watching. To learn algebra you must be an active participant. In other words, you have to get on the playing field. You must read the text book, pay attention in class, and most important, you must do your homework. The more exercise you do, the better you will be. **Do the problem sets at the end of the chapter.**

This text was written with you in mind. Short, clear sentences are used and many examples are given to illustrate specific points. It is our goal that you come to realize that algebra is not just another math course that you are required to take, but a course that offers a wealth of useful information and applications.

You may wish to form a study group with other students in your class. Many students find that working in small groups provides an excellent way to learn the material.

You may be thinking to yourself, "I hate Math," or "I wish I did not have to take this class." You may have picked up or heard of the term, "Math Anxiety," and feel you fit this category. In order to be successful in this class you have to change your attitude to a more positive one. As authors of this book as well as instructors for this type of course, we will help you achieve this new positive attitude.

There are two very important commitments that you must make to be successful in this course. They are attending class and doing your homework regularly. You need to practice what you have heard in class. It is through doing homework that you truly learn the material. Ask questions in class about homework problems you don't understand. You should not feel satisfied until you understand all the concepts needed to successfully work each and every assigned problem.

You should plan to attend every class. There is a positive relationship between grades and attending class. Every time you miss a class, you miss important information. There is a saying that for every missed class, it takes about three classes to make it up. If you need to miss a class, contact your instructor ahead of time, and get the homework and reading assignment.

When you are in class, take careful notes. Write both numbers and letters clearly, so that you can read them later. Be sure to get help as soon as you feel you need it. Do not wait.

Where should you seek help? There are a number of resources on campus. You should know your instructor's office hours, e-mail address, and you should not hesitate to seek help from your instructor when you need it. Make sure you have read the assigned material and tried the homework before meeting with your instructor. Always come prepared with specific questions to ask. The worst thing that you could do is "throw up your hands" and say, "I don't understand this, help". You must make an attempt. This goes back to having a positive attitude.

There are often other sources of help available. Many colleges have a mathematics lab or a mathematics learning center, where tutors are available. Ask you instructor early in the semester if tutoring is available. Find out how to arrange for tutorial help and work with a tutor as needed.

Remember, follow these hints and not only will you be successful in math but you will also find math to be fun.

45.   The Real Number System

During our study of Algebra we will only work with **Real Numbers**. I know that you have heard of and have seen this term many times.

THE REAL NUMBERS

- A **Set** is a collection of objects. Sets that are parts of other sets are called *subsets*.
- **Natural Numbers:** {1, 2, 3...} These are sets of numbers used for counting.
- **Whole Numbers:** {0, 1, 2, 3...} This is the set of natural numbers with 0 included.
- **Integers:** Integers are whole numbers, not fractions.
- What are *Real Numbers*? They are a set of all rational numbers and irrational numbers. All these numbers can be represented on a number line.
- **Rational Numbers:** Any number that can be represented as a single fraction with a non-zero divisor.
- **Irrational Numbers:** They are real numbers that are not rational: $\sqrt{3}$ or $\sqrt{5}$.
- **The Number Line:** Is used to represent all positive numbers and all negative numbers.

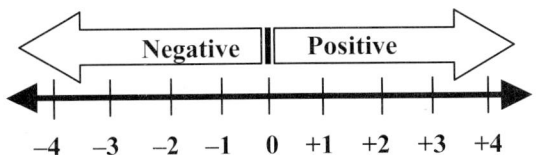

When representing a number on the number line, the distance of that number from 0 is called the absolute value. Thus, the absolute value of +2 is 2, and the absolute value of –2 is 2. The absolute value of a number is its distance from 0 on the number line. The number is represented by the symbol ||.

LET US EXPLORE THESE REAL NUMBERS.

Integer: An integer is a whole number, which can be either negative (–) or positive (+) and zero (0).

Examples: 5, –2, 300, 6, 0.

- **Rational Number:** A fraction $\dfrac{a}{b}$, where both a and b are integers and b ≠ 0.

Examples: $\dfrac{3}{4}, -\dfrac{5}{2}, -\dfrac{10}{3}, \dfrac{12}{5}, \dfrac{2}{3}$.

What about the number 6? We can express 6 as $\frac{6}{1}$. So what does this mean? The number 6 is a rational number because we can write it as a fraction: $\frac{6}{1}$. **All Integers are rational numbers, but not all rational numbers are integers.**

What about $\frac{6}{0}$? In the definition of a rational number, we can see that there can **never** be a 0 in the denominator. So $\frac{6}{0}$ is what we call **undefined**. It is correct, however, to have a 0 in the numerator. For example $\frac{0}{6} = 0$. What about $\frac{0}{0}$? I bet you would like to say that the answer is 1. You know that you can **never** have a 0 in the denominator. So $\frac{0}{0}$ is **undefined**.

Fractions can also be expressed as a decimal. For example:

$$\frac{2}{5} = .4 \qquad\qquad \frac{3}{4} = .75 \qquad\qquad \frac{1}{4} = .25$$

These decimals are called **terminating** decimals. These are also rational.

Now, what about $\frac{1}{3}$, $\frac{1}{9}$, and $\frac{2}{3}$?

$$\frac{1}{3} = .3333... = .\overline{3}$$
$$\frac{1}{9} = .1111... = .\overline{1}$$
$$\frac{2}{3} = .6666... = .\overline{6}$$

These decimals are called repeating decimals. Decimals can repeat in 1 digit, 2 digits, or as many digits as possible. These decimals are also called rational numbers. So is that it? Are there any other numbers in the **Real Number System**? You bet.

Irrational Number: Most books would probably define this as a number that is not rational. Let me do a little better job of defining an irrational number. We can say that an irrational number is a decimal that does not repeat and does not terminate. Is this a little better? The classic irrational number is π. It is 3.14....In order to terminate the decimal, we must round it off. So π or any combination of π, such as 2π or $\pi/3$ is a non-repeating, non-terminating decimal. The easiest way to identify any other irrational number is that they are all non-perfect squares.

Example: $\sqrt{4} = 2$, $\sqrt{9} = 3$, $\sqrt{25} = 5$

These numbers are perfect squares that happen to be integers and rational numbers.

How about these numbers?

$$\sqrt{2} = 1.41421356237...$$
$$\sqrt{3} = 1.73205080756...$$
$$\sqrt{8} = 2.82842712474...$$

So you see these numbers never end and never repeat themselves. These are called irrational numbers.

LET US SUMMARIZE

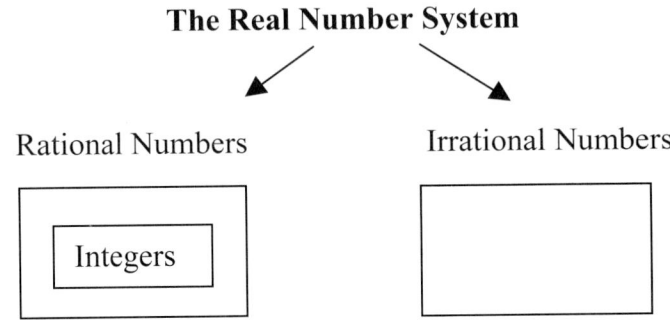

The Real Number System

Rational Numbers   Irrational Numbers

Integers

46. Properties of Real Numbers

The properties of real numbers are defined extensively in other college mathematics courses. In this text we will explain through examples those properties of real numbers that are most important in the study of algebra; namely, the **commutative**, **associative**, **distributive**, **inverse**, and **identity** laws.

THE COMMUTATIVE LAW

This property of real numbers states that the sum and product of any two real numbers is the same, regardless of the way in which you add or multiply.

$$6 + 3 = 3 + 6$$
$$3 \times 4 = 4 \times 3$$
$$.6 + .4 = .4 + .6$$
$$.6 \times .4 = .4 \times .6$$

So here is the rule:

$$a + b = b + a$$
$$a \times b = b \times a$$
$$ab = ba$$

The key word is **order**. If you want to change the order without changing the value, you can then use the Commutative Law. Also, what about: 5(2A + B) = 5(B + 2A) = (2A + B)5? Notice, all we did here is change the order. We never changed the **parentheses**.

THE ASSOCIATIVE LAW

The associative property of real numbers states that the sum or product of any three real numbers is the same, regardless of the order in which you add or multiply.

$$6 + (4 + 3) = (6 + 4) + 3$$
$$6 \times (4 \times 3) = (6 \times 4) \times 3$$

So there is the rule:

$$a + (b + c) = (a + b) + c$$
$$a \times (b \times c) = (a \times b) \times c$$
$$a(bc) = (ab)c$$

The key word is **regroup**. The easiest way to remember the Associative Law is to keep in mind three things:

1. Regroup; change parentheses.
2. Keep the same order.
3. Associate only over the same operation.

For example, 5A + (3B + 2A). Our goal as you will see later is to put like things together. That means I would like to get the 5A with the 2A. Here is why these rules are important.

Let us follow:

$$5A + (3B + 2A) = 5A + (2A + 3B)$$

What did I do here? If you remember, all I did was change the order. We call that the **Commutative Law**. Then I want to **regroup**.

$$5A + (2A + 3B) = (5A + 2A) + 3B$$

We call this the **Associative Law** and then we can say that 5A + 2A = 7A by adding. So what do we get?

$$(5A + 2A) + 3B = 7A + 3B$$

We will explore this later.

THE DISTRIBUTIVE LAW

This property actually involves the two operations of multiplication and addition or multiplication and subtraction. We might say that multiplication is "distributed" over a sum, or multiplication is "distributed" over a subtraction (difference).

$$2(4 + 2) = 2(4) + 2(2) = 8 + 4 = 12$$
$$2(4 - 2) = 2(4) - 2(2) = 8 - 4 = 4$$

Why distribute if I know that:

$$2(4 + 2) = 2(6) = 12$$
$$2(4 - 2) = 2(2) = 4.$$

This seems easier and you happen to be right. However what about this?

$$5(2A + 3B) = 5(2A) + 5(3B) = 10A + 15B$$
$$5(2A - 3B) = 5(2A) - 5(3B) = 10A - 15B$$

As you can see above, you cannot add or subtract inside the parentheses because you do not have like terms. So you must use the distributive law. So the key word in the distributive property is **parentheses**. When you see a parentheses you want to multiply and use the **Distributive Law**.

IDENTITY LAW

There is an identity property for addition and for multiplication. The number 0 (zero) is called the identity of addition (or subtraction), since adding (or subtracting) zero does not change the identity of a number.

Examples: $5 + 0 = 5$, and $5 - 0 = 5$.

The number 1 (one) is the identity for multiplication (or division), since multiplying (or dividing) by 1 (one) does not change the identity of a number.

Examples: $5(1) = 5$, and $5/1 = 5$.

Remember that the number 1 (one) may also be expressed as 6/6, 3/3, 1.5/1.5. In general, $a/a = 1$.
So what are the key words here? The key words are **change the look**. Multiplying or dividing by 1 (one), or adding or subtracting by 0 (zero) does not change the value.

INVERSE LAW

This property is used to solve an equation. There is the inverse law for addition and for multiplication.

Additive Inverses are numbers whose sum is 0 (zero).

Examples: $a + (-a) = 0$
$$5 + (-5) = 0$$
$$-5 + 5 = 0$$

MULTIPLICATIVE INVERSES:

Reciprocals are numbers whose product is 1 (one).

Examples: $a \cdot \dfrac{1}{a} = 1$

$$5 \cdot \dfrac{1}{5} = 1$$

So again, the key here is for solving an equation. We will explore this later.

LET US SUMMARIZE

	Key Word
1) **Commutative Law** $a + b = b + a$ $a(b) = b(a)$	Order
2) **Associative Law** $a + (b + c) = (a + b) + c$ $a(bc) = (ab)c$	Regroup
3) **Distributive Law** $a(b + c) = ab + ac$ $a(b - c) = ab - ac$	Remove Parentheses
4) **Identity Law** $a + 0 = a$ $a - 0 = a$ $a \cdot 1 = a$ $a \div 1 = a$	Change the Look
5) **Inverse Law** $a + (-a) = 0$ $a \cdot \dfrac{1}{a} = 1$	Solve an Equation

PROBLEM SET #1

I. Fill out the following Real Number Table:

Number	Real	Integer	Rational	Irrational	None of these
Example: 5.2	✓		✓		
1. $\frac{3}{5}$					
2. 6.285					
4. $\sqrt{18}$					
5. 2π					
6. $2\sqrt{25}$					
7. 8%					
8. 200%					
9. 5/0					
10. $-\sqrt{49}$					
11. $\sqrt{-4}$					

II State the property of real numbers (commutative, associative, distributive, identity, inverse) illustrated by each of the following:

1. $20 + 30 = 30 + 20$

2. $6 + (3 + 2) = (6 + 3) + 2$

3. $3(5 \times 4) = 3(5) + 3(4)$

4. $5 + 0 = 0 + 5$

5. $2A + 3B = 3B + 2A$

6. $5(0) = 0(5)$

7. $6 \bullet 1 = 1 \bullet 6$

8. $4 + 0 = 4$

9. $4 \bullet 1 = 4$

10. $5 \times \dfrac{1}{5} = 1$

11. $4 + (-4) = 0$

12. $5(4 \times 2) = 5(2 \times 4)$

47. Operations Involving Real Numbers

What we want to show you is how to simplify a numerical expression. What is a numerical expression? It is an expression that includes numbers and operations. Where do we make our errors? The key word here is **Signs**. Let us look at some easy rules.

RULES FOR SIGNED NUMBERS: ADDITION, SUBTRACTION, MULTIPLICATION, AND DIVISION

ADDITION OF SIGNED NUMBERS

1. When adding numbers with the same signs, keep the sign and add the numbers.

2. When adding numbers with the opposite signs, keep the sign of the larger number and take the difference.

Example 1: (−3) + (−5)

    Answer: −8

Example 2: (−6) + (8)

    Answer: 2

Example 3: −4 −7 = -11

Example 4: 6 + 2 = 8

Hint: You add when the signs are the same. Look of examples 3 and 4.

SUBTRACTION OF SIGNED NUMBERS

When subtracting numbers, change the sign of the subtrahend (the number after the subtraction sign) to the opposite sign and then follow rules for addition.

Example 1: 6 −(−5)

    Solution: The opposite of −5 is 5.
                     −(−5) = 5
                     6 −(−5) = 6 + 5 = 11

    Answer: 11

Example 2: −6 −(−5)

    Solution: The opposite of −5 is 5
                     −(−5) = 5
                     −6 −(−5) = −6 + 5 = −1

    Answer: −1

Example 3: −2 + 8 = 6

    Answer: 6

Example 4: 6 − 10 = −4

    Answer: −4

Hint: You subtract when the signs are the opposite. You take the smaller number from the larger number and keep the sign of the larger number. Look at examples 3 and 4.

PART A
Fill in the correct answer in the space provided:

1. $(-3) + (-4)$ Answer _____

2. $-2 + (+7)$ Answer _____

3. $(-9) + (12)$ Answer _____

4. $(7) + (-4)$ Answer _____

5. $-3 + (-8)$ Answer _____

6. $6 + (-7)$ Answer _____

7. $-8 + 4 - 7 + 6 - 3 + 8$ Answer _____

8. $-2 - 7 + 6 - 3 + 2 + 1$ Answer _____

PART B
Fill in the correct answer in the space provided:

1. $(-2) - (-6)$ Answer _____

2. $(-3) - (-7)$ Answer _____

3. $-2 - (-7)$ Answer _____

4. $4 - (7)$ Answer _____

5. $6 - (-3)$ Answer _____

6. $-6 - (-2)$ Answer _____

7. $9 - (-5)$ Answer _____

8. $-8 - (-6)$ Answer _____

9. $-1 - (10)$ Answer _____

10. $-3 - (-4)$ Answer _____

11. $(-2) - (-7)$ Answer _____

12. $3 - (-8)$ Answer _____

MULTIPLICATION AND DIVISION OF SIGNED NUMBERS

1. When multiplying or dividing *two* numbers with the *same* signs, the result is positive.
2. When multiplying or dividing *two* numbers with the *opposite* signs, the result is negative.
3. The product of an odd number of negative numbers is negative.
4. The product of an even number of negative numbers is positive.

For Example:

$6 \times 7 = 7 \times 6 = 42.$

$(3 \times 4) \times 5 = 3 \times (4 \times 5) = 60.$

Example 1: $3(-7)$

Solution: $3(-7) = -21$
Answer: -21

Example 2: $(-3)(-4)$

Solution: $(-3)(-4) = 12$
Answer: 12

Example 3: $(-2)(-7)(-1)(-5)(-6)$

Solution: Multiplication. An odd number of negative signs—the answer is negative.
Answer: -420

Example 4: $(-3)(-4)(-1)(-5)(-2)(-6)$

Solution: Multiplication. An even number of negative signs—the answer is positive.
Answer: 720

Division facts:

1. $a \div a = 1$ A number divided by itself equals 1.
2. $a \div 1 = a$ A number divided by 1 equals the number.
3. $0 \div a = 0$ Zero divided by a number equals zero.
4. $a \div 0 = \infty$ Undefined. A number divided by zero is undefined—not defined.

Example 1: $-6 \div 2$

      Solution: $-6 \div 2$

      Answer: -3

> Numerator and Denominator: Opposite signs in division. The result is negative (no sign by the number 2 indicates it is positive.)

Example 2: $-9 \div -3$

      Solution: $-9 \div -3$

      Answer: 3

> Numerator and Denominator: Same signs in division means the result is positive.

Hint: When you divide or multiply and the signs are the same, then the answer is Positive. When you divide or multiply and the signs are opposite, then the answer is negative.

Fill in the correct answer in the space provided:

1. $(3)(-4)$ Answer _____

2. $7(-5)$ Answer _____

3. $-6(-2)$ Answer _____

4. $(-3)(5)$ Answer _____

5. $(-1)(-2)(-4)(-1)(-7)$ Answer _____

6. $(-3)(-1)(-4)(-1)(-5)(-1)$ Answer _____

7. $\dfrac{-63}{-7}$ Answer _____

8. $\dfrac{-15}{5}$ Answer _____

9. $\dfrac{32}{-8}$ Answer _____

10. $\dfrac{-9}{-3}$ Answer _____

11. $\dfrac{-14}{2}$ Answer _____

12. $\dfrac{63}{-7}$ Answer _____

Now that we all know how to add, subtract, multiply and divide, let us put it all together.

$$6 + \frac{10}{2}$$

Do you think that you can do this? I think the answer is 8 or maybe 11. Should we flip a coin? I hope **not**. So how do we do this? Do we work left to right or right to left, or maybe inside out. Well, let us not guess or flip coins. What we need to look at is what we call the order of operations.

48. Order of Operations

RULES FOR ORDER OF OPERATIONS

1. Perform indicated operations inside the parentheses.
2. Evaluate the roots and the powers.
3. Multiply or divide from left to right.
4. If necessary, add or subtract.

- **Squaring a Number:** A number multiplied by itself.
- **Power:** It is the number of times a basis is used as a factor.
- **Exponent:** It is the number of times a factor is used.
- **Base:** The number that serves as a starting point.

Base^{Power}

1. 3^4:   3 base   4 power

2. 6^7:   6 base   7 power

For example:
1. $a^3 = a \cdot a \cdot a$
2. $2^3 = 2 \cdot 2 \cdot 2 = 8$
3. $a^5 = a \cdot a \cdot a \cdot a \cdot a$
4. $3^5 = 3 \cdot 3 \cdot 3 \cdot 3 \cdot 3 = 243$

A dot between two variables or numerals indicates multiplication.

4. $3^5 = 3 \cdot 3 \cdot 3 \cdot 3 \cdot 3 = 243$

Example 1: $3(-2 + 4)$

Solution: $3(2)$

Answer: 6

Perform operation within parentheses

Example 2: $3 - 2(4 + 5)^2$

Solution: $3 - 2(9)^2$
$3 - 2(81)$
$3 - 162$
-159

Answer: -159

Perform operation within parentheses
Powers.
Multiplication (2 numbers opposite signs, the result is negative).
Addition (2 numbers opposite signs, keep the sign of the larger number and take the difference.)

Example 3: $4(-5)^2 + 3(-7)$

Solution: $4(25) + 3(-7)$
$100 - 21$
79

Answer: 79

Power
Multiplication (left to right): Two numbers same signs, the result is positive. Two numbers opposite signs, the result is negative.
Addition: Signs are different, keep the sign of the larger number and take the difference.

PROBLEM SET #2

Simplify each of the following using the order of operations, rules for adding, subtracting, dividing, multiplying. You should also try to use the properties for real numbers.

1. -3^2

2. $(-3)^2$

3. $6(7 + 1)$

4. $8(4 - 2)$

5. $-2(8 - 4)$

6. $6(3-7)$

7. $2 - 3(7 - 4)$

8. $6 + 2(8 + 4)$

9. $3(8 + 1) + 4$

10. $7(4 + 3) - 3(5 + 9)$

11. $4(6)^2$

12. $-3(4 + 5)^2$

13. $-3 + (4 + 5)^2$

14. $6 - 7(5)^2$

15. $-3(-4)^2$

16. $-6(-3 - 4)$

17. $3 + 2(4 + 5)^2$

18. $(-3)^2 + 4(-5)$

19. $(-4 - 5)^2$

20. $(-2)^2 - 4(-3)^2$

21. $-7(4 - 2)$

22. $-3(4 + 7)^2$

23. $-3 + 2(4 + 7)^2$

24. $-4(9 + 1) - 7$

25. $7 - 8(6)^2$

26. $(-4)^2 + 3(-6)$

27. $(-2 - 3)^2$

28. $4 + 3(5 + 6)^2$

29. $-2(-4 - 5)^2$

30. $5(7)^2$

31. $6 - 2(-3)^2$

32. $-3(-4)^2 - 5(-6)^2$

49. Algebraic Expressions

An **algebraic expression** is a statement that contains any or all of the following:
    a. literal part(s)
    b. numeric part(s)
    c. signs indicating operations
    d. grouping symbols.

The **literal** part of an algebraic expression may change in value; thus it is called a **variable**. The **numeric** part remains unchanged; (IE: 3 is always 3); thus, it is called a **constant**.

    Example: The **term** $3x^2$ contains the variable x and the constants 3 and 2. This **single termed expression** is called a **monomial**.

    Example: The expression $3x^2 - 4$ contains the variable x, and the constants 2 (the exponent), 3, and 4. It also contains the operational sign. This **two-termed expression** is called a **binomial**.

    Example: The expression $3x^4 - (x^3 + 2)$ contains the variable x, the constants 3 and 2, the exponent, which is the constant 4, the operational sign, -, and the grouping symbol, ( ).

    Remembering that subtraction is the inverse of addition, and $(-x^3 - 2)$ is the additive inverse of $x^3 + 2$, we may write: $3x^4 - (x^3 + 2)$ as $3x^4 - x^3 - x^3 - 2$
    This **three-termed expression** is called a **trinomial**.

Any algebraic expression which contains **more than one term** is called a **polynomial**.

50. Interpreting Algebraic Expressions

VARIABLE
A symbol that stands for a number.

Example 1: Suppose that "b" represents a number.
        a) 2 less than a number
        b) 5 more than a number
        c) 3 times a number
        d) the number divided by 4

    Solution: a) Less than represents –, b–2
              b) More than represents +, b + 5 or 5 + b
              c) 3 times a number, 3•b or 3b
              d) The number divided by 4, b ÷ 4 or b/4

Example 2: Find the value in cents of n nickels and d dimes.

Solution: One nickel is valued at 5 cents.
n nickels = 5 x n = 5n

One dime is valued at 10 cents.
d dimes = 10 x d = 10d

n nickels and d dimes
5n + 10d

Answer: 5n + 10d

Interpret each of the following algebraic expressions in terms of "x":
Fill in the correct answer in the space provided:

1.   5 more than a number   Answer _____

2.   a number minus 7   Answer _____

3.   a number decreased by 6   Answer _____

4.   a number plus 5   Answer _____

5.   7 times a number   Answer _____

6.   4 less than a number   Answer _____

7.   a number increased by 14   Answer _____

8.   4 more than one-half a number   Answer _____

9.   3 more than 4 times a number   Answer _____

10. 6 less than 3 times a number   Answer _____

Interpret each of the following algebraic expressions. Fill in the correct answer in the space provided:

Value of Money:

1. One nickel = 5 cents
   "n" nickels = 5n
2. One dime = 10 cents
   "d" dimes = 10d
3. One quarter = 25 cents
   "q" quarters = 25q

1. Find the value in cents of "n" nickels and "q" quarters.   Answer _____

2. Find the value in cents of "d" dimes and "q" quarters.   Answer _____

3. Find the value in cents of "d" dimes and "n" nickels.   Answer _____

4. Find the value in cents of "q" quarters, "n" nickels, and "d' dimes.   Answer _____

51. Addition and Subtraction of Algebraic Expressions

> **Rules:**
> Addition and Subtraction of Algebraic Expressions

Add or subtract coefficients (numbers in front) of like terms.

LIKE TERMS
   A. Same variables.
   B. Same exponents for the same variables.

Example 1: Which are like terms?
   a) $6x^2$, $3x^2$ b) $4a^2$, $6a^3$

   Solution: a) Like Terms: Both terms have the same variable and the same exponent:
      $6x^2$, $3x^2$.

   b.) Unlike Terms: Both terms have the same variable. However, they have different exponents: $4a^2$, $6a^3$.

Example 2: $(3a + 4b) + (5a - 7b)$

Solution: Line up like terms and **add** in columns:
$3a + 4b$
$\underline{5a - 7b}$
$8a - 3b$

Answer: $8a - 3b$

Example 3: Find the sum of $3x^2 - 7x$ and $2 - 5x$

Solution: Line up like terms:
$3x^2 - 7x$
$\underline{ -5x \quad + 2}$
$3x^2 - 12x + 2$

Answer: $3x^2 - 12x + 2$

Example 4: Subtract $6x^2 - 9$ from $3x^2 - 7$.

Solution: 1) Line up like terms:
$3x^2 - 7$
$\underline{6x^2 - 9}$

2) Change signs of subtrahend (bottom number to the opposite) and then follow rules for addition.
$3x^2 - 7$
$\underline{-6x^2 + 9}$
$-3x^2 + 2$

Answer: $-3x^2 + 2$

LET US LOOK AT ANOTHER APPROACH WHEN WE COMBINE LIKE TERMS.

BACK TO EXAMPLE 3

Example 3: Find the sum of $3x^2 - 7x$ and $2 - 5x$.

Let us rewrite this statement: $(3x^2 - 7x) + (2 - 5x)$.
Since an imaginary 1 (one) is in front of both parentheses, we get $1(3x^2 - 7x) + 1(2 - 5x)$. We can use the **distributive law**. This will give us $3x^2 - 7x + 2 - 5x$. Then combine like terms. The only terms that are alike are the $-7x$ and $-5x$. Since the signs are the same we keep the sign and add. Now we will get $-7x - 5x = -12x$.
The final answer is: $3x^2 - 12x + 2$.

BACK TO EXAMPLE 4

Example 4:   Subtract $6x^2 - 9$ from $3x^2 - 7$.

Let us rewrite this statement: $(3x^2 - 7) - (6x^2 - 9)$. The **from** part **always** goes first. In other words, you will get **from** $- (\quad)$. Since there is an maginary 1 (one) in front of both parentheses, you then get $1(3x^2 - 7) - 1(6x^2 - 9)$. Let us use the **distributive law** again: $3x^2 - 7 - 6x^2 + 9$. Now combine like terms: $3x^2 - 6x^2$ and $-7 + 9$.

Remember—same signs you add and opposite signs you subtract.
$3x^2 - 6x^2 = -3x^2$
$-7 + 9 = 2$

Your Answer is $= -3x^2 + 2$

Fill in the correct answer in the space provided:

1. Add $3x + 7y$ and $6x + 8y$ Answer _____

2. Add $3a - 7b$ and $4a - 2b$ Answer _____

3. Add $6x^2 + 5x$ and $8x^3 - 7x$ Answer _____

4. Add $7b - 2$ and $3b + 7$ Answer _____

5. Find the sum of $4x^2 - 7x + 6$ and $-3x + 2$ Answer _____

6. Find the sum of $7y^2 + 3y$ and $3y^2 + 7y - 8$ Answer _____

7. Add $3a^2 - 7a + 6$ and $-7a^2 + 4a - 8$ Answer _____

8. Subtract $-3x + 6$ from $x - 8$ Answer _____

9. Subtract $-7x^2 + 8x$ from $x^2 - 8x$ Answer _____

10. Subtract $-3x^2 - 7x$ from $x - 7$ Answer _____

11. Subtract $7y - 3$ from $-7y - 3$ Answer _____

12. Subtract $-7x^2 + 3x - 7$ from $x^2 - 8x + 9$ Answer _____

13. Subtract $3x - 4$ from $x - 7$ Answer _____

14. Subtract $3x^2 - 7x + 6$ from $-3x^2 + 7x - 6$ Answer _____

15. Simplify $(7x^2 + 3x - 6) - (-x^2 + 6)$ Answer _____

16. Simplify $(-3x^2 + 6) + (3x - 9)$ Answer _____

17. Simplify $(2x^2 - 7x) + (-3x - 6)$ Answer _____

18. Simplify $(-3x^2 + 6x - 9) - (3x^2 + 6x - 9)$ Answer _____

19. $(4x + 8y) + (7x + 9y)$ Answer _____

20. Add $4a - 8b$ and $5a - 3b$ Answer _____

21. Add $7x^2 - 12x$ and $9x^3 - 11$ Answer _____

22. $(4a^2 - 7a) + (-3a + 9a^2)$ Answer _____

23. Add $-6x^2 + 9$ and $-3x + 11$ Answer _____

24. $(7b^2 - 6a) + (-3b^2 + 9a)$ Answer _____

25. Subtract $8y - 4$ from $-8y - 4$ Answer _____

26. Subtract $4x - 5$ from $x - 8$ Answer _____

27. Simplify $(-4x^2 + 7x + 10) - (-4x^2 + 7x - 10)$ Answer _____

28. Simplify $(-7x^2 - 7x - 10) - (7x^2 + 7x + 10)$ Answer _____

52. Exponent Rule for Multiplication and Monomial Multiplication

EXPONENT RULE FOR MULTIPLICATION

1. When multiplying numbers with the same base, keep the base and add the exponents.

   $(A^m)(A^n) = A^{m+n}$

2. If no exponent is written, it is understood to be 1.

> **Monomial:** Is a polynomial with only one term.
> **Binomial:** Is a polynomial with two terms.
> **Trinomial:** Is a polynomial with three terms.
> **Polynomial:** Is an algebraic expression in which all the exponents are whole numbers and in which there is no division by a variable (no variable in the denominator of a fraction).

Example 1: $c^7 \cdot c^2$

   Solution: $c^7 \cdot c^2 = c^{7+2} = c^9$

   Answer: c^9

Example 2: $a^7 \cdot a$

   Solution: Notice $a = a^1$
   $a^7 \cdot a = a^7 \cdot a^1 = a^{7+1} = a^8$

   Answer: a^8

Fill in the correct answer in the space provided:

1. $(x^2)(x^3)$ Answer _____

2. $(x^2)(y^3)$ Answer _____

3. $(a^2)(a)$ Answer _____

4. $(a^7)(a^2)$ Answer _____

5. $(2^6)(2^5)$ Answer _____

6. $(a^3)(a)$ Answer _____

7. $(y^2)(y^7)$ Answer _____

8. $(y^8)(x)$ Answer _____

9. $(y^3)(x)$ Answer _____

10. $(y^2)(y^7)$ Answer _____

53. Multiplication of a Monomial by a Monomial

RULES FOR MULTIPLICATION OF A MONOMIAL BY A MONOMIAL

1. Determine the sign of the product.
2. Multiply all the coefficients (the numbers in front of the unknowns).
3. Multiply the variables by adding exponents, if the bases are the same.

Example 1: $(-6x^2y^7)(3x^4y^2)$

Solution: STEP 1: Sign of answer –
             STEP 2: Multiply coefficients (numbers in front of the variables).
                      18
             STEP 3: Multiplication: Same base – add exponents.
                      $x^2 \cdot x^4 = x^6$
                      $y^7 \cdot y^2 = y^9$
                      $-18x^6y^9$

Answer: $-18x^6y^9$

Fill in the correct answer in the space provided:

1. $(-3x^2y)(-4xy^2)$ Answer _____

2. $(7xy^2)(-2x^4y^6)$ Answer _____

3. $(7rst)(-2rst)$ Answer _____

4. $(-6x^2y^3)(2x^3y^{8)}$ Answer _____

5. $(3ab^2c)(-4abc)$ Answer _____

6. $(-4x^3)(-8x^2)$ Answer _____

7. $(7xy^2z)(-2xyz)$ Answer _____

8. $(3ab^2c)(-4a^2bc^2)$ Answer _____

9. $(7rst^2)(-2r^2st)$ Answer _____

10. $(-6x^2y^2z)(-2x^2y^2z^2)$ Answer _____

54. Multiplication of a Monomial by a Binomial

Distributive Law of Multiplication:

This law holds for multiplication over addition.
For any three numbers a, b, and c, multiplication
before addition: $a(b+c) = ab + ac$.

Example 1: $3x^2(4x^3 - 6x)$

Solution: $3x^2(4x^3 - 6x)$
$3x^2 \bullet 4x^3$ Distributive Law

Answer: $12x^5 - 18x^3$

Example 2: $3a(a^2b + 4ab^2)$

Solution: $3a \bullet a^2b + 3a \bullet 4ab^2$

Answer: $3a^3b + 12a^2b^2$

133

For each of the products, fill in the correct answer in the space provided:

1. $3(x - 2)$ Answer_____

2. $-2(y - 4)$ Answer_____

3. $a(a + 4)$ Answer_____

4. $-b(b - 7)$ Answer_____

5. $-3x(x - 6)$ Answer_____

6. $4y(-y + 7)$ Answer_____

7. $-5z(2z^2 - 7z)$ Answer_____

8. $8x(-7x^2 - 8x)$ Answer_____

9. $5s^2(-2s + 7)$ Answer_____

10. $-4ab^2(-2a + 7)$ Answer_____

11. $7xy^2(3x^2y - 1)$ Answer_____

12. $-4ab^2(3a^2b + 3ab^2)$ Answer_____

13. $7a^2b(-4ab^2 + 3a^2b)$ Answer_____

14. $-2xy^3(3x^3y^3 - 2x^2y^2)$ Answer_____

15. $7x^2y(-3x^2 + 9y)$ Answer_____

16. $-3xy(-4x^2y - 5y^2x)$ Answer_____

17. $-4x(x - 7)$ Answer_____

18. $3x^2(6x - 7)$ Answer_____

55. Multiplication of a Binomial by a Binomial

> **Rules for Multiplication of a Binomial by a Binomial:**
>
> **Hint:** Multiply each term in the first binomial with each term in the second binomial.

Example 1: $(3x - 5)(2x - 1)$

Solution: 1. Multiply first term of each binomial to find the first term of the answer.
$$(3x)(2x) = 6x^2$$

2. The middle term of the answer is found by adding the products of the two outside terms with the two inside terms in each binominal.

$$3x(-1) = -3x \text{ outside}$$
$$-5(2x) = \underline{-10x} \text{ inside}$$
$$-13x$$

3. The last term of the answer is found by multiplying the last term of each binomial.

$$(-5)(-1) = 5$$

Answer: $6x^2 - 13x + 5$

This method is called the FOIL Method. The FOIL Method can only be used when you multiply a binomial by a binomial. What is FOIL?

F = First Terms

O = Outside Terms

I = Inside Terms

L = Last Terms

Let us look at Example 1 again:

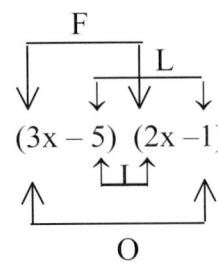

$$F = (3x)(2x) = 6x^2$$

$$O = (3x)(-1) = -3x$$

$$I = (-5)(2x) = -10x$$

$$L = (-5)(-1) = 5$$

Let us put this together:

$6x^2 - \underline{3x - 10x} + 5$

Now combine like terms: $6x^2 - 13x + 5$ is the answer.

For each of the following products fill in the correct answer in the space provided:

1. $(x - 1)(x + 3)$ Answer_____

2. $(x - 4)(x + 5)$ Answer_____

3. $(2x - 3)(2x + 4)$ Answer_____

4. $(3x - 2)(2x + 1)$ Answer_____

5. $(y - 2)(y + 2)$ Answer_____

6. $(y - 5)(y + 5)$ Answer_____

7. $(x - 7)(x + 3)$ Answer_____

8. $(x - 5)(x + 6)$ Answer_____

9. $(3x - 6)(3x + 6)$ Answer_____

10. $(2x - 4)(3x + 6)$ Answer_____

11. $(x - 2)^2$ Answer_____

12. $(x + 5)^2$ Answer_____

56. Multiplication of Polynomials

Rules for Multiplication of Polynomials:

Hint: To find the product of two polynomials, use the column method just like in long multiplication with whole numbers.

Example: $(2x + 4)(3x^2 + 2x + 2)$

Solution: $3x^2 + 2x + 2$
$\underline{\qquad\quad 2x + 4}$

$12x^2 + 8x + 8 \qquad \leftarrow 4(3x^2 + 2x + 2)$
$\underline{6x^3 + 4x^2 + 4x \qquad \leftarrow 2x(3x^2 + 2x + 2)}$

Answer: $6x^3 + 16x^2 + 12x + 8$

For each of the products, fill in the correct answer in the space provided:

1. $(x + 2)(x^2 + 3x + 4)$ Answer_____

2. $(y - 4)(y^2 + 2y + 6)$ Answer_____

3. $(2x + 1)(x^2 - 2x + 4)$ Answer_____

4. $(y + 3)(y^2 - 3y + 9)$ Answer_____

5. $(x - 2)(x^2 + 4x + 6)$ Answer_____

6. $(y - 3)(y^2 - y + 4)$ Answer_____

7. $(5y^2 + 2y + 2)(y^2 - 3y + 5)$ Answer_____

8. $(2x^2 + x + 1)(x^2 - 4x + 3)$ Answer_____

9. $(y - 5)(y^2 + 3y + 7)$ Answer_____

10. $(3x - 6)(x^2 - 4x + 7)$ Answer_____

57. Evaluating Algebraic Expressions
Rules for Evaluating Algebraic Expressions

1.	Substitute the value for the unknowns in the given expression.
2.	Evaluate the roots and powers.
3.	Multiply or divide from left to right.
4.	If necessary, add or subtract.

Example 1: Find the value of $3a - 1$ when $a = 6$.

Solution: $3a - 1$
$3(6) - 1$
$18 - 1$

Answer: 17

> Substitute $a = 6$
> Order of operations

Example 2: Find the value of $a^2 + 7a$, when $a = -2$.

Solution: $a^2 + 7a$
$(-2)^2 + 7(-2)$
$4 + (-14)$
-10

Answer: -10

> Substitute $a = -2$
> Order of operations

Example 3: Find the value of $y^2 + 3x^2$, when $x = -1$ and $y = 2$.

Solution: $y^2 + 3x^2$
$(2)^2 + 3(-1)^2$
$4 + 3(1)$
$4 + 3$
7

Answer: 7

> Substitute $x = -1$ and $y = 2$
> Order of operations

Example 4: Find the value of $x^3y + 4x$, when $x = -2$ and $y = 5$.

Solution: $x^3y + 4x$
$(-2)^3(5) + 4(-2)$
$(-8)(5) + 4(-2)$
$-40 + (-8)$
-48

Answer: -48

> Substitute $x = -2$
> and $y = 5$
> Order of operations

Example 5: If $a = -3bc$, find a, when $b = -2$ and $c = -3$.

Solution: $a = -3bc$
$a = -3(-2)(-3)$
$a = 6(-3)$
$a = -18$

Answer: -18

> Substitute $b = -2$
> and $c = -3$
> Order of operations

16. $5x + x(x - 9)$ Answer_____

17. $7x^2 + 4x^2(-x - 7)$ Answer_____

18. $3y^2 + 5y^2(y + 5)$ Answer_____

19. $3x^2 - 2x(x + 4)$ Answer_____

20. $4y^2 + 6y^2(y + 6)$ Answer_____

PROBLEM SET #3
Interpret each of the following algebraic expressions:

1.   Six more than a number

2.   A number minus eight

3.   A number decreased by six

4.   A number plus seven

5.   8 times a number

6.   5 less than a number

7.   A number increased by 14

8.   4 more than one third a number

9.   5 more than 6 times a number

10.   7 less than 4 times a number

11.   Find the value in cents of "q" quarters and "d" dimes.

12.   Find the value in cents of "n" nickels and "q" quarters.

PROBLEM SET #4
Add the polynomials:

1. $(3x + 12) + (-3x - 2)$

2. $(5x - 2y) + (3x + 8y)$

3. $(8x^3 + 5y^2 - 10z) + (3x^2 + 2y^2 + 8z)$

4. $(y^2 - y - 5) + (3y - 2y^2 + 1)$

5. $(4x^3 + 5x - 7 - 4x^2) + (4x^2 - 2x^3 + 4x - 1)$

6. $(4a^2b + 6a - 7) + (4a - 2a^2b + 5ab^2)$

PROBLEM SET #5
Subtract the polynomials:

1. $(2x - 3y + 2) - (x + y - 7)$

2. $(x^2 - 4x) - (x - 2)$

3. $(5x^2 + 2) - (3 - 2c^2)$

4. $3xy - (4x - 2xy)$

5. $(5x^3 - 6x^2 + 2x - 7) - (2x^3 - 6x - 1)$

6. $(-10xy^2 + 5x^2y) - (4xy^2 - 3x^2y)$

PROBLEM SET #6
Multiply the following:

1. $6(a - b)$

2. $2(x^2 - y - 3z)$

3. $xy(x - 2y)$

4. $7x^2(x^2 - 3x - 5)$

5. $-xy^2(2x^2y - 3x^2)$

6. $-5xyz(-2xy - 3xz - 4y^2)$

7. $(x - 3)(2x + 4)$

8. $(6x - 3)(3 - x)$

9. $(4x - 1)(3x + 5)$

10. $(x - 3)^2$

11. $(3x - y)^2$

12. $(x + 2y)(x - 3y)$

13. $(x - y)^2$

14. $(x + 3)(x^2 + 4x + 5)$

15. $(x - 5)(x^2 + 3x - 7)$

16. $(x - 4)(x^2 - x - 4)$

PROBLEM SET #7
Evaluate each algebraic expression:

1.   Find the value of $3x - 5$ when $x = -3$.

2.   Find the value of $A^2 - 8A$, when $A = -5$.

3.   Evaluate $-b^2$ when $b = -6$.

4.   Find the value of $4A + 5B$ when $A = -6$ and $B = -7$.

5.   Find the value of $x^2 + 7xy$ when $x = 4$ and $y = 5$.

6.   Find the value of $4x^3 + 7x^2$ when $x = -1$.

7.   Evaluate $-3x^2$ when $x = -4$.

8.   Evaluate $-3x^3y^2$ when $x = -2$ and $y = -3$.

9.   Find the value of $x^2 + 6y$ when $x = 5$ and $y = 6$.

10.   Evaluate $-5x^2$ when $x = -6$.

PROBLEM SET #8
Evaluate each algebraic expression after setting $x = 2$, $y = -3$, $z = -4$:

1. $x - y - (x - z)$

2. $x^2 - 3xy - z$

3. $2xy - 3(x - z)$

4. $xz^2 - (y - z)$

5. $x^2 - 4xy$

6. $x - (y - z)^2$

PROBLEM SET #9
Using the order of operations in algebra simplify each expression:

1. $4y + y(y + 8)$

2. $3x + x(x - 5)$

3. $4x + x^2(x - 7)$

4. $5y + 5y^2(-y + 10)$

5. $7x^2 - 8x(x - 5)$

6. $4x^2 + 5x^2(-x - 8)$

7. $2x + x(x - 9)$

8. $3x^2 + 6x(x - 7)$

59. More On the Rules for Exponents—Exponent Rule

EXPONENT RULE: RAISING A NUMBER TO A POWER

To raise a number to a power, multiply the exponents.

$$(x^m)^n = x^{mn}$$

Example 1: $(a^4)^2$

      Solution: $(a^4)^2 = a^4 \bullet a^4 = a^8$
      Answer: a^8

Example 2: $(x^2y^4)^3$

      Solution: $(x^2y^4)^3 = x^{2 \cdot 3}y^{4 \cdot 3} = x^6y^{12}$
      Answer: x^6y^{12}

Example 3: $(5x^2y^4)^3$

      Solution: $(5x^2y^4)^3 = 5^3x^{2 \cdot 3}y^{4 \cdot 3} = 125x^6y^{12}$
      Answer: $125x^6y^{12}$

Fill in the letter of the correct answer in the space provided:

1. $(x^4)^3$

    (a) x (b) x^7 (c) x^{12}
    (d) x^5 (e) x^{64} Answer_____

2. $(y^{12})^2$

    (a) y^{10} (b) y^{24} (c) y^{14}
    (d) y^{144} (e) y^{36} Answer_____

3. $(x^7)^2$

    (a) x^{14} (b) x^{49} (c) x^9
    (d) x^5 (e) x^{17} Answer_____

4. $(y^{15})^4$

    (a) y^{19} (b) y^{11} (c) y^{10}
    (d) y^{24} (e) y^{60} Answer_____

5. $(ab^2)^3$

    (a) a^2b (b) a^3b^8 (c) ab^6
    (d) a^2b^2 (e) a^3b^6 Answer_____

6. $(c^2d^4)^5$

    (a) $c^{10}d^{20}$ (b) $c^{15}d^7$ (c) c^3d

    (d) c^3d^9 (e) c^4d^7 Answer_____

7. $(c^5d^7)^3$

    (a) c^2d^4 (b) $c^{15}d^7$ (c) c^5d^4

    (d) c^2d^{21} (e) $c^{15}d^{21}$ Answer_____

8. $(4b^2)^3$

    (a) $16b^4$ (b) $64b^4$ (c) $12b^5$

    (d) $4b^5$ (e) $12b^6$ Answer_____

9. $(2x^2y^3)^4$

    (a) $16x^8y^{12}$ (b) $16x^6y^7$ (c) $64x^8y^{12}$

    (d) $64x^2y^{12}$ (e) $16x^8y^7$ Answer_____

60. Division of Algebraic Expressions

EXPONENT RULE FOR DIVISION

When dividing numbers with the same base, keep the base and subtract the exponents (exponent in the numerator minus exponent in the denominator).

Example 1: $\dfrac{c^7}{c^2}$

    Solution:

$$\frac{c^7}{c^2} = c^{7-2} = c^5$$

    Answer: c^5

Example 2: $\dfrac{a^7}{a}$

    Solution: Notice: $a = a^1$

$$\frac{a^7}{a} = \frac{a^7}{a^1} = a^{7-1} = a^6 \quad \text{Notice } a = a^1$$

    Answer: a^6

Fill in the correct answer in the space provided:

1. $\dfrac{x^4}{x^2}$ Answer_____

5. $\dfrac{x^3}{x^7}$ Answer_____

2. $\dfrac{a^7}{a^2}$ Answer_____

6. $\dfrac{a^6}{a}$ Answer_____

3. $\dfrac{b^7}{b}$ Answer_____

7. $\dfrac{b^6}{b^2}$ Answer_____

4. $\dfrac{x^7}{y}$ Answer_____

8. $\dfrac{x^8}{y^2}$ Answer_____

RULES FOR DIVISION IN ALGEBRA BY A MONOMIAL

> 1. Divide each part of the numerator by the denominator.
> 2. Determine the sign of the quotient.
> 3. Divide the coefficients.
> 4. Divide the variables by subtracting the exponents, if the bases are the same.

Example 1: $\dfrac{8a^2}{4a}$

Solution: Divide coefficients and then subtract exponents provided the bases are the same.

$$\frac{8a^2}{4a} = 2a$$

Answer: 2a

Example 2: $\dfrac{6b^4 - 12}{3}$

Solution: $\dfrac{6b^4 - 12}{3} = \dfrac{6b^4}{3} - \dfrac{12}{3} = 2b^4 - 4$

Answer: $2b^4 - 4$

Example 3: $\dfrac{15x^7 - 5x}{5x}$

Solution: $\dfrac{15x^7 - 5x}{5x} = \dfrac{15x^7}{5x} - \dfrac{5x}{5x} = 3x^6 - 1$

Answer: $3x^6 - 1$

Fill in the correct answer in the space provided:

1. $\dfrac{6x^2}{2x}$　　　Answer_____

2. $\dfrac{-4x^2}{-x^2}$　　　Answer_____

3. $\dfrac{6a-12}{3}$　　　Answer_____

4. $\dfrac{10y-20}{-5}$　　Answer_____

5. $\dfrac{6a^2-3a}{-3a}$　　Answer_____

6. $\dfrac{8y^3-6y^2}{-4y}$　　Answer_____

So far we have looked at some simple examples of exponents. Let us raise the bar. Simplify $x^2 \div x^4$ or x^2/x^4. Remember when you divide, you must subtract the exponents. The rule again is $x^a \div x^b = x^{a-b}$. So therefore $x^2/x^4 = x^{2-4} = x^{-2}$. It just so happens that we can never leave the final answer with a negative exponent. So $x^{-2} = \dfrac{1}{x^2}$.

Let us look at some more examples.

Example 1: $\dfrac{x^2 y^3}{x^5 y} = x^{2-5}y^{3-1} = x^{-3}y^2$

　　　Final Answer is: $\dfrac{y^2}{x^3}$

Example 2: $\dfrac{5x^{-2}}{6y^{-4}} = \dfrac{5y^4}{6x^2}$

Example 3: $\dfrac{5x^2y - 2xy^4}{x^3y^2}$

Here is what we should do. Let us rewrite the expression:

$\dfrac{5x^2y}{x^3y^2} - \dfrac{2xy^2}{x^3y^2}$　　　then

$5x^{2-3}y^{1-2} - 2x^{1-3}y^{2-2}$　　then　　　$5x^{-1}y^{-1} - 2x^{-2}y^0$

then $\dfrac{5}{xy} - \dfrac{2}{x^2}$　since $y^0 = 1$.

Remember anything raised to a zero power is 1.

Let us summarize the rules of exponents.

1. $x^a \bullet x^b = x^{a+b}$

2. $(x^a)^b = x^{ab}$

3. $x^a / x^b = x^{a-b}$

4. $x^{-1} = 1/x$ and $1/x^{-1} = x$

5. $x^0 = 1$

PROBLEM SET #10
A. Multiply and simplify the following:

1. $(x^5)^3$

2. $(y^{17})^6$

3. $(xy^3)^4$

4. $(a^2b)^4$

5. $(c^2d^5)^6$

6. $(6x^2)^3$

7. $(-3x^2y^4)^5$

8. $(3x^3y^2)^2$

9. $(-2x^2y^7)^6$

10. $(a^3b^4)^5$

11. $(2xy^4)^3$

12. $(-3xy^4)^4$

PROBLEM SET #11
B. Divide each of the following and simplify:

1. $\dfrac{8x^3}{2x}$

2. $\dfrac{-7x^2}{-x^2}$

3. $\dfrac{12b-24}{-6b}$

4. $\dfrac{20y-40}{-5}$

5. $\dfrac{9y^2-18}{-3}$

6. $\dfrac{6x^4-3x^2}{3x^2}$

7. $\dfrac{16x^7-4x^5}{-2x}$

8. $\dfrac{12x^3y^7}{-6x^2}$

9. $\dfrac{18x^7y^8}{-2xy}$

14. $\dfrac{x^{-2}y^{-3}}{x^5y^{-1}}$

15. $\dfrac{x^3y^{-2}}{x^5y^{-4}}$

16. $\dfrac{2x^{-3}z^2}{5x^{-3}z^{-2}}$

17. $\dfrac{10xy^{-4}}{2x^3y^2}$

18. $\dfrac{21x^2-18x}{-3x^2}$

19. $\dfrac{ax^2+bx}{x}$

20. $\dfrac{-28x^3+16x^2-6x}{-2x}$

21. $\dfrac{7xy-8xz}{2x}$

22. $\dfrac{3xyx+6xy}{-2xy}$

10. $\dfrac{16y^3 - 6y^2}{-2y}$

23. $\dfrac{-7x^4 - 6x^3}{2x}$

11. $\dfrac{18x^7 - 3x^2}{3x^2}$

24. $\dfrac{25x^2 - 30x}{5x^2}$

12. $\dfrac{14x^4y^7 - 2x^5y}{-2x^3y}$

25. $\dfrac{4 - 12x + 8x^2}{4}$

13. $\dfrac{7xy + 8xz}{2xy}$

61. Factoring A Polynomial

WHAT IS FACTORING?

If a polynomial can be expressed as the product of two or more algebraic expressions, then each expression of the product is called a **factor** of the given polynomial. Let us **try** that again. Thus to **factor a polynomial** is to **find two** or more algebraic expressions whose **product** is the given polynomial.

COMMON FACTORS

RULES FOR COMMON FACTORS

1.	Find the largest number that divides evenly into the coefficients.
2.	To factor out a variable as a common factor, the variable must appear in each part of the expression. Factor out the variables to the lowest exponent that appears.
3.	Divide each segment of the expression by the common factor.

Example 1: Factor completely $6x^2 - 2$
Solution: $6x^2 - 2$
STEP 1: Largest number that divides evenly into the coefficients is 2.
STEP 2: Divide each segment of the binomial by 2.
$$\dfrac{6x^2}{2} - \dfrac{2}{2} = 2(3x^2 - 1)$$
Answer: $2(3x^2 - 1)$

Example 2: Factor completely $10a^3 + 15a^2$

Solution: $10a^3 + 15a^2$

STEP 1: Largest number that divides evenly into the coefficients is 5.
STEP 2: Provided the same variable is present in each segment of the binomial, factor it out to the lowest exponent that is present (a^2).
STEP 3: Common factor is $5a^2$.

$$\frac{10a^3}{5a^2} + \frac{15^2}{5a^2} = 5a^2(2a + 3)$$

Answer: $5a^2(2a+3)$

For each of the following examples write the common factor in the space provided:

1. $3x^2 + 6$ Answer_____

2. $12a - 24$ Answer_____

3. $6x^2 - 16$ Answer_____

4. $x^2 + 6x$ Answer_____

5. $a^4 + 7a^3$ Answer_____

6. $6x^2 + 12x$ Answer_____

7. $3x^2 - 6x$ Answer_____

8. $9x^2 - 18$ Answer_____

9. $3x^2y + 6x$ Answer_____

10. $10x^2y + 20y^2$ Answer_____

11. $18x^7y - 9x^6y^6$ Answer_____

12. $6x^3y^7 - 12x^2y^6$ Answer_____

13. $x^2 - 4x$ Answer_____

14. $6a^2 + 3b^2$ Answer_____

15. $6ab - 12a^2b^2$ Answer_____

16. $7x^2y^4 - 14x^{14}y^3$ Answer_____

17. $9x^2 + 18y^2$ Answer_____

18. $7x^2 + 14xy$ Answer_____

62. Factors: The Difference of Two Squares

RULES FOR FACTORING THE DIFFERENCE OF TWO SQUARES

1.	The first term of the expression is a perfect square and the last term of the expression is a perfect square separated by a negative sign.
2.	Factor out the highest common factor.
3.	Find the square root of the first term and then find the square root of the second term. One set of factors is separated by a positive sign and the second set of factors by a negative sign.

Example 1: Factor completely $a^2 - 36$

    Solution: $a^2 - 36$

                STEP 1: Determine if the expression is the difference of perfect squares.

                STEP 2: Factor out common factors first.

                STEP 3: Take the square root of the terms. One factor has a positive sign and the other a negative sign.
                      $(a+6)(a-6)$

    Answer: $(a+6)(a-6)$

Example 2: Factor completely $x^2 + 36$

    Solution: Not factorable—as there are no common factors and it is not a difference of perfect squares (+ sign separate the x^2 and the 36).

    Answer: Cannot be factored.

Example 3: Factor completely $16a^2 - 64$

    Solution: $16a^2 - 64$

          $\dfrac{16a^2}{16} - \dfrac{64}{16} = 16(a^2 - 4)$ Common Factor.

          $16a^2 - 4 = 16(a+2)(a-2)$ Use method of difference of perfect squares.

    Answer: $16(a+2)(a-2)$

Hint: Let us summarize this rule for you. This is what we must look for:
1. Two terms.
2. Both terms are perfect squares.
3. A minus sign in between the two terms.

For each of the following examples, write the factors in the space provided:

1. $x^2 - 25$ Answer_____

2. $y^2 - 64$ Answer_____

3. $4x^2 + 36$ Answer_____

4. $x^2 - 49$ Answer_____

5. $9x^2 - 16y^2$ Answer_____

6. $49y^2 - 25x^2$ Answer_____

7. $3x^2 - 48$ Answer_____

8. $2x^2 - 18$ Answer_____

9. $9 - x^2$ Answer_____

10. $16 - y^2$ Answer_____

11. $x^2 - 16$ Answer_____

12. $x^6 - 36$ Answer_____

13. $x^8 - 81$ Answer_____

14. $9x^4 - 81$ Answer_____

63. Trinomial Factors

RULES FOR FACTORING TRINOMIALS IN WHICH THE COEFFICIENT OF x^2 IS 1

1. Factor out the highest common factor.
2. To factor one must find two numbers whose product is the last term (constant term) and the sum of the same two numbers is the middle term.

Example 1:   Factor completely $x^2 + 7x + 10$

    Solution: Two numbers are needed whose product is 10 and the sum of the same two numbers is 7. The numbers are 5 and 2.

    Answer: $(x + 5)(x + 2)$.

Example 2:   Factor completely $x^2 - 5x - 6$

Solution: Two numbers are needed whose product is 6 and the sum of the same two numbers with opposite signs is –5. The numbers are –6 and 1.

Answer: $(x - 6)(x + 1)$

Hint: Do you remember the **FOIL Method**? Well, you are using the FOIL Method in **Reverse**. Always check your answer. Let us look at an example of the **Reverse FOIL**.

To factor the trinomial $x^2 + 5x + 6$, you must consider:

1.   The factors of the first term
2.   The factors of the last term
3.   The sign of the last term, and
4.   The sign and coefficient of the middle term.

In the above expression,

1.   The factors of the first term are x•x.
2.   The factors of the last term are either 6•1 or 3•2.
3.   The sign of the last term is positive, so (-6)(-1) and (-2)(-3) are also possible factors.
4.   The sign of the middle term is positive, and it has coefficient 5.
5.   The combination +2 and +3 will add to +5, and at the same time multiply to +6.
6.   The result of factoring $x^2 + 5x + 6$ is $(x + 2)(x + 3)$.

To check the answer, multiply:

   $(x + 2)(x + 3) = x^2 + 3x + 2x + 6 = x^2 + 5x + 6$.

The result is the original expression.

Example: Factor $x^2 - 9x + 20$

1.   The factor of the first term are x • x.

2.   The factor of the last term are 20 • 1 or 10 • 2 or 5 • 4.

3.   The sign of the last term is positive so (–20)(–1), (–10)(–2) or (–5)(–4) are also possible factors.

4.   The sign of the middle term is negative and has coefficient 9, so we want the combination of –5 and –4 for our factors, since they add to –9 while multiplying to +20.

   Therefore in factored form: $x^2 - 9x + 20 = (x - 5)(x - 4)$

Answer: $(x - 5)(x - 4) = x^2 - 4x - 5x + 20 = x^2 - 9x + 20$

For each of the following expressions write the factors in the space provided:

1. $x^2 + 5x + 4$ Answer_____

2. $x^2 + 7x + 12$ Answer_____

3. $x^2 - 3x + 2$ Answer_____

4. $x^2 - 4x - 5$ Answer_____

5. $y^2 + y - 12$ Answer_____

6. $y^2 - 9y + 20$ Answer_____

7. $x^2 + 7x + 6$ Answer_____

8. $x^2 + 13x + 42$ Answer_____

9. $y^2 + 3y - 18$ Answer_____

10. $x^2 + 15x + 56$ Answer_____

Hint: Common Factor First

11. $2x^2 + 6x + 4$ Answer_____

12. $2y^3 + 4y^2 + 30y$ Answer_____

13. $2y^2 + 18y + 28$ Answer_____

14. $5x^3 + 45x^2 + 100x$ Answer_____

PROBLEM SET #12
Factor completely each of the following:

1. $y^2 + 7y$ 21. $18x^6y^2 - 9x^5y^5$

2. $x^2 - 36$ 22. $4x^2 - 16y^2$

3. $4x^2 - 8x$ 23. $x^2 + 3x + 2$

4. $x^2 + 6x + 5$ 24. $x^2 - 15x + 54$

5. $y^2 + y - 6$ 25. $x^6 - 81$

6. $3A^2 - 48$ 26. $x^8 - 36$

7. $x^2 - 144$ 27. $4x^4 - 81$

8. $A^2 + 6A + 4$

9. $6x - 24x^3$

10. $x^2 - 5x + 6$

11. $6x^3 - 54x$

12. $x^2 - 9x + 20$

13. $x^2 - 7x + 12$

14. $5B^2 + 45B^2 + 100B$

15. $20x^2y - 30x$

16. $49A^2 - 64B^2$

17. $x^2 - 5x + 4$

18. $x^2 + 9x + 20$

19. $2x^2 + 18x + 28$

20. $36x^2 - 81y^2$

28. $7x^3y^2 - 14x^5y^2$

29. $x^2 + 4x - 5$

30. $16 - x^2$

31. $196x^2 - 4y^2$

32. $7x^2 + 21x$

33. $6x^2 + 4b$

34. $x^2 - 3x - 10$

35. $x^2 - 2x - 8$

36. $x^2 - 4x - 32$

37. $x^2 + 3x - 54$

38. $x^2 + 13x + 30$

39. $x^2 + 13x - 30$

40. $x^2 - 6x - 40$

64. An Additional Factoring Problem

TRINOMIALS WHERE THE FIRST TERM IS GREATER THAN 1

In the last section, we looked at the method for factoring trinomials with the first term equal to one. For example, $x^2 - 7x + 5 = (x - 2)(x - 5)$. Now we would like to look at a trinomial where the **first term** $\neq 1$.

Let us look at $2x^2 + 13x + 15$. You can see that the first term is $2x^2$ not x^2. So how do we factor this? We are going to use **factoring by trial and error**. Recall that factoring is the reverse of multiplying. Consider the product of the following two binomials:

$$\begin{array}{cccc} \text{F} & \text{O} & \text{I} & \text{L} \end{array}$$

$$\begin{aligned} (2x + 3)(x + 5) &= (2x)(x) + (2x)(5) + 3(x) + 3(5) \\ &= 2x^2 + 10x + 3x + 15 \\ &= 2x^2 + 13x + 15 \end{aligned}$$

Notice that the product of the first terms of the binomials gives the x-squared term of the trinomial, $2x^2$. Take note that the product of the last terms of the binomials gives the last term, or constant, of the trinomial, $+15$. Finally, notice that the sum of the products of the outer terms and inner terms of the binomials gives the middle term of the trinomial, $+13x$. When we factor a trinomial using trial and error, we make use of these important facts. Note that $2x^2 + 13x + 15$ in factored form is $(2x + 3)(x + 5)$.

$$2x^2 + 13x + 15 = (2x + 3)(x + 5)$$

Let us look at another example:

$$2x^2 + 11x + 15$$

The factors of the **first term**, $2x^2$, are **2x** and **x**.

The factors of the **last term**, **15**, are **15** and **1**, or **5** and **3**. We have to find the correct combination of the **first** and **last term**, so that the middle term is **11x**.

Let us see how it works:

Trinomial	Possible Factors	Product of First Terms	Product of Last Terms	Sum of the products of Outer and Inner Terms
	$(2x + 15)(x + 1)$	$2x^2$	15	$2x(1) + 15(x) = 17$
	$(2x + 1)(x + 15)$	$2x^2$	15	$2x(15) + 1(x) = 31$
$2x^2 + 11x + 15$	**$(2x + 5)(x + 3)$**	$2x^2$	15	$2x(3) + 5(x) = \mathbf{11}$
	$(2x + 3)(x + 5)$	$2x^2$	15	$2x(5) + 3(x) = 13$

Since $(2x + 5)(x + 3)$ yields the correct x term, $11x$, the trinomial $2x^2 + 11x + 15$ factors into $(2x^2 + 5)(x + 3)$.
$$2x^2 + 11x + 15 = (2x + 5)(x + 3)$$

Remember, we can check this factoring using the FOIL method.

$$\text{Check: } (2x + 5)(x + 3) = 2x(x) + 2x(3) + 5(x) + 5(3)$$

$$= 2x^2 + 6x + 5x + 15$$

$$= \mathbf{2x^2 + 11x + 15}$$

Since we obtained the original trinomial, our factoring is correct.

Hints:

1. Determine if there is any common factor to all three terms. If so, factor it out.
2. Write all pairs of factors of the coefficient of the squared term (First Term).
3. Write all parts of factors of the constant term (Last Term).
4. Try all the combinations of these factors until the correct middle term is found.

PROBLEM SET #13

Factor completely if possible each of the following problems:

1. $3x^2 - 37x + 12$
2. $2x^2 - x - 2$
3. $8x^2 - 2x - 3$
4. $15x^2 - 23x + 4$
5. $6x^2 + 11x - 35$
6. $8x^2 + 11x + 3$
7. $3x^2 - 10x + 3$
8. $6x^2 + 41x - 7$
9. $7y^2 - 40y - 12$
10. $22x^2 + 5x - 3$
11. $12x^2 - 11x + 2$
12. $6x^2 - 7x + 3$
13. $6a^2 - 7a + 6$
14. $10x^2 - x - 9$
15. $2x^2 + 11x + 15$
16. $2x^2 - x - 15$
17. $2x^2 + 5x - 12$
18. $6x^2 - 17x + 12$
19. $2x^2 - 9x + 10$
20. $3x^2 + 2x - 5$
21. $3x^2 + 5x + 2$
22. $3x^2 - 2x - 8$
23. $3x^2 - 11x - 6$
24. $6x^2 + 7x - 10$
25. $8x^2 + 13x - 6$

65. Solving Linear Equations

RULES: REMEMBER WE SAW THIS EARLIER

1. An equation is a statement of equality. There are three parts to an equation: the right side, the left side, and the equal sign.
2. To solve an equation, use the Addition Property. Additive Inverse: for every number A, there is exactly one number—A, such that:

$$A + (-A) = 0, \quad X - 2 = 3$$

$$X = 5 \text{ (Add 2 to both sides)}.$$

3. If necessary, in the last step, use the Multiplication Property. Multiplicative Inverse: It is the product of two numerals or two variables that $= 1$.

$$n \cdot {}^1/_n = 1$$

$$2x = 6$$

$$x = 3$$

(Multiply both sides by the multiplicative inverse of 2, which is ½.)

Example 1: $3x - 6 = 12$

Solution: $3x - 6 = 12$
$3x - 6 + 6 = 12 + 6$ Additive Inverse
${}^1/_3 \cdot 3x = 18 \cdot {}^1/_3$ Multiplicative Inverse

Answer: $x = 6$

Example 2: $3(x + 7) = 21$

Solution: $3(x + 7) = 21$
$3x + 21 = 21$ Distributive Law of Multiplication
$3x + 21 - 21 = 21 + 21$ Additive Inverse
${}^1/_3 \cdot 3x = 42 \cdot {}^1/_3$ Multiplicative Inverse

Answer: $x = 14$

Example 3: $3x + 6 + 2x = 31$
$5x + 6 = 31$ Addition of Like Terms
$5x + 6 - 6 = 31 - 6$ Additive Inverse
${}^1/_5 \cdot 5x = 25 \cdot {}^1/_5$ Multiplicative Inverse

Answer: $x = 5$

Example 4: $6x + 1 = 2x + 45$
$6x + 1 - 1 = 2x + 45 - 1$ Additive Inverse
$6x = 2x + 44$ Additive Inverse
$6x - 2x = 2x - 2x + 44$
$¼ \cdot 4x = 44 \cdot ¼$ Multiplicative Inverse
$x = 11$

Answer: $x = 11$

Solve each of the following equations:
Write the correct answer in the space provided:

1. $x - 5 = 2$ Answer_____

2. $x + 7 = 4$ Answer_____

3. $2x = 6$ Answer_____

4. $-3y = 9$ Answer_____

5. $2y - 7 = 9$ Answer_____

6. $-3x - 6 = 9$ Answer_____

7. $-3x + 6 = 12$ Answer_____

8. $4 - x = 0$ Answer_____

9. $3y + 4 = 2y + 6$ Answer_____

10. $y - 7 = 1$ Answer_____

11. $2x - 6 = -12$ Answer_____

66. Solving Equations With Fractions

RULES:
1. Multiply each and every number and variable on both sides of the equation by the lowest common denominator (LCD).
2. Now follow the rules used for solving equations.

Example 1: $\dfrac{a}{6} + 12 = \dfrac{a}{3}$

Solution: The LCD for $\dfrac{a}{3}$ and $\dfrac{a}{6}$ is 6.

Multiply both sides by 6.

$\dfrac{a}{6} + 12 = \dfrac{a}{3}$.

$6 \cdot (\dfrac{a}{6}) + 6(12) = 6(\dfrac{a}{3})$ Use the Distributive Law of Multiplication.

$a + 72 = 2a$

$a - a + 72 = 2a - a$ Additive Inverse

$72 = a$

Answer: $a = 72$

Example 2: $\dfrac{x}{3} + \dfrac{x}{4} = 12$

Solution: The LCD for $\dfrac{x}{3}$ and $\dfrac{x}{4}$ is 12.

Multiply both sides by 12.

$$\dfrac{x}{3} + \dfrac{x}{4} = 12$$

$$12 \cdot \left(\dfrac{x}{3} + \dfrac{x}{4} \right) = 12 \cdot 12 \qquad \text{Use the Distributive Law of Multiplication.}$$

$$4x + 3x = 144 \qquad \text{Addition of like terms}$$

$$^1/_7 \cdot 7x = 144 \cdot {}^1/_7 \qquad \text{Multiplicative Inverse}$$

$$x = \dfrac{144}{7}$$

Answer: $x = \dfrac{144}{7}$

Solve each of the following equations. Write the answer in the space provided:

1. $\dfrac{x+1}{2} = \dfrac{3x+6}{4}$ Answer_____

2. $\dfrac{x-4}{3} = \dfrac{2x+1}{5}$ Answer_____

3. $\dfrac{x}{2} + \dfrac{x}{4} = 3$ Answer_____

4. $\dfrac{x}{3} + \dfrac{x}{9} = 4$ Answer_____

5. $\dfrac{x}{12} + 1 = \dfrac{x}{10}$ Answer_____

6. $\dfrac{x}{2} + 3 = \dfrac{x}{4}$ Answer_____

7. $\dfrac{u}{10} = \dfrac{u}{5} - 2$ Answer_____

8. $\dfrac{x}{7} + 2 = \dfrac{x}{14}$ Answer_____

9. $\dfrac{x}{2} + \dfrac{x}{3} = 5$ Answer_____

HINTS TO SOLVING AN EQUATION

1. Remove all denominators by multiplying each term by the LCM (Least Common Multiple).
2. Remove all parentheses by using the Distributive Law.
3. **Simplify** both sides of the equation.
4. Bring the **letter** to one side of the equation and bring the **number** to the opposite side of equation and simplify both sides. (This is the inverse law for addition).
5. Divide both sides of the equation by **whatever** is in front of the letter. (This is the inverse for multiplication.) You just solved for the unknown letter. See how easy this is.

PROBLEM SET #14
Solve each of the following equations:

1. $x - 6 = 4$

2. $x + 8 = 6$

3. $-3x = 12$

4. $-4y = -16$

5. $2y - 9 = 15$

6. $-3x - 6 = -12$

7. $5 - y = 0$

8. $6 - 7y = 20$

9. $3x - 6 = 2x + 15$

10. $4x - 7 = x + 8$

11. $3x + 6 + 2x = 31$

12. $4x - 7 - x = 2$

13. $2y - 9 = 5$

14. $-3(x-6) = 18$

15. $-2(x + 4) = -8$

16. $7x - 9 = x + 15$

17. $7x - 2 = 2x + 23$

18. $3(x - 7) = -3$

19. $3x + 4 = 2x + 6$

20. $2y - 6 = -12$

21. $3x - 7 = 2x + 5$

29. $5(y - 2) = -2(y - 2)$

30. $6x + 3x - 12 = 2x$

31. $9x + 3(2x - 1) = 12$

32. $3(y - 2) - 2 = 5(y + 3) - 7(y - 1)$

33. $2(x - 1) + 2 + 3(x - \frac{1}{3}) + 1 = -4(x - \frac{9}{4})$

34. $-2x - 3(2x - 4) = 4x + 8$

35. $\frac{1}{3}x - 3 = 4$

36. $y - \frac{1}{4} = 5\frac{3}{4}$

37. $2(x + 1) = 7x - 8$

38. $z - \frac{5}{4} = \frac{12}{2}$

39. $\frac{3x}{4} - 6 = \frac{x}{12}$

40. $\frac{x}{3} + \frac{x}{4} = 22$

41. $\frac{x}{3}x - \frac{3x}{8} = 5 + \frac{3x}{4}$

42. $\frac{3x - 2}{5} = 1$

43. $\frac{1 - 2x}{4} = 2$

44. $\frac{y}{9} + \frac{y}{3} = 4$

45. $\frac{y}{2} + 3 = \frac{y}{4}$

46. $\frac{x}{3} + 2 = 6$

47. $\frac{x}{5} = \frac{x}{10} - 4$

48. $\frac{y}{3} + \frac{y}{2} = 5$

49. $\frac{y}{24} + 2 = \frac{y}{20}$

161

22. $3x - 5 = 7$	50. $\dfrac{x}{3} + 1 = \dfrac{x}{2} + 6$
23. $3(x - 5) = 7$	51. $\dfrac{y+1}{4} = \dfrac{3y+6}{2}$
24. $70 = 6x + 10$	52. $\dfrac{x+7}{4} = \dfrac{3x-6}{2}$
25. $-5y + 17 = 47$	53. $\dfrac{x}{3} + \dfrac{x}{4} = 12$
26. $x + 3 = 4x + 1$	54. $\dfrac{x-7}{3} = \dfrac{2x+7}{4}$
27. $2x - 5 = x - 8$	55. $\dfrac{x}{4} - 7 = 14$
28. $2(x + 5) = 10 - x$	

67. Solving Literal Equations

Rules:
1. A literal equation is an equation with two or more variables.
2. Isolate the variable to be solved.
3. Follow the rules used to solve linear equations.

Example 1: If $3y - 7 = x$, solve for y.

      Solution: To solve for y, the variable y must be isolated.

$$3y - 7 = x$$
$$3y - 7 + 7 = x + 7 \qquad \text{Additive Inverse}$$
$$\frac{1}{3} \bullet 3y = \frac{1}{3}(x + 7) \qquad \text{Multiplicative Inverse}$$
$$y = \frac{x + 7}{3}$$

      Answer: $y = \dfrac{x = 7}{3}$

Example 2: If $bx + a = 3c$, solve for x.

      Solution: Isolate x on the left side. Use Additive Inverse by adding –a to both sides of the equation.

$$bx + a = 3c$$
$$bx + a - a = 3c - a \qquad \text{Additive Inverse}$$
$$\frac{1}{b} \cdot bx = \frac{1}{b} \cdot (3c - a) \qquad \text{Multiplicative Inverse}$$

      Answer: $x = \dfrac{3c - a}{b}$

Solve each of the following equations for the variable indicated. Write the correct answer in the space provided:

1. $x - y = 7$ Solve for x: Answer_____
2. $x - y = 3$ Solve for y: Answer_____
3. $a - 7b = 0$ Solve for a: Answer_____
4. $a - 2b = 0$ Solve for b: Answer_____
5. $3x - 2 = y$ Solve for x: Answer_____
6. $4x - 5y = 6$ Solve for y: Answer_____

7. $\dfrac{x}{2} + 4 = y$ Solve for x: Answer_____

8. $\dfrac{x}{3} - 7 = y$ Solve for x: Answer_____

9. $x + y + z = 6$ Solve for z: Answer_____
10. $3x - 4y + 7z = 9$ Solve for y: Answer_____

11. $\dfrac{a - b}{4} = c$ Solve for a: Answer_____

12. $3(x + y) = 6$ Solve for x: Answer_____
13. $-2(x - y + z) = 12$ Solve for x: Answer_____

PROBLEM SET #15
Solving Literal Equations:

1. $x - y = 9$ Solve for x: Answer_____
2. $a + 8b = 0$ Solve for a: Answer_____
3. $4x - 5 = y$ Solve for x: Answer_____
4. $5x - 6y = 7$ Solve for y: Answer_____

5. $\dfrac{x}{3} + 4 = y$ Solve for x: Answer_____

6. $\dfrac{x}{4} - 8 = y$ Solve for x: Answer_____

7. $x - 2y = 0$ Solve for y: Answer_____
8. $A + B + C = 0$ Solve for B: Answer_____
9. $4x - 5y + 8z = 3$ Solve for x: Answer_____
10. $4(x + y) = 6$ Solve for y: Answer_____

11. $\dfrac{x - y}{3} = c$ Solve for x: Answer_____

12. $\dfrac{A - B}{2} = d$ Solve for a: Answer_____

13. $\dfrac{x}{4} - 8 = y$ Solve for x: Answer_____

14. $2a - 3b = 4c$ Solve for a: Answer_____
15. $F = MA$ Solve for M: Answer_____
16. $r^2 = x^2 + y^2$ Solve for y^2:   Answer_____

17. $z = \dfrac{x - m}{s}$ Solve for x: Answer_____

18.	$y = mx + b$	Solve for b:	Answer_____
19.	$A = P(1 + r)$	Solve for P:	Answer_____
20.	$V = \pi r^2 h$	Solve for h:	Answer_____
21.	$a(c - d) = b$	Solve for a:	Answer_____
22.	$P = 2L + w$	Solve for L:	Answer_____
23.	$A = \frac{1}{2}(bh)$	Solve for h:	Answer_____

68. Solving Verbal Problems—Number Problems

RULES

English	Algebra
The sum of x and y	$x + y$
The product of x and y	xy
The quotient of x and y	$\dfrac{x}{y}$
A number	x
6 more than a number	$6 + x$
4 times a number	$4x$
The difference of x and y	$x - y$

Example: The sum of twice a number and four is eight.
Find the number.

Solution: 1. Let x = the number.
2. The sum of twice a number and four is represented as: $2x + 4$.
3. The word "is" translates as =.
4. Eight is 8.
5. Equation: $2x + 4 = 8$
6. Solve for x.

$$2x + 4 = 8 \qquad \text{Add } -4 \text{ to both sides}$$
Additive Inverse

$$2x = 4 \qquad \text{Multiply both sides by } \tfrac{1}{2}$$
Multiplicative Inverse

$$x = 2.$$

Answer: x = 2

Some other **key** words are:

    is means equal to

    of means to multiply

    what is the thing you are solving for

Let us look at an example using these words:

Example 1:   What is 20% of 80?

$x = 20\%$ of 80

$x = .20 \,(80)$

$\boxed{x = 16}$

Example 2:   Forty is what percent of eighty?

$40 = x\,(80)$

Let us clean this up. You then get:

$$\frac{80x}{80} = \frac{40}{80}$$

$x = \tfrac{1}{2}$

$\boxed{x = 50\%}$

Example 3:   Fifty percent of what number is 200?

$50\%\,(x) = 200$

$50\%\, x = 200$

$.50x\, /.50 = 200/.50 \quad \dfrac{.50x}{.50} = \dfrac{200}{.50}$

$\boxed{x = 400}$

Solve the following problems. Write the correct answer in the space provided:

1.   The sum of twice a number and six is twelve. Find the number.

    Answer:_____

2.   Four times the sum of a number and seven is thirty. Find the number.

    Answer:_____

3.   One number is four less than another. Their sum is eight. Find both numbers.

    Answer:_____

4.   The sum of twice a number and eight is four. Find the number.

    Answer:_____

5. If twice the difference of a number and three were decreased by five, the result would be three. Find the number.

Answer:_____

6. One number is 6 less than another. Their sum is twelve. Find the larger number.

Answer:_____

7. Five times the sum of a number and six is forty. Find the number.

Answer:_____

8. The sum of twice a number and nine is fifteen. Find the number.

Answer:_____

PROBLEM SET #16

Solve the following problems. Set up an equation for each problem. Only algebraic solution accepted. Show all work.

1.   The sum of four times a number and seven is sixty-seven. Find the number.

2.   One number is six less than another. Their sum is twelve. Find both numbers.

3.   The sum of twice a number and sixteen is twenty-four. Find the number.

4.   Six times a number and seven is forty-three. Find the number.

5.   One number is eight less than another. The sum is twenty-four. Find the larger number.

6.   A number divided by ten is thirty. Find the number.

7.   Two more than five times a number is thirty-seven. Find the number.

8.   One number is ten less than another; their sum is fifty. Find the smaller number.

9.   At a baseball game, each ticket costs $10. If expenses total $3,000, how many tickets must be sold in order to have a profit of $2,000?

10.   It costs a manufacturer $20 to produce each video game. In addition, there is a general overhead of $30,000. He produces 6,000 games. If he received $50 per game from a wholesaler, how many games must he sell to break even?

11.   A number increased by 3 is 15. Find the number.

12.   A number decreased by 5 is 25. Find the number.

13.   A number increased by 10 is 32. What is the number?

14.   A number diminished by 4 is 28. Find the number.

15.   12 more than a number is 32. What is the number?

16.   When 15 is added to a number, the result is 27. What is the number?

17.   When 15 is subtracted from a number, the result is 27. What is the number?

18.   The total cost of a shirt and necktie is $16. If the shirt costs three times as much as the necktie, what is the cost of each?

19.   The sum of three consecutive integers is 69. Find the three integers.

20.   A man distributed $310 among his three friends, Tom, Sammy, and Mike. He gave Sammy 3 times as much as Tom, and Mike $10 more than Tom. How much money did each receive?

21.   The greater of two numbers is two more than three times the smaller. Four times the greater exceeds five times the smaller by 22. Find the numbers.

22.   Mrs. Jones bought two kinds of candy for a party; one kind costing 40 cents a pound, and the other 70 cents a pound. If she pays $3.40 for 7 pounds of candy, how many pounds of each kind did she buy?

23.   Perry is twice as old as Jim. Three years ago Perry was three times as old as Jim was then. What are the present ages of both boys?

24.   John sold 500 tickets a football game and collected a total of $600. If he charged students 75 cents per ticket and non-students $1.50 per ticket, how many students did he sell tickets to?

69. Ratios and Proportions—Verbal Problems

1.	**Ratio:**	If x and y are any two numbers, where $y \neq 0$, then the ratio of x and y is: $\dfrac{x}{y}$.
2.	**Proportion:**	Is a statement that two ratios are equal. Means—Extremes Property
		If a, b, c, and d are real numbers, when $b \neq 0$ and $d \neq 0$, then:
		if $\dfrac{a}{b} = \dfrac{c}{d}$, then ad = bc.
	In words:	In any proportion, the product of the means is equal to the product of the extremes.

Example 1: Solve $\dfrac{3}{x} = \dfrac{6}{7}$

Solution: 1. $\dfrac{3}{x} = \dfrac{6}{7}$ Extremes are 3 and 6.

                              Means are x and 7.

           2. $6x = 21$ Products of means = product of extremes.

           3. $x = \dfrac{21}{6}$ Multiply both sides by 1/6.

                   Multiplicative Inverse

           4. $nnx = \dfrac{7}{2}$ Reduce

Answer: $x = \dfrac{7}{2}$

Example 2: A baseball player gets 6 hits in the first 18 games. If he continues hitting at the same rate, how many hits will he get in the first 45 games?

Solution:

1. Ratio 1 = Ratio 2

2. $\dfrac{Hits}{Games} = \dfrac{Hits}{Games}$

3. $\dfrac{6}{18} = \dfrac{x}{45}$

4. $270 = 18x$. Product of extremes = product of means

5. $15 = x$. Multiply both sides by $\dfrac{1}{18}$. Multiplicative Inverse.

Answer: $x = 15$.

Solve each of the following proportions.
Write the correct answer in the space provided:

1. $\dfrac{x}{3} = \dfrac{6}{9}$ Answer:_____

2. $\dfrac{4}{x} = \dfrac{2}{3}$ Answer:_____

3. $\dfrac{15}{60} = \dfrac{60}{x}$ Answer:_____

4. $\dfrac{2}{7} = \dfrac{x}{14}$ Answer:_____

5. $\dfrac{x+2}{3} = \dfrac{2}{5}$ Answer:_____

6. $\dfrac{x+1}{4} = \dfrac{2}{9}$ Answer:_____

PROBLEM SET #17
Solve each of the following verbal problems by the method of ratios and proportions.

1. If 200 grams of ice creams contain 26 grams of fat, how much fat is in 700 grams of ice cream?

2. A map is drawn so that 2 inches represents 350 miles. If the distance between 2 cities is 875 miles, how far apart are they on the map?

3. An airplane flies 1950 miles in 6 hours. How far will it travel in 7 hours?

4. A man drives his car 630 miles in 10 hours. At this rate, how far will he travel in 12 hours?

5. A 5-ounce serving of grapefruit juice contains 125 grams of water. How many grams of water are there in an 8-ounce serving of grapefruit juice?

6. A basketball player makes 8 out of 12 free throws in the first game of the season. If she shoots with the same accuracy in the second game, how many of the 15 free throws she attempts will she make?

7. If 400 grams of candy contains 68 grams of fat, how many grams of fat are there in 700 grams of candy?

8. Zelma drives her car 720 miles in 8 hours. At this rate, how far will she travel in 11 hours?

9. A map is drawn so that 2 inches represents 700 miles. If the distance between 2 cities is 3,850 miles, how far apart are they on a map?

10. A 7-ounce serving of orange juice contains 105 grams of water. How many grams of water are in a 12 –ounce serving of orange juice?

11. A baseball player makes 2 hits every 9 times a bat. If he hits the ball with the same accuracy, how many hits would he get if he were at bat 450 times?

70. Solving Simultaneous Equations

SIMULTANEOUS EQUATIONS ARE TWO EQUATIONS WITH TWO DIFFERENT VARIABLES

Rules: Category # 1

1. If the equation is in the following form:
   $$x + y = 6$$
   $$x - y = 2$$

   Add both equations to eliminate one of the variables. Then solve for the other variable.

2. Substitute the value found for the variable in either equation and solve the equation for the other variable.

Example 1:   Solve the system of equations $x + y = 6$ and $x - y = 2$.

Solution:
$$x + y = 6$$
$$\underline{x - y = 2}$$
$$2x \quad = 8$$

Eliminate the $+y$ and the $-y$ in both equations by addition.

$$(\frac{1}{2})2x = \frac{1}{2}(8)$$

Solve for x by using the multiplicative inverse of 2 which is 1/2.

$$x = 4$$
$$4 + y = 6$$
$$4 - 4 + y = 6 - 4$$
$$y = 2$$

Substitute 4 for x in either equation to find y.
Additive Inverse of $+4$ is -4.

Answer: $x = 4, y = 2$

Hint: You are given 2 equations with 2 unknowns (x and y). What is your **goal**?

You want to find out this question:

For what value(s) of x and y satisfy both equations? When you learn about graphing linear equations, you will be able to see graphically what you are solving. What you will be **seeing** on the graph is where these 2 lines intersect. The **intersection** point is the value for x and y that satisfies these 2 equations.

Solve each of the following simultaneous equations.
Fill in the correct answer in the space provided:

1. $x - y = 2$
   $x + y = 4$ Answer:_____

2. $a - b = 5$
   $a + b = 3$ Answer:_____

3. $x - 2b = 5$
   $x + 2b = 3$ Answer:_____

4. $-2x + y = 6$
   $2x + 2y = 6$ Answer:_____

5. $a - b = 6$
   $a + b = 2$ Answer:_____

Rules: Category # 2

1. If the equation is in the following form:
   $$2x - y = 6$$
   $$x + 3y = 3$$

   Solve by the following procedure:

2. Multiply each and every number on both sides of the first equation by 3 or multiply the second equation by –2.

3. Add both equations to eliminate one set of variables and solve for the other variable.

4. Substitute the value found for the variable in one of the equations and solve for other variable.

Example 1: Solve the system of equations 2x – y = 6 and x + 3y = 3.

Solution:

$$2x - y = 6$$
$$\underline{x + 3y = 3}$$
$$6x - 3y = 18$$ Multiply top equation on both sides by 3.

$$\underline{x + 3y\ = 3}$$
$$7x\quad = 21$$ Eliminate the –3y and the +3y in both equations by addition.

$$\frac{1}{7} \bullet 7x = \frac{1}{7} \bullet 21$$ Multiplicative inverse of 7 is 1/7.

$$x = 3$$

$$3 + 3y = 3$$ Substitute 3 for x in to find y.

$$3 - 3 + 3y = 3 - 3$$ Additive Inverse of +3 is –3.

$$3y = 0$$

$$\frac{1}{3} \bullet 3y = \frac{1}{3} \bullet 0$$ Multiplicative Inverse of 3 is 1/3.

Answer: x = 3, y = 0.

Solve each of the following simultaneous equations. Fill in the correct answer in the space provided:

1. $2x -\ y = 8$
       $\underline{x + 3y = 4}$ Answer_____

2. $2x - 6y = 4$
       $\underline{x + 2y = 3}$ Answer_____

3. $4x - y\ =\ 6$
       $\underline{x + 2y = 15}$ Answer_____

4. $2a - 3b = -3$
       $\underline{a + 4b =\ 4}$ Answer_____

5. $3x - 2y\ =\ -8$
       $\underline{x + 4y\ =\ 2}$ Answer_____

1.   Some simultaneous equations can be solved by substitution.

$$2x + 3y \quad = \quad 7$$
$$\underline{\qquad y \qquad = \qquad x - 1}$$

In the above problem, substitute "x – 1" for "y" in the top equation, and then solve for x.

$$2x + 3(x - 1) = 7$$

2.   Substitute the value found for the variable in either one of the equations, and solve for the other variable.

Example 1: Solve the system of equations $2x + 3y = 7$ and $y = x - 1$.

Solution:

$2x + 3y$	$=$	7
y	$=$	$x - 1$
$2x + 3(x - 1)$	$=$	7

Substitute x – 1 for y in the top equation.

$2x + 3x - 3 \quad = \quad 7$ Distributive Law of Multiplication.

$5x - 3 \quad = \quad 7$ Addition of like terms.

$5x - 3 + 3 \quad = \quad 7 + 3$ Additive Inverse of –3 is + 3.

$5x \quad = 10$

$\dfrac{1}{5} \bullet 5x = \dfrac{1}{5} \bullet 10$ Multiplicative inverse of 5 is 1/5.

$x \quad = \quad 2$
$y \quad = \quad 2 - 1$ Substitute 2 for x in the bottom
$y \quad = \quad 1$ equation to find y.

Answer: $x = 2, y = 1.$

Solve each of the follow simultaneous equations.
Fill in the correct answer in the space provided:

1. $3x \; + \; 4y \quad = \quad 6$
$\underline{\qquad\qquad y \quad = \quad x - 1}$ Answer_____

2. $4x \; + \; 2y \quad = \quad 6$
$\underline{\qquad\qquad x \quad = \quad y}$ Answer_____

3. $2x \; + \; 3y \quad = \quad 7$
$\underline{\qquad\qquad y \quad = \quad x + 4}$ Answer_____

4. $2x \; + \; 4y \quad = \quad 6$
$\underline{\qquad\qquad x \quad = \quad y + 3}$ Answer_____

5. $3x + 6y = 6$
   $\underline{\hspace{3em} x = 2y + 6}$ Answer_____

6. $4x + 6y = 16$
   $\underline{\hspace{3em} y = 2x + 8}$ Answer_____

7. $2x + y = 6$
   $\underline{\hspace{3em} y = x}$ Answer_____

PROBLEM SET #18
Solve each of the following simultaneous equations:

1. $x - y = 7$
   $x + y = 1$

2. $x + 3y = 4$
   $2x - y = 8$

3. $2x + 4y = 6$
   $x = y + 3$

4. $-3x + 2y = 6$
   $3x + y = 3$

5. $A + 2B = 6$
   $A - 3B = 1$

6. $3A - 4B = 0$
   $A = 7 - B$

7. $3A + B = 10$
   $2A + 3B = 9$

8. $A + B = 6$
   $2A - B = 3$

9. $2x + 3y = 9$
   $3x + y = 10$

10. $2A - B = 6$
    $3A + B = 1$

11. $3x + y = 6$
    $y = x + 2$

12. $4A + 3B = 2$
    $A + B = 0$

13. $2A - B = 7$
    $A + B = 2$

14. $3x - y = 4$
    $y = x$

15. $2x + 5y = 9$
    $4x - 3y = 5$

16. $x - 2b = 10$
    $x + 2b = 6$

17. $4A - B = 12$
    $A + 2B = 30$

18. $4x + 8y = 12$
    $x = y$

19. $-4x + 2y = 12$
    $4x + 4y = 12$

20. $2A + 3B = 7$
    $A = B - 4$

21. $4x + 12y = 8$
    $2x + 4y = 6$

71. Solving Quadratic Equations

Rules:

1. Any equation that can be put into the form $ax^2 + bx + c = 0$ is called a quadratic equation. There are two solutions for each equation.
2. Set equation equal to zero.
3. Factor.
4. Set each factor equal to zero.
5. Solve for each of the factors.

Example 1: $x^2 + 7x = -6$

Solution:
1. Set equation equal to zero.
$$x^2 + 7x + 6 = 0$$
2. Factor
$$(x + 6)(x + 1) = 0$$
3. Set each factor equal to zero.
$$x + 6 = 0 \text{ or } x + 1 = 0$$
4. Solve
$$x = -6 \text{ or } x = -1$$

Answer: $(-6, -1)$ solution set

Solve each of the following quadratic equations.

1. $y^2 + 7y + 10 = 0$ Answer_____

2. $x^2 + 12y + 11 = 0$ Answer_____

3. $x^2 + 5x = -4$ Answer_____

4. $y^2 - 9y = -20$ Answer_____

5. $x^2 + 2x = 3$ Answer_____

6. $x^2 = 16$ Answer_____

7. $x^2 - x = 6$ Answer_____

8. $x^2 = 25$ Answer_____

9. $x^2 - 7x = -12$ Answer_____

10. $y^2 + 4y = -3$ Answer_____

11. $x^2 + 5x = -6$ Answer_____

12. $x^2 + 8x = -15$ Answer_____

PROBLEM SET #19
Solve each of the following quadratic equations:

1. $x^2 + 9x = -20$

2. $y^2 - 4y = -3$

3. $x^2 + 9x = -8$

4. $x^2 = 36$

5. $x^2 - 8x = -15$

6. $x^2 - x = 20$

7. $x^2 + 3x = 4$

8. $x^2 + 8x = -7$

9. $x^2 + 6x = -8$

10. $A^2 - 7A = 18$

11. $x^2 + 9x = 10$

12. $A^2 + 7A = 18$

13. $y^2 - 3y = -2$

14. $y^2 - 6y = 16$

15. $x^2 - 9x = -14$

16. $x^2 - 25 = 0$

17. $9x^2 - 36 = 0$

18. $x^2 - 7x = 0$

19. $4x^2 + 5x = 0$

20. $x^2 - 4x - 21 = 0$

21. $2x^2 - 9x + 10 = 0$

22. $3x^2 = 21$

23. $3x^2 + 24x = 0$

24. $x^2 + 8x = -15$

72. Graph of a Straight Line

A graph is a picture used to show some information. The center of the graph is the origin. At the origin, the center of the graph, both the x and y values are zero. The horizontal line represents the x-axis, and the vertical line represents the y-axis.

To draw a graph of a straight line, one must find points that are solutions to the equation. For example, in the equation x = y + 1, one must assume values of one of the variables and solve for the other variable. If one assumes y = 1, substitute the value in the equation and solve for x; (x = 2). Choose several values for y and find the values for x. Locate them on the graph. The points should connect to a straight line.

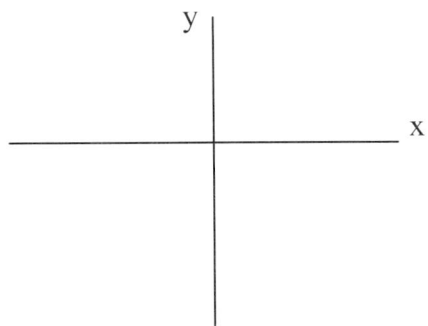

Rules To Graph:

1. Choose at Least Three Different Values for One Variable.
2. Substitute in the Equation and Find the Value of the Other Variable.
3. Plot the (x, y) Values for Each Point.
4. Connect the Points as a Straight Line.

In writing a point, use the following notation: (x, y). The x value is written first, and then the y value separated by a comma and enclosed by a parenthesis. The point (–3, –5) has an x value of –3 and a y of –5.

TO DETERMINE IF A POINT LIES ON A GRAPH

Rules:

1. Substitute in the equation the values given.
2. If both sides of the equation have the same value, the point is a solution to the equation.

Example 1: Which of these points lies on the graph $4x + y = 6$?

a). $(2\ 7)$ b). $(-3, -5)$

c). $(1, 2)$ d). $(6, 7)$

Solution: Solve equation by substituting the value of each point for x and y in the equation. Start with choice (a) until you find the correct answer.

1. Substitute $(2, 7)$. 2 for x and 7 for y.

$$4x + y = 6$$
$$4(2) + 7 = 6$$
$$8 + 7 = 6 \qquad \textbf{False}$$

2. Substitute $(-3, -5)$. -3 for x and -5 for y.

$$4x + y = 6$$
$$4(-3) + (-5) = 6$$
$$-12 - 5 = 6 \quad \textbf{False}$$

3. Substitute $(1, 2)$. 1 for x and 2 for y.

$$4x + y = 6$$
$$4(1) + 2 = 6$$
$$4 + 2 = 6 \qquad \textbf{True}$$

Answer: $(1, 2)$

Fill in the letter of the correct answer in the space provided:

1. Which one of the following points lies on the graph: $y = 3x + 1$?

a) $(3, 4)$ b) $(-2, -7)$

c) $(-3, -4)$ d) $(2, 7)$ Answer_____

2. Which one of the following points lies on the graph: $2x + 3y = 5$?

a) $(3, 4)$ b) $(1, 1)$

c) $(-3, -4)$ d) $(2, 9)$ Answer_____

3. Which one of the following points lies on the graph: $y = x - 2$?

a) $(3, 7)$ b) $(2, 1)$

c) $(4, 2)$ d) $(7, 3)$

e) $(7, 4)$ Answer_____

4. Which one of the following points lies on the graph: $6x - 5y = 1$?

    a) $(2, 4)$ b) $(1, 1)$

    c) $(6, 2)$ d) $(3, 4)$ Answer_____

5. Which one of the following points lies on the graph: $x - y = 1$?

    a) $(5, 7)$ b) $(4, 6)$

    c) $(3, 2)$ d) $(-4, -3)$ Answer_____

6. Which one of the following points lies on the graph: $y = 4 - x$?

    a) $(3, 4)$ b) $(4, 0)$

    c) $(-2, 4)$ d) $(-4, -5)$ Answer_____

7. Which one of the following points lies on the graph: $5x + y = 0$?

    a) $(3, 4)$ b) $(1, -5)$

    c) $(-2, 4)$ d) $(-4, -3)$ Answer_____

73. Plotting Points on the Graph

The figure below is a representation of the Cartesian Plane, so named after the mathematician Des Cartes. The x and y axes are divided into equal units, similar to the real number line.

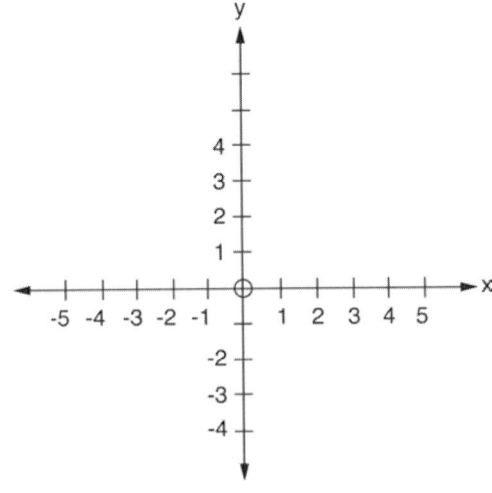

Numbers to the **right** of zero on the x axis are **positive**. Numbers to the **left** of zero on the x axis are **negative**.

Numbers which are on the y axis and **above** the x axis are **positive**. Numbers which are on the y axis and below the x axis are **negative**.

> **Note:** If you move right or left but NOT up or down, the point is on the x axis; if you move up or down but NOT right or left, the point is on the y axis.

> **Points on the Cartesian Plan are represented by ordered pairs of numbers, so called because the FIRST number represents the X coordinate and the SECOND number represents the Y coordinate.**

The pairs of numbers are written in parentheses and separated by commas: (x, y), $(3, -1)$, $(0, 6)$, etc.

The sign of each number indicates "direction"; that is:

> if x is positive, the point is to the right of zero
> if x is negative, the point is to the left of zero
> if y is positive, the point is above zero
> if y is negative, the point is below zero.

Example: Plot (locate) the following points in the Cartesian Plane:
A = (3, 5)   B = (−3, 5)   C = (−3, -5)   D = (3, −5)

For A: start at origin and move 3 units to the right along the x axis, then up 5 units.
For B: start at origin; move 3 units left and 5 units up.
For C: start at origin; move 3 units left and 5 units down.
For D: move 3 units right and 5 units down from zero.

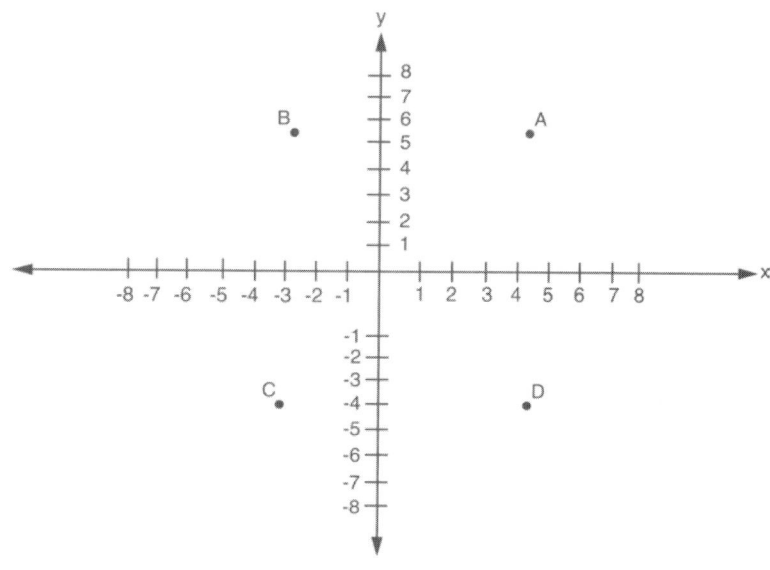

74. To Find "x" Intercept and the "y" Intercept

Rules Used to Find Intercepts:

x—Intercept: Is the point where the line crosses the x axis.

y—Intercept: Is the point where the line crosses the y axis.

1.   To find the x intercept, set the y value equal to zero.

Example: $2x + 3y = 6$

Solution: $2x + 3y = 6$
                    $y = 0$
Then, $2x = 6$
                    $x = 3$
Answer: $x = 3$

2.   To find the y intercept, set the x value equal to zero.

Example: $3x + 7y = 14$

Solution: $3x + 7y = 14$
                    $x = 0$
Then, $7y = 14$
                    $y = 2$
Answer: $y = 2$

Fill in the correct answer in the space provided:

1.   Find the x intercept for the equation $2x - y = 6$.   Answer_____

2.   Find the x intercept for the equation $-2x - 3y = -6$.   Answer_____

3.   Find the x intercept for the equation $-7x - 7y = 14$.   Answer_____

4.   Find the x intercept for the equation $3x + 6y = 12$.   Answer_____

5.   Where does the graph $2x - 3y = 6$ intercept the x axis?   Answer_____

6.   Where does the graph $-2x - 7y = 14$ intercept the y axis? Answer_____

7.   Where does the graph $3x + 6y = 1$ intercept the x axis?   Answer_____

8.   Where does the graph $-4x - 6y = -3$ intercept the y axis? Answer_____

75. To Write an Equation of a Straight Line Knowing the "X" Intercept And The "Y" Intercept

1.	Use the formula:
	$\dfrac{x}{a} + \dfrac{y}{b} = 1$, where "a" is the value of the "x" intercept
	and "b" is the value of the "y" intercept.
2.	Remove the fractions by using the lowest common multiplier (LCD).

Example 1: Write an equation for the line.

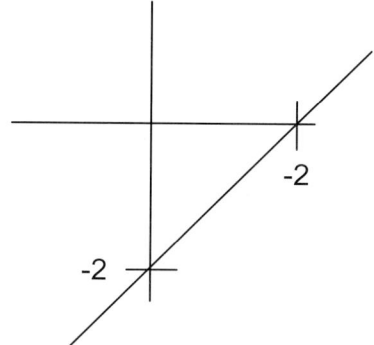

-2

-2

Solution:

$\dfrac{x}{a} + \dfrac{y}{b} = 1$

> Write the formula.

$\dfrac{x}{2} + \dfrac{y}{-2} = 1$

> Substitute:
>
> a = x – intercept = 2, and
>
> b = y – intercept = -2.

$2(\dfrac{x}{2}) + 2(\dfrac{y}{-2}) = 2(1)$

$x - y = 2$

> Use LCD = 2 to clear fractions by multiplying both sides by 2

Answer: $x - y = 2$

Write the correct answer in the space provided:

1. Write an equation for the line:

a)

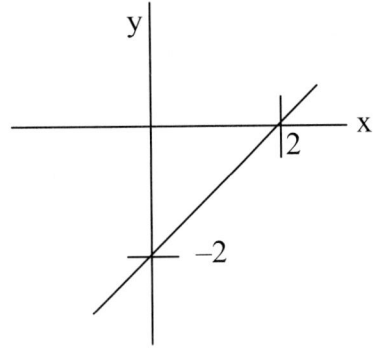

Answer_____

b)

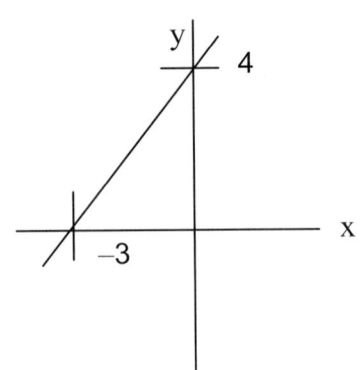

Answer_____

2. Write an equation for the line:

a)

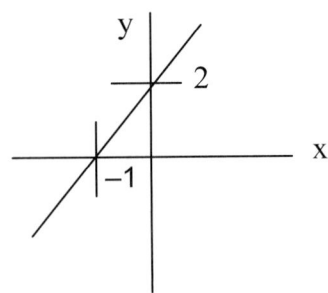

Answer_____

b)

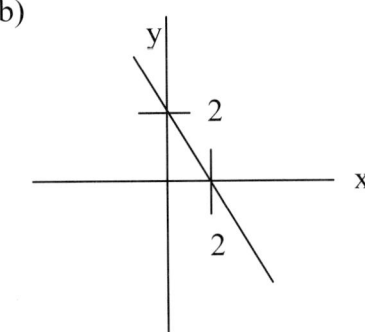

Answer_____

76. To Find The Slope Given Two Points

Rules:

Slope: It is the ratio of the change in the vertical distance to the change in the horizontal distance.

Definition: If points (x_1, y_1) and (x_2, y_2) are any two points, then the slope of the line on which they lie is:

$$\text{Slope} = m = \frac{y_2 - y_1}{x_2 - x_1}$$

1.   Label the points (x_1, y_1) and (x_2, y_2).
2.   Write the formula for slope.
3.   Substitute the values into the formula.
4.   Evaluate.

Example: Find the slope of the line between the points
            (4,3) (6,5)

Solution :   1.   Label the points:
                        $(x_1, y_1) = (4,3)$
                        $(x_2, y_2) = (6,5)$

                2.   Substitute the formula and evaluate.
                        $$m = \frac{y_2 - y_1}{x_2 - x_1} = \frac{5 - 3}{6 - 4} = \frac{2}{2} = 1$$

Answer: m = 1

Find the slope for each set of points. Write the correct answer in the space provided:

1.   (3,1), (5,4)   Answer_____

2.   (2,1), (5,5)   Answer_____

3.   (1,3), (5,2)   Answer_____

4.   (−1, −1), (−2, −2)   Answer_____

5.   (1, −3), (4,2)   Answer_____

6.   (2, −4), (3, −1)   Answer_____

7.   (4,5), (5,6)   Answer_____

8.   (−3, −2) (1,3)   Answer_____

9.   (2, −5), (3, −2)   Answer_____

10.   (−3, 3), (3, -1)   Answer_____

77. Slope Intercept Form of the Equation of a Line

The equation of a line with slope "m" and y intercept, "b" is always given by the following: $y = mx + b$.

Rules:

1. Write the equation: $Y = mx + b$
2. Substitute in the equation the value of the slope and the value of the y-intercept.

Example: Write the equation of a line with slope 2 and y-intercept 5.

Solution: Substitute m = 2 and b = 5 in the following equation:

$$y = mx + b$$
$$y = 2x + 5$$

Answer : $y = 2x + 5$

For each of the following problems, write an equation:
Write the correct answer in the space provided:

1. m = 4, b = 1   Answer_____

2. m = 3, b = –6   Answer_____

3. m = –2, b = 4   Answer_____

4. m = –5, b = –6   Answer_____

5. m = –1, b = –1   Answer_____

6. m = 2, b =2   Answer_____

7. $m = \dfrac{2}{3}, b = 6$ Answer_____

8. $m \dfrac{-2}{5}, b = \dfrac{3}{4}$ Answer_____

78. To Find the Slope and the "y" Intercept Given an Equation

Rules:

1. Write the equation in the form y = mx + b (Slope—Intercept form).
2. Solve the equation for y.

Example: Find the slope and the y-intercept for 4x + 2y = 8.

Solution: Write the equation in the form y = mx + b (solve for y).

1.   4x + 2y = 8   Original equation

2.   2y = –4x + 8   Add a – 4x to each side.
                          Additive Inverse

3. $\frac{1}{2}$ (2y) = $\frac{1}{2}$ (–4x + 8) Multiplicative Inverse. Multiply by $\frac{1}{2}$.

4.   y = –2x + 4   Simplify.

5.   Slope = m = –2
     y-intercept = b = 4

Answer: m = –2, b = 4.

Find the slope and the y-intercept for each of the following equations. Write the correct answer in the space provided:

1.   4x + y = 6   Answer_____

2.   3x + y = 4   Answer_____

3.   2x – y = 5   Answer_____

4.   5x – y = 6   Answer_____

5.   6x + 3y = 9   Answer_____

6.   2x + 4y = 6   Answer_____

7.   x – y = 2   Answer_____

8.   2x + 3y = 6   Answer_____

79. Find The Equation of a Line Given One Point (X_1, Y_1) on the Line and he Slope of the Line

Let us now introduce the point-slope form of a liner equation.

When the slope of a line and a point on the line are known, we can use the point slope form to determine the equation of the line. The point–slope form can be obtained by beginning with the slope between any selected point (x,y) and a fixed point (x_1, y_1) on a line.

> Point–slope form of a Linear Equation

$y - y_1 = m(x - x_1)$, where m is the slope of the line and (x_1, y_1) is a point on the line.

Example: Write an equation of the line that goes through the point (2,3) and has a slope of 4.

Solution: The slope m is 4. The point on the line is (2,3); use this point for (x_1, y_1) in the formula. Substitute 4 for m, 2 for x_1, and 3 for y_1 in the point–slope form of a linear equation.

$$y - y_1 = m(x - x_1)$$
$$y - 3 = 4(x - 2)$$
$$y - 3 = 4x - 8$$
$$y = 4x - 5$$

The graph of $y = 4x - 5$ has a slope of 4 and passes through the point (2,3).

Find the equation of the line with slope m and going through the point (x_1, y_1):

1.   m = 3; point (3, 4)   Answer_____

2.   m = –2; point (–2, 4)   Answer_____

3.   m = 5;   point (–1, –3)   Answer_____

4.   m = –1; point (5, –2)   Answer_____

5.   m = -6; Point (3, –4)   Answer_____

PROBLEM SET #20
Solve the following verbal problems:

1. Find the x-intercept for the equation $3x - y = 9$. Answer_____
2. Find the y-intercept for the equation $3x - 7y = -14$. Answer_____
3. Find the x-intercept for the equation $3x - 7y = 12$: Answer_____
4. Find the y-intercept for the equation $-6x - 9y = 18$. Answer_____
5. Where does the graph $3x + 7y = -15$ intercept the x-axis? Answer_____
6. Where does the graph $-4x - 6y = -12$ intercept the y-axis? Answer_____
7. Where does the graph $3x + 6y = 24$ intercept the x- axis? Answer_____
8. Where does the graph $7x - 9y = 18$ intercept the y-axis? Answer_____

PROBLEM SET #21
Find the slope for each of the following sets of points:

1. (3,2) (5, 6)
2. (3, 1) (5, 9)
3. (-6, -2) (-4, -9)
4. (-9, 2) (-3, 4)
5. (7, -6) (-3,4)
6. (-3, -7) (28, -1)
7. (2,5) (7, 9)
8. (3, -6) (-2, 9)

9. (-2, 1) (-4, 8)
10. (-3, -7) (-4, -1)
11. (-3, 7) (4, -9)
12. (4, -9) (-3,7)
13. (7, 1) (1,7)
14. (-3, -4) (-4, -3)
15. (6,1) (7,4)

PROBLEM SET #22
For each of the following problems, write an equation:

1. $m = 5, b = 2$
2. $m = 3, b = -7$
3. $m = -2, b = 5$
4. $m = -5, b = -7$
5. $m = -2, b = -1$

6. $m = 2, b = 3$
7. $m = \dfrac{-2}{3}, b = 9$
8. $m = \dfrac{-3}{5}, b = \dfrac{1}{4}$
9. $m = \dfrac{2}{9}, b = \dfrac{4}{5}$

189

PROBLEM SET #23
Solve the following verbal problems:

1. Which one of the following points lies on the graph: $y = 2x + 1$?
    a) $(-3, 7)$ b) $(1, 3)$ c) $(2, 9)$ d) $(3, 4)$

2. Which one of the following points lies on the graph: $2x + y = 5$?
    a) $(-3, -5)$ b) $(4, 1)$ c) $(2, 1)$ d) $(-7, -5)$

3. Which one of the following points lies on the graph: $y = x - 1$?
    a) $(2, 9)$ b) $(6, -5)$ c) $(3, -4)$ d) $(4, 3)$

4. Which one of the following points lies on the graph: $7x - 6y = 1$?
    a) $(3, 7)$ b) $(1, 1)$ c) $(-2, -7)$ d) $(-3, -4)$

5. Which one of the following points lies on the graph: $x - y = 2$?
    a) $(4, 2)$ b) $(3, 7)$ c) $(-6, -9)$ d) $(2, 9)$

6. Which one of the following points lies on the graph $y = 5 - x$?
    a) $(2, 7)$ b) $(6, 9)$ c) $(-3, -7)$ d) $(3, 2)$

7. Which one of the following points lies on the graph: $6x + 2y = 0$?
    a) $(-3, -7)$ (b) $(2, 7)$ c) $(1, -3)$ d) $(-2, 9)$

PROBLEM SET #24
Find the slope and the y-intercept for each of the following equations:

1. $x + 4y = 8$ 7. $x - y = 4$

2. $y + 3x = 12$ 8. $y = 9 - 3x$

3. $y = -3x + 6$ 9. $3x - 7y = 21$

4. $x = 6 - y$ 10. $y = 3x$

5. $2x + 3y = 12$ 11. $6 = 3x + y$

6. $2y + 4x = 8$ 12. $7 = -x - y$

Write the equation of the line with the given properties using the point-slope form:

1.   Slope = 5, through (0, 4)

2.   Slope = –2, through (–4, 5)

3.   Slope = 4, through (2, 3)

4.   Slope = –1, through (6, 0)

5.   Slope = $\frac{1}{2}$, through (–1, –5)

6.   Slope = $-\frac{2}{3}$, through (–1, -2)

7.   Slope = $-\frac{1}{2}$, through (–2, –4)

8.   Slope = $\frac{3}{4}$, through (8, -4)

80. An Introduction To Geometry

Geometry is the study of shapes, sizes and relationships of figures such as squares, rectangles, triangles, and circles. Important geometric definitions include the following:

Point: A point has no length or width. It only marks a position. It is represented by a dot. A capital letter is placed near the dot.

Line: A line is an infinite set of points. It has length but no width.

The above line can be referred to as line RS or SR.

Plane: A plane is a flat surface that extends in all directions. It has no end.

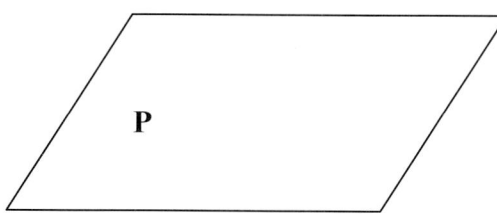

This figure represents plane P. Technically it is only part of a plane and it has no boundaries.

INFORMATION ABOUT LINES

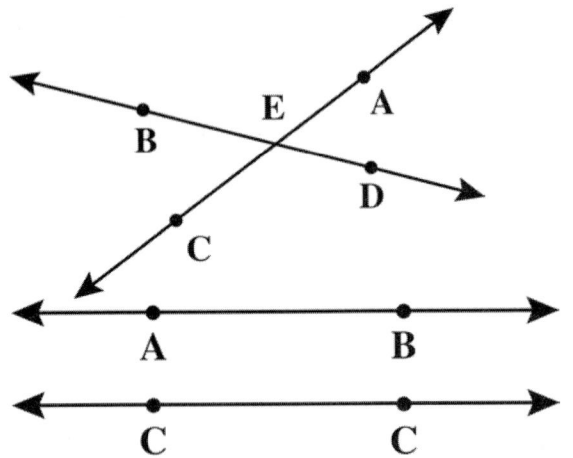

Intersecting Lines are two straight lines that meet or cross each other. They intersect at only one point.

Parallel Lines are two lines in the same plane that never intersect.

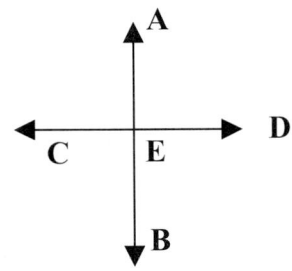

Perpendicular Lines are two straight lines that intersect to form right angles (90°). If AB is perpendicular to CD, then the four angles at E are right angles.

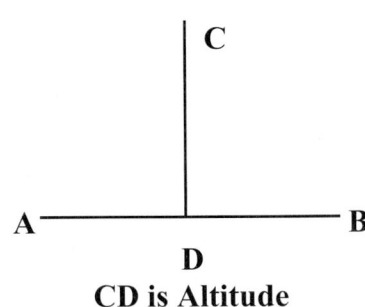

CD is Altitude

Altitude is a line drawn to another line forming right angles. An attitude of a triangle is a line drawn from a vertex perpendicular to the opposite side. It is a measure of the height of a geometric figure, such as a triangle or a rectangle.

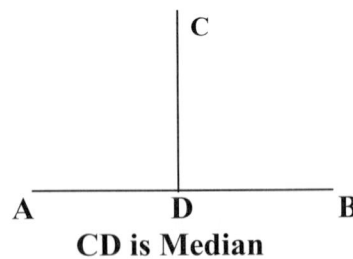

CD is Median

Median is a line drawn to another line that divides it into two equal line segments. In a triangle, it is a line drawn from a vertex to the midpoint of the opposite side.

81. Angle Theorems and Applications

ANGLES

- **Angle**: An angle is the union of two rays that extend from a common end point.

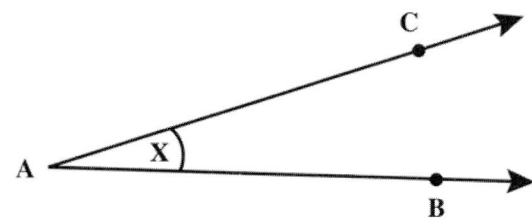

The symbol for an angle is ∠. The vertex is at "A". To name an angle, the vertex letter must be in the middle, if three letters are used. There are four ways to name the above angle.

   1. ∠ CAB   2. ∠ BAC   3. ∠ A   4. ∠ X

The Vertex is the interesting point of two sides. Angles are measured in degrees.

- **Right Angle:** Right angle is an angle that measures exactly 90°.
- **Straight Angle**: Straight angle is an angle that measures exactly 180°.
- **Obtuse Angle:** Obtuse angle is an angle that measures less than 180° & more than 90°.
- **Bisector**: Bisector is a ray that divides the angle into two equal segments.

ANGLE THEOREMS

- **Supplementary Angles**: Supplementary angles are two or more angles that add up to 180°.
- **Complementary Angles:** Complementary angles are two or more angles that add up to 90°.
- **Vertical Angles**: Vertical Angles are formed when two lines intersect. The opposite angles are equal. They are called vertical angles.

Example 1: An angle is eight times its supplement. Find both angles.
    Solution: Let x = smaller angle.

                 Let 8x = larger angle.

                 $8x + x = 180^\circ$ definition of Supplementary.

                 $9x = 180^\circ =$ Add like terms.

       $x = 20^\circ$ Answer Smaller angle.
       $8x = 160^\circ$ Answer Larger angle.

Example 2: An angle is 60^0 more than its complement.
Find the larger angle.
Solution: Let x = Smaller angle.

Let $x + 60^0$ = larger angle

$x + x + 60° = 90^0$ definition of Complementary.

$2x + 60^0 = 90^0$ Add like terms.

$2x = 30^0$ Solve.

$x = 15°$ Answer Smaller angle.
$x + 60^0 = 75^0$ Answer Larger angle.

Answer each of the following questions. Write the correct answer in the space provided:

1. Find the complement of an angle that is 29^0.   Answer_____

2. Find the supplement of an angle that is 59^0.   Answer_____

3. An angle is five times its supplement. Find the larger angle.   Answer_____

4. An angle is four times its complement. Find both angles.   Answer_____

5. An angle is 60^0 more than its supplement. Find both angles.   Answer_____

6. An angle is 12^0 less than its complement. Find
both smaller angles.   Answer_____

7. An angle exceeds its supplement by 60^0 Find the larger angle. Answer_____

8. An angle is twice its supplement. Find both angles.   Answer_____

82. Triangle Theorems and Applications

TRIANGLE THEOREMS

A triangle is a polygon with three sides and three angles. (A polygon is a closed figure formed by three or more sides.) The symbol for a triangle is Δ.

- **Equilateral Triangle:** is a triangle with three equal sides of equal lengths.
- **Isosceles Triangle:** is a triangle with two sides of equal length
- **Scalene Triangle:** is a triangle with no two sides of equal length.
- **Right Triangle:** is a triangle with a right angle.

The sum of the angles of a triangle is 180^0.

Example 1: The vertex angle of an isosceles triangle is 40^0.
Find the number of degrees in each base angle.

Solution: Let x = the number of degrees in each base angle.

$x + x + 40^0 = 180^0$ the sum of the angles of a triangle.

$2x + 40^0 = 180^0$. Add like terms.

$2x = 140°$. Solve.

$x = 70^0$

Answer: Each base angle is 70^0.

Example 2: The three angles of a triangle are in the ratio of the 3:4:5. Find the number of degrees in each angle.

Solution: Let 3x, 4x, and 5x represent three angles.

$3x + 4x + 5x = 180^0$ sum of the angles of a triangle.

$12x = 180^0$. Add like Terms

$x = 15^0$. Solve the equation

$3x = 45^0$

$4x = 60^0$

$5x = 75^0$

Answer: The three angles are 45^0, 60^0, and 75^0.

Answer each of the following questions: Write the correct answer in the space provided:

1. The vertex angle of an isosceles triangle is 70^0.
Find the value of each base angle. Answer_____

2. The three angles of a triangle are in the ratio of 1:2:3.
Find the value of the larger angle. Answer_____

3. The vertex angle of and isosceles triangle is 80^0.
Find the value of each base angle. Answer_____

4. The vertex of an isosceles triangle is twice the base
angle. Find the value of the vertex angle. Answer_____

83. Circle Theorems—Circumference—Area

CIRCLE THEOREMS

A circle is a plane figure bounded by a curved line, every point of which is the same distance from the center of the figure. The circumference of a circle is the line that forms its outer boundary. It is like the perimeter of a circle. A radius of a circle is a line segment joining the center to any point on the circumference. A diameter is a line segment joining two points on the circumference and passing through the center. A diameter is equal to two radii.

$$C = 2\pi r \quad \text{Circumference}$$
$$A = \pi r^2 \quad \text{Area}$$
$$\pi = \frac{22}{7} = 3.14$$

Example 1: Find the circumference of a circle whose diameter is 14 cm.

Solution: The radius of a circle is half the diameter.
Two radii make up one diameter.

$C = 2\pi r$ Formula

$C = 2\left(\dfrac{22}{7}\right)(7)$ Substitute

$C = 44$ cm. Evaluate

Answer: The circumference of the circle is 44 cm.

Example 2: Find the area of a circle whose radius is 6 cm.

Solution: $A = \pi r^2$

$A = 3.14\,(6)^2$ Substitute

$A = 3.14\,(36)$ Evaluate

$A = 113$ sq. cm.

Answer: The area of the circle is 113 sq.cm

Answer each of the following questions. Write the correct answer in the space provided:

1. Find the circumference of a circle whose radius is 14 cm. Answer_____

2. Find the radius of a circle whose circumference is 11 cm. Answer_____

3. Find the area of a circle whose diameter is 14 cm. Answer_____

4. Find the circumference of a circle whose radius is 7 cm. Answer_____

5. Find the radius of a circle whose circumference is 22 cm. Answer_____

6. Find the area of a circle whose radius is 8 cm. Answer_____

84. Area and Perimeter of Geometric Figures

IMPORTANT GEOMETRIC FORMS

- **Polygon**: is a closed figure formed by three or more straight lines, all of which intersect in a plane.
- **Triangle**: is a polygon with three sides and with three angles.
- **Quadrilateral:** is a polygon with four sides.
- **Parallelogram**: is a quadrilateral in which both pairs of opposite sides are right angles.
- **Rectangle:** is a parallelogram in which all angles are right angles.
- **Square:** is a rectangle in which all sides are equal.
- **Rhombus**: is a parallelogram in which all the sides are equal in length.
- **Trapezoid:** is a quadrilateral in which only one pair of opposite sides are parallel.

IMPORTANT FORMULAS: AREA AND PERIMETER

- **Area:** is the amount of the plane enclosed by a polygon.
- **Perimeter:** is the distance around the polygon.

AREA OF A RECTANGLE	AREA OF A SQUARE
Area = length x width A = l x w	Area = side squared A = S^2

AREA OF A TRIANGLE	AREA OF A TRAPEZOID
Area = ½ (base x height) A = ½ (b x h)	Area of Trapezoid = $\frac{1}{2}$ height (Sum of the bases) $A = \frac{1}{2} h (b_1 + b_2)$

PERIMETER OF A RECTANGLE	PERIMETER OF A SQUARE
Perimeter = 2 x length + 2 x width P = 21 + 2W	Perimeter = 4 times the side P = 4S

Example 1:   Find the area of a rectangle whose length is 10 cm. and whose width is 5 cm.

Solution: A = 1 x w Formula

A = 10 x 5 Substitute

A = 50 sq. cm. Evaluate

Answer: The area is 50 sq. cm.

Example 2:   Find the perimeter of a square whose side is 14 inches.

Solution: P = 4S   Formula

P = 4 (14)   Substitute

P = 56 in.   Evaluate

Answer: The perimeter is 56 in.

Example 3: Find the side of a square whose area is 64 sq. cm.

Solution: $A = s^2$ Formula

$64 = s^2$ Substitute

8 = s   Evaluate (take the square root of both sides.)

Answer: The side is 8 cm.

Example 4: Find the area of a trapezoid whose altitude is 8 cm.
and whose bases are 12 cm. and 14 cm.

Solution: $A = 1/2\ h\ (b_1 + b_2)$ Formula

$A = 1/2\ 8\ (12 + 14)$ Substitute

$A = 4\ (26)$ Evaluate

$A = 104$ sq. cm.

Answer: The area is 104 sq. cm.

Answer each of the following questions. Write the correct answer in the space provided:

1.   Find the perimeter of a rectangle whose
       dimensions are 14 cm. and 12 cm.   Answer_____

2.   If the perimeter of a square is 48 meters, what
       is the value of the side of a square?   Answer_____

3.   The area of a triangle is 48 sq. cm. If the base is
       24cm., find the value of the altitude.   Answer_____

4.   Find the side of square whose area is 64 sq.cm.   Answer_____

5.   Find the area of square whose perimeter
       is 24 feet.   Answer_____

6.   The area of a trapezoid is 72 sq. cm. and the sum of
       its bases is 36 cm. Find the altitude.   Answer_____

85. Pythagorean Theorem

> **Rules for the Pythagorean Theorem:**
>
> 1. This theorem applies only to a right triangle. A right triangle is a triangle with a 90 degree angle. The side opposite the right angle is called the hypotenuse. The other two sides are called legs. The hypotenuse is the longest side.
> 2. This theorem states:
>
> $$\text{Leg}^2 + \text{Leg}^2 = \text{Hypotenuse}^2$$
>
> $$a^2 + b^2 = c^2$$

Example 1: In the right triangle shown, find x.

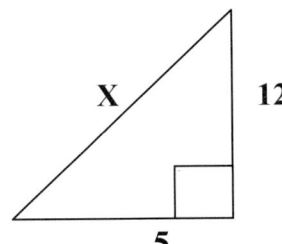

Solution: $a^2 + b^2 = c^2$

| Write the formula. Substitute. |

$12^2 + 5^2 = x^2$

$144 + 25 = x^2$

| Perform order of operations and solve |

$\sqrt{169} = \sqrt{x^2}$

Answer: $x = 13$

Example 2: In the right triangle shown, find x.

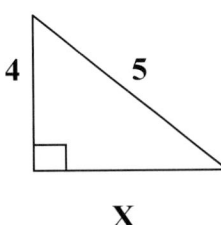

Solution: $a^2 + b^2 = c^2$

| Write the formula. Substitute. |

$x^2 + 4^2 = 5^2$
$x^2 + 16 = 25$
$x^2 + 16 - 16 = 25 - 16$

| Perform order of operations and solve |

$\sqrt{x^2} = \sqrt{9}$

Answer: $x = 3$

Write the length of the missing side in the space provided:

1.

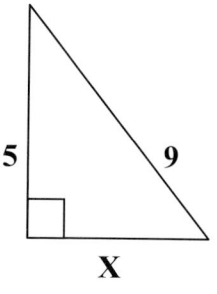

Answer_____

4.

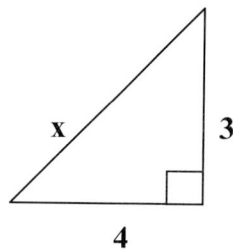

Answer_____

2.

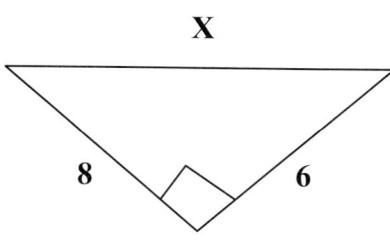

Answer_____

5.

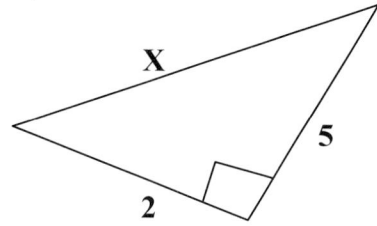

Answer_____

3.

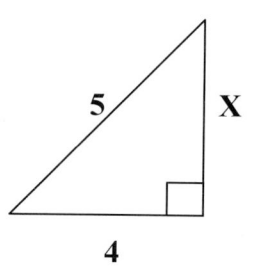

Answer_____

6.

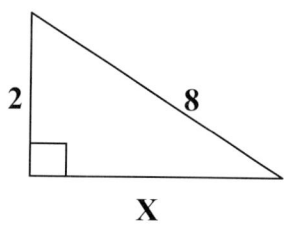

Answer_____

PROBLEM SET #26
Answer each of the following questions:

1. Find the complement of an angle that is $61°$.

2. Find the supplement of an angle that is $121°$.

3. An angle is eight times its supplement. Find the smaller angle.

4. An angle is five times its complement. Find the larger angle.

5. An angle is $80°$ more than its supplement. Find both angles.

6. An angle is $24°$ less than its complement. Find the smaller angle.

7. An angle exceeds its supplement by $120°$. Find the larger angle.

8. An angle is twice its complement. Find the larger angle.

PROBLEM SET #27
Answer each of the following verbal problems:

1. The vertex angle of an isosceles triangle is 50°. Find the value of each base angle.

2. The three angles of a triangle are in the ratio 2:3:4. Find the value of the larger angle.

3. The vertex angle on an isosceles triangle is 40°. Find the value of each base angle.

4. The vertex angles of an isosceles triangle is three times the base angle. Find the value of the vertex angle.

PROBLEM SET #28
Answer each of the following verbal questions:

1. Find the circumference of a circle whose radius is 22 cm.

2. Find the radius of a circle whose circumference is 28 cm.

3. Find the area of a circle whose diameter is 28 cm.

4. Find the circumference of a circle whose diameter is 14 cm.

5. Find the radius of a circle whose circumference is 44 cm.

6. Find the area of a circle whose radius is 16 cm.

PROBLEM SET #29
Answer each of the following verbal problems:

1. Find the perimeter of a rectangle whose dimensions are 14 cm. and 12 cm..

2. If the perimeter of a square is 60 cm., what is the value of the side of the square?

3. The area of a triangle is 60 sq. cm. If the base is 12 cm., find the value of its altitude.

4. Find the side of a square whose perimeter is 48 ft.

5. The area of a trapezoid is 144 sq. cm. and the sum of the bases is 72 cm. Find the altitude.

6. Find the area of a rectangle whose perimeter is 60 ft. and whose length is 20 ft.

7. Find the perimeter of a rectangle whose area is 300 sq. ft. and whose length is 125 ft.

8. Find the area of a rectangle whose length is 30 cm. and whose width is 12 cm.

PROBLEM SET #30
Answer each of the following verbal problems:

1. Find the perimeter of a rectangle whose dimensions are 14 cm. and 12 cm.

2. If the perimeter of a square is 60 cm., what is the value of the side of the square?

3. The area of a triangle is 60 sq. cm. If the basis is 12 cm., find the value of its altitude.

4. Find the side of a square whose perimeter is 48 ft.

5. The area of a trapezoid is 144 sq. cm. And the sum of the bases is 72 cm. Find the altitude.

6. Find the area of a rectangle whose perimeter is 60 ft. and whose length is 20 ft.

7. Find the perimeter of a rectangle whose area is 300 sq. ft and whose length is 125 feet.

8. Find the area of rectangle whose length is 30 cm. and whose width is 12 cm.

86. Sample Examinations and Answers

SAMPLE EXAM #1

A. Write the letter of the correct answer in the space provided:

1. Write six million three hundred fifty-four.

   a) 600,354   b) 6,000,354   c) 60,000,354
   d) 60,254   d) 6,003,540   Answer_____

2. $671 - 89$

   a) 760   b) 572   c) 682
   d) 581   e) 582   Answer_____

3. A play starts at 6:45 p.m. and ends at 9:30 p.m. How long is the play?

   a) 3 hours 45 minutes   b) 2 hours 30 minutes
   c) 2 hours 45 minutes   d) 1 hour 30 minutes
   e) 4 hours 45 minutes   Answer_____

4. $\dfrac{2}{7} + \dfrac{1}{6}$

   a) $\dfrac{19}{42}$ b) $\dfrac{3}{13}$ c) $\dfrac{3}{42}$

   d) $\dfrac{1}{14}$ e) $\dfrac{1}{7}$ Answer_____

5. $4.08 + .48 + 40$

   a) 4.96   b) 44.56   c) .496
   d) 4.456   e) .4456   Answer_____

6. What is 30% of 90?

   a) 27   b) 270   c) .27
   d) 300   e) 3,000   Answer_____

7. $4(-1)^2 - 3(7)$

   a) -25 b) 25   c) 17
   d) -17 e) 5   Answer_____

8. Change $\dfrac{2}{9}$ to a decimal, rounded to the nearest hundredth.

   a) .22   b) .23   c) .222
   d) .02   e) .022   Answer_____

9. Which number is the smallest?

a) .04   b) .041   c) .004
d) .0045 e) .401

Answer_____

10. $12.2 - 3.49$

a) 15.69   b) 1.569   c) 8.71
c) 87.1   e) .871

Answer_____

11. Which of the fractions is the smallest?

a) $\frac{5}{9}$ b) $\frac{2}{7}$ c) $\frac{3}{5}$

d) $\frac{1}{5}$ e) $\frac{2}{9}$

Answer _____

12. $2424 \div 12$

a) 22   b) 101   c) 11
d) 202   c) 200

Answer_____

13. $1\frac{3}{4} \div 7$

a) $\frac{1}{7}$ b) $\frac{1}{4}$ c) $\frac{2}{3}$

d) $\frac{1}{6}$ e) $\frac{3}{7}$

Answer_____

14. Jose has a 92 average on three chemistry tests. On his first two tests he received a 97 and 91. What must his grade be on the third test?

a) 94   b) 91   c) 87
d) 88   e) 89

Answer_____

15. If 20% of number is 4, find the number.

a) .8   b) 8   c) 80
d) 2   e) 20

Answer_____

16. $3\frac{5}{6} - 1\frac{1}{3}$

a) $2\frac{1}{2}$ b) $3\frac{1}{2}$ c) $5\frac{1}{6}$

d) $2\frac{1}{3}$ e) $3\frac{2}{3}$

Answer_____

17. A $30 blouse is reduced by 10%. What is the sale price?

a) $3   b) $24   c) $33
d) $27   e) $36

Answer_____

18. What is the cost to carpet a room 8 yards by 6 yards at $5 per square yard?

a) $400   b) $300   c) $240
d) $140   e) $280   Answer_____

19. 3.1 x .004

a) .124   b) 12.4   c) 1.24
d) 124   e) .0124   Answer_____

20. .022 ÷ .02 equals

a) 1.1   b) 11   c) .11
d) .011   e) 110   Answer_____

21. Add $2a^2 - 7a$ and $3 - a$

a) $6a^2 - 7a + 3$ b) $2a^3 - 7a - 3$
c) $2a^2 - 8a + 3$ d) $6a^2 - 6a + 3$
e) $2a^3 + 8a - 3$ Answer_____

22. Simplify $\dfrac{12x^2 - 6x}{2x}$

a) $6x - 3$ b) $6x^2 - 3x$ c) $6x^3 - 3x^2$
d) $6x^2 - 3$ e) $6x^3 - 6x$ Answer_____

23. Find the value of "q" quarters and "n" nickels.

a) $q + n$ b) $25(q + n)$ c) qn
d) $5(q + n)$ e) $25q + 5n$ Answer_____

24. Solve for x: $3x - 6 = x + 4$

a) –5   b) 3   c) –3
d) 5   e) 2   Answer_____

25. Solve for x: $\dfrac{x}{2} + \dfrac{x}{4} = 3$

a) 3   b) –3   c) 4
d) –4   e) 5   Answer_____

26. Simplify $(2x^3 y^4)^3$

a) $8x^6y^7$ b) $8x^9y^4$ c) $6x^9y^{12}$
d) $8x^9y^{12}$ e) $8x^6y^{12}$ Answer_____

27. If $a = 3$ and $b = 4$, find the value $3a^2 - 2b^2$.

a) 5   b) – 59   c) –5
d) 59   e) 30   Answer_____

28.   Factor $6x^2 - 3x$.

a) $3(2x^2 - x)$ b) $3x(2x - 1)$ c) $3x(2x - 3)$
d) $3(2x^2 - 3x)$ e) $3(6x^2 - x)$ Answer_____

29.   Find the product of $3x^2y^3$ and $-2xy$.

a) $6xy^2$ b) $-6x^3y^4$ c) $-6xy$
d) $6x^3y^4$ e) $6x^2y$ Answer_____

30.   Simply $6a^2 - 2a(a + 3)$.

a) $4a^2 - 6a$ b) $8a^2 - 6a$ c) $2a^2 - 3a$
d) $4a^2 - 3a$ e) $3a^4 + 6a$ Answer_____

31.   Subtract $3x^2 - 6$ from $6x^2 - 7$.

a) $9x^2 - 1$ b) $-3x^2 + 1$ c) $3x^2 - 1$
d) $9x^2 + 1$ e) $3x^4 - 1$ Answer_____

32.   If $2x - y = 6$ and $4x + y = 6$ then,

a) $x = 2, y = 1$ b) $x = 2, y = -2$ c) $x = 2, y = 4$
d) $x = 4, y = -1$ e) $x = 3, y = 3$ Answer_____

33.   In the following right triangle, find the value of x.

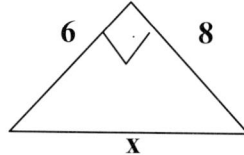

a) 4   b) 100   c) 8
d) 5   e) 10   Answer_____

34.   Which of the following points lies on the graph $2x + y = 6$?

a) $(3, 3)$ b) $(-3, -3)$ c) $(2, 2)$
d) $(-2, -2)$ e) $(6, 1)$ Answer_____

35.   Solve for x: $2x + 3y = 7$

a) $7 - 3y$ b) $7 + 3y$ c) $\dfrac{7 - 2x}{3}$

d) $\dfrac{7 - 3y}{2}$ e) $\dfrac{7 + 3y}{2}$ Answer_____

36. Write an equation for the line.

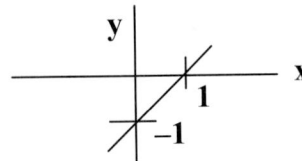

a) $x + 7 = 1$ b) $x - y = 1$ c) $x = y + 2$
d) $x + y = 2$ e) $x + 2y = 2$

Answer_____

37. There are 80 mathematics professors at City College in which 25% are women. Without firing anyone, how many additional women must be hired in order to bring the percentage of women up to 50%?

a) 20   b) 30   c) 40
d) 50   e) 60

Answer_____

38. Solve for x : $\frac{x}{2} - 1 = \frac{x+3}{4}$.

a) –7   b) 4   c) –4
d) 1   e) 7

Answer_____

39. A toy storeowner finds that 2 out of 7 toys sold are returned. If 350 toys are sold in a week, how many are expected to be returned?

a) 50   b) 100   c) 150
d) 200   e) 250

Answer_____

40. If (0, b) lies on the graph, $y = 3x - 8$ then, b =

a) 3   b) –3   c) 8
d) 6   e) –8

Answer_____

ANSWERS : SAMPLE EXAM #1

1.	b	21.	c
2.	e	22.	a
3.	c	23.	e
4.	a	24.	d
5.	b	25.	c
6.	a	26.	d
7.	d	27.	c
8.	a	28.	b
9.	c	29.	b
10.	c	30.	a
11.	d	31.	c
12.	d	32.	b
13.	b	33.	e
14.	d	34.	c
15.	e	35.	d
16.	a	36.	b
17.	d	37.	c
18.	c	38.	e
19.	e	39.	b
20.	a	40.	e

SAMPLE EXAM # 2
B. Write the letter of the correct answer in the space provided:

1. Write three million forty-five.

    a) 300,045   b) 3,000,045   c) 3,000,450
    d) 30,045   e) 300,450   Answer_____

2. 421 – 37
    a) 484   b) 458   c) 358
    d) 494   e) 384   Answer_____

3. A movie starts at 6:15 p.m. and ends at 9:05 p.m.
    How long was the movie?

    a) 3 hours 50 minutes   b) 2 hours 45 minutes
    c) 4 hours 20 minutes   d) 4 hours 50 minutes
    e) 2 hours 50 minutes   Answer_____

4. $\dfrac{4}{9} + \dfrac{1}{3}$

    a) $\dfrac{5}{12}$ b) $\dfrac{5}{9}$ c) $\dfrac{4}{27}$

    d) $\dfrac{7}{9}$ e) $\dfrac{2}{3}$ Answer_____

5. 4.7 – 1.89
    a) 6.59   b) 65.9   c) 2.81
    d) 28.1   e) .281   Answer_____

6. Change $\dfrac{7}{9}$ to a decimal rounded to the nearest hundredth.

    a) .78   b) .79   c) .777
    d) .709   e) .785   Answer_____

7. $6(-2)^2 - 3(6)$

    a) 6   b) –6   c) 42
    d) –4   e) 12   Answer_____

8. What is 40% of 70?

    a) .28   b) 175   c) 28
    d) 1.75   e) 1.19   Answer_____

9. Which fraction is the smallest?
    a) $\dfrac{2}{7}$ b) $\dfrac{1}{3}$ c) $\dfrac{4}{9}$

    d) $\dfrac{3}{8}$ e) $\dfrac{2}{5}$ Answer_____

10. $\frac{2}{3} \div 6$

    a) 4   b) $\frac{1}{9}$ c) $\frac{1}{4}$

    d) $\frac{5}{9}$ e) $\frac{2}{3}$ Answer_____

11. Zelma has a 94 average on three mathematics tests. On her first two tests, she received 89 and 95. What must her grade be on the third test?

    a) 95   b) 96   c) 97
    d) 98   e) 99   Answer_____

12. If 40% of a number is 60, find the number.

    a) 250   b) 100   c) 150
    d) 240   e) 24   Answer_____

13. Which number is the smallest?
    a) .076   b) .7   c) .07
    d) .071   e) .075   Answer_____

14. $6.1 + .61 + 61$

    a) 7.32   b) 6.771   c) 73.2
    d) .6771   e) 67.71   Answer_____

15. Express 40% as a fraction?

    a) 2/5   b) 7/10   c) 3/5
    d) 4/5   e) 3/10   Answer_____

16. $4\frac{5}{9} - 2\frac{1}{3}$
    a) $4\frac{2}{9}$ b) $3\frac{2}{9}$ c) $2\frac{2}{9}$
    d) $2\frac{2}{3}$ e) $3\frac{1}{3}$ Answer_____

17. If pencils sell for \$.12 each, how many can be purchased for \$24?

    a) 48   b) 480   c) 20
    d) 40   e) 200   Answer_____

18. A \$45 jacket is reduced by 20%. What is the discount?

    a) \$9   b) \$36   c) \$25
    d) \$50   e) \$60   Answer_____

19. Find the cost to carpet a room 7 yards by 6 yards at \$4 per square yard.

    a) \$28   b) \$24   c) \$42
    d) \$168   e) \$104   Answer_____

20. $3.6 \div 36$ equals

    a) 10   b) 1   c) .01

    d) .1   e) 100   Answer_____

21. Solve for x: $4x - 2 = x + 7$

    a) -3 b) 2   c) -2

    d) 4   e) 3   Answer_____

22. Simplify $(3x^2 y^3)^4$.

    a) $12x^8y^{12}$ b) $81x^8y^{12}$ c) $12x^6y^7$

    d) $81x^6y^7$ e) $12x^6y^7$ Answer_____

23. Find the value of "d" dimes and "n" nickels.

    a) $d + n$ b) $10(d + n)$ c) 5

    d) $5(d + n)$ e) $10d + 5n$ Answer_____

24. Solve for x: $\frac{x}{3} + \frac{x}{5} = 8$

    a) 15   b) -15 c) 8

    d) -8 e) 6   Answer_____

25. If $x = 4$ and $y = 5$, find the value of $3x^2 + 4y^2$

    a) 32   b) 27   c) 144

    d) 29   e) 148   Answer_____

26. Simplify $\dfrac{16x^2 - 32x}{8x}$

    a) $2x - 4$ b) $2x + 4$ c) $2x^3 - 4x^2$

    d) $2x^2 - 4x$ e) $2x^3 - 4x$ Answer_____

27. Factor $9y^2 - 6y$

    a) $3(3y^2 - 2y)$ b) $y(9y - 6)$ c) $3y(3y - 2)$

    d) $3y(7y - 6)$ e) $y(3y - 6)$ Answer_____

28. Add $3x^2 - 6x$ and $4 - x$.

    a) $3x^2 - 6x + 4$ b) $3x^2 - 7x + 4$ c) $3x^2 - 6x - 4$

    d) $3x^2 - 3x$ e) $7x^2 - 7x$ Answer_____

29. Simplify $3x^2 - 2x(x+3)$

    a) $x^2 - 6x$ b) $x^2 + 6x$ c) $5x^2 - 6x$

    d) $5x^2 + 6x$ e) $-x^2 - 6x$ Answer_____

30. Find the product of $4a^2b^3$ and $-3ab$

    a) $-12a^2b^3$ b) $-12a^3b^4$ c) $64a^2b^3$

    d) $-64a^2b^3$ e) $12a^2b^3$ Answer_____

31.   If $3x - y = 4$ and $x + y = 8$, then,

        a) $x = 5$, $y = 2$ b) $x = 3$, $y = 5$
        c) $x = 2$, $y = 3$ d) $x = 4$, $y = 1$
        e) $x = 6$, $y = 2$ Answer_____

32.   Subtract $3a^2 - 6b^2$ from $6b^2 - 3a^2$

        a) 0 b) $-12b^2 - 6a$ c) $3a^2 - 12b^2$
        d) $9a^2 - 9b^2$ e) $-6a^2 + 12b^2$ Answer_____

33.   In the following right triangle, find the value of x.

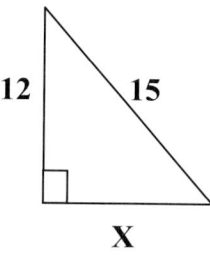

        a) 9   b) 369   c) 11
        d) 15   e) 17   Answer_____

34.   Which of the following points lies on the graph:
    $3x + 2y = 5$?

        a) $(-1, -1)$ b) $(2, -4)$ c) $(-2, 4)$
        d) $(3, 7)$ e) $(1, 1)$ Answer_____

35.   Solve for y: $2x - 4y = 14$,

        a) $7 + x$ b) $\dfrac{7-x}{2}$ c) $-7 - x$

        d) $\dfrac{7+x}{2}$ e) $\dfrac{-7+x}{2}$ Answer_____

36.   Write an equation for the line.

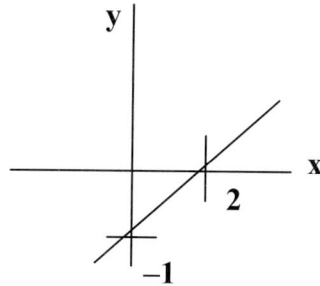

        a) $x - 2y = 2$ b) $x - y = 2$
        c) $x - 2y = -2$ d) $x - 2y = 1$
        e) $x - y = -1$ Answer_____

37. Solve for x: $\dfrac{x}{3} - 2 = \dfrac{x+6}{6}$

    a) 18   b) – 18   c) 9
    d) –9   e) 8   Answer _____

38. Martin Luther King High School has 60 psychologists
    in which 20% are women. Without firing anyone, how
    many additional women must be hired in order to bring
    the percentage of women up to 50%?

    a) 24   b) 35   c) 12
    d) 25   e) 36   Answer_____

39. A secretary earns $60 in 8 hours. At this rate of pay,
    how much will she earn in 20 hours?

    a) $100   b) $150   c) $200
    d) $ 75   e) $50   Answer_____

40. If a = 3bc^2, find "a" when b = 4 and c = 5

    a) 240   b) 120   c) 70
    d) 60   e) 300   Answer_____

ANSWERS : SAMPLE EXAM # 2

1.	b	21.	e
2.	e	22.	b
3.	e	23.	e
4.	d	24.	a
5.	c	25.	e
6.	a	26.	a
7.	a.	27.	c
8.	c	28.	b
9.	a	29.	a
10.	b	30.	b
11.	d	31.	b
12.	c	32.	e
13.	c	33.	a
14.	e	34.	e
15.	a	35.	e
16.	c	36.	a
17.	e	37.	a
18.	a.	38.	e
19.	d	39.	b
20.	d	40.	e

87. ANSWER KEY

PAGE 4

1. a) {5,6,7,8.......}
   b) {3,4,5,6,7,8}
   c) {1,2,3,4,5}
   d) {2,4,6,8}

2. a) Hundreds
   b) Ones
   c) Tens
   d) Thousands

3. a) 754
   b) 4,059
   c) 340
   d) 8,600

4. a) Six thousand three hundred fifty-nine
   b) Nine thousand three hundred eights
   c) Three hundred forty-nine
   d) Eight thousand six hundred

PAGE 8

1. Commutative Property of Addition
2. Identity Element of Addition
3. Identity Element for Multiplication
4. Associative Property for Multiplication
5. Associative Property for Addition
6. Commutative Property for Multiplication
7. Distributive Property for Multiplication

PAGES 13-14

1. 169
2. 591
3. 253
4. 3,301
5. 6,970
6. 1,634
7. 8,298
8. 8,638
9. 1,434
10. 4,024
11. 1,347
12. 7,967
13. 6,591
14. 7,692
15. 7,925
16. 7,404
17. 5,638
18. 46,536
19. 79,092
20. 11,793

PAGES 14-15

1. 712
2. 59
3. 8
4. 3,333
5. 11
6. 462
7. 74
8. 109
9. 3,761
10. 1,748
11. 33
12. 258
13. 102
14. 6,002
15. 750
16. 55
17. 547
18. 362
19. 358
20. 31

PAGE 15

1. 234
2. 84
3. 2,886
4. 1,273
5. 20,000
6. 360,000
7. 186,963
8. 100,100
9. 400,400
10. 10,875
11. 160,000
12. 4,000,000
13. 4,773
14. 57,290
15. 18,000,000
16. 28,000,000
17. 10,233
18. 173,546
19. 81,003
20. 358,248

PAGE 16

1. 32
2. 75
3. 15
4. 3
5. 12
6. 4
7. 3
8. 42
9. 103
10. 27
11. 101
12. 1,001
13. 30
14. 25
15. ∞
16. 0
17. ∞
18. 0
19. 101
20. 501

PAGE 17

1. 9,826
2. 38,677
3. 7,134
4. 11
5. 2
6. 661
7. 33,558
8. 26,325
9. 73,290
10. 101
11. 39
12. 560
13. 21,528
14. 55
15. 6,033
16. 101
17. 3,648
18. 99
19. 4,347
20. 3,880
21. 3,135
22. 228
23. 56
24. 71,063
25. 119

PAGES 18, 19

1. C
2. E
3. A
4. B
5. D
6. A
7. B
8. E
9. B

PAGE 20

1. 9 hrs. 6 mins.
2. 6 yds. 1 ft. 4 in.
3. 1 hr. 57 min.
4. 7 in.
5. 1 hr. 55 min
6. 1 ft. 7 in
7. 2 hrs. 40 min.
8. 3 hrs. 47 min
9. 37 min.
10. 1 hr. 5 min.

PAGES 21, 22

1. 36.7
2. 60
3. 80
4. 14
5. 20
6. 90
7. 100
8. 12
9. 40
10. 10

PAGE 23

1. 20
2. 26
3. 103
4. 10
5. 40
6. 12
7. 16
8. 1
9. 49
10. 147
11. 588
12. 199
13. 21
14. 77
15. 9

PAGE 25

1. 7
2. 6
3. 3
4. 3
5. 8
6. 3
7. 3
8. 4
9. 9
10. 6

PAGE 27

1. a) Ones
   b) Hundredths
   c) Tenths
   d) Ten Thousandths
   e) Tenths
   f) Tens

2. a) Forty-three and fifty-four hundredths
   b) Sixty-eight and nine tenths
   c) Twelve and three hundred twenty-five thousandths
   d) Sixteen and two hundred ninety-five ten thousandths
   e) One hundred and two tenths
   f) Three hundred and twenty-five hundredths

3. a) 7.003
   b) 32.12
   c) 200.07
   d) .159
   e) 3000.6
   f) 27.0010

PAGE 29: PART A
1. E
2. B
3. B
4. A
5. E
6. C

PAGE 29: PART B
1. B
2. D
3. E
4. E
5. C
6. A

PAGE 31: PART A
1. .38
2. .22
3. .86
4. .21
5. .29
6. .18
7. .89
8. .83

PAGE 31: PART B
1. .273
2. .769
3. .286
4. .375
5. .471
6. .579
7. .571
8. .778

PAGE 32: PART A
1. 29.981
2. 41.996
3. 17.802
4. 9.865
5. 23.45
6. 8.325
7. 97.989
8. 27.84
9. 79.92
10. 79.665

PAGE 32: PART B
1. 25.1
2. 9.35
3. 2.922
4. 12.75
5. 3.89
6. 71.28
7. 1.3
8. 5.911
9. 235.22
10. 548.33

PAGE 33: PART A
1. .20
2. .234
3. .96
4. .017
5. .081
6. 2109.12
7. .0032
8. 14.4
9. 1.26
10. .0048
11. 82.62
12. 5152.17

PAGE 33: PART B
1. $2.94
2. $26.40
3. $3.95
4. $205.80
5. $45.00

PAGE 35: PART A
1. 60
2. 2,400
3. 200
4. .07
5. .5
6. 12,000
7. .14
8. 12
9. 50
10. 1.01
11. 200
12. .6

PAGE 35: PART B
1. 40
2. 24
3. 20
4. 16

PAGE 37

1. 7.6
2. $21.75
3. 203.75
4. 3.25
5. $47.52
6. .0414
7. 319.50
8. $2,921.50
9. $715
10. 13.5
11. 3.14
12. 28.8
13. .001
14. $18.56
15. $3.38
16. 10

PAGE 39

1. 300
2. 2,000
3. $1,000
4. $2,500
5. 5,000
6. 333.33
7. 200
8. 200
9. 4,800
10. $7,600

PAGE 40

1. 50%
2. 62.5%
3. 75%
4. 40%
5. 12.5%
6. 50%
7. 25%
8. 33%
9. 33%
10. 16%

PAGE 40 WORKBOOK

1. 14.25
2. 270
3. 1.5
4. 20%
5. $36.25
6. 900
7. 2,000
8. $.08
9. $3,000
10. 20%
11. 40
12. $104.65
13. 3,000
14. 40%
15. $8.33

PAGE 41

1. .49
2. 39.5
3. 8.951
4. 3.86
5. 3.95
6. 60
7. .198
8. .0379
9. 6.2
10. 300
11. .0122
12. .079

PAGE 42: PART A

1. .24
2. .65
3. .045
4. .03
5. 4.5
6. .35
7. .36
8. 1.75

PAGE 43: PART B

1. $\dfrac{7}{20}$

2. $\dfrac{1}{50}$

3. $\dfrac{1}{40}$

4. $1\dfrac{1}{5}$

5. $4\dfrac{7}{20}$

6. $\dfrac{9}{200}$

7. $\dfrac{4}{25}$

8. $6\dfrac{2}{5}$

9. $\dfrac{89}{1000}$

10. $\dfrac{29}{40}$

PAGE 43: PART C

1. $\dfrac{7}{20}$

2. $\dfrac{2}{25}$

3. $\dfrac{19}{100}$

4. $\dfrac{6}{25}$

5. $1\dfrac{1}{2}$

6. $\dfrac{7}{10}$

7. $\dfrac{79}{100}$

8. $2\dfrac{9}{20}$

9. $\dfrac{9}{25}$

10. $\dfrac{1}{25}$

PAGE 44: PART D

1. .39
2. .07
3. 1.25
4. .008
5. .06
6. .54
7. 4.29
8. .007
9. .04
10. .16

PAGE 45

1. $5.25
2. $4.12
3. $111.00
4. $170.00
5. $1,003.00
6. $3,675.00
7. $3.44
8. $1,820.00
9. $10.65
10. $3.70

PAGES 47, 48

1. C
2. A
3. E
4. D
5. A
6. D
7. A
8. B
9. E
10. A
11. B
12. A
13. A
14. A
15. A
16. E

PAGE 49

1. $97.20
2. $30,740.00
3. $38.00
4. $45.00
5. $8,320,000.00
6. $16.80
7. $20.87

PAGE 50
1. $386.75
2. $71.20
3. 7,440,000
4. $22,000.00
5. $34.91
6. $16.25
7. $1.68
8. 1,980,000

PAGE 52
1. 40 SQ. YDS.
2. 1,950 SQ. IN.
3. $504.00
4. $315.00
5. 30 FT
6. 110 FT
7. $840.00
8. $378.00
9. $864.00
10. 12 IN.

PAGE 57

Improper Fractions

1. $\dfrac{9}{2}$
2. $\dfrac{11}{3}$
3. $\dfrac{18}{4}$
4. $\dfrac{19}{5}$
5. $\dfrac{17}{3}$
6. $\dfrac{7}{4}$
7. $\dfrac{15}{2}$
8. $\dfrac{29}{3}$
9. $\dfrac{22}{4}$
10. $\dfrac{26}{6}$
11. $\dfrac{32}{4}$
12. $\dfrac{29}{4}$
13. $\dfrac{63}{5}$

Changed to Mixed Numbers

1. $1\dfrac{4}{5}$
2. $2\dfrac{3}{4}$
3. $3\dfrac{1}{4}$
4. $2\dfrac{1}{7}$
5. $3\dfrac{2}{4}$
6. 2
7. 4
8. $2\dfrac{3}{8}$
9. $1\dfrac{8}{14}$
10. $1\dfrac{15}{17}$
11. $11\dfrac{11}{20}$
12. $1\dfrac{5}{19}$
13. $4\dfrac{1}{4}$

1. $\dfrac{1}{2}$

2. $\dfrac{3}{4}$

3. $\dfrac{1}{3}$

4. $\dfrac{1}{2}$

5. $\dfrac{1}{2}$

6. $\dfrac{1}{4}$

7. $\dfrac{4}{5}$

8. $\dfrac{3}{5}$

9. $\dfrac{1}{2}$

10. $\dfrac{1}{2}$

11. $\dfrac{13}{24}$

12. $\dfrac{8}{9}$

13. $3\dfrac{1}{2}$

14. $\dfrac{1}{3}$

15. $\dfrac{1}{5}$

16. $\dfrac{1}{2}$

17. $\dfrac{1}{4}$

18. $\dfrac{3}{10}$

19. $\dfrac{1}{7}$

20. $\dfrac{1}{5}$

PAGE 60

1. $\dfrac{8}{12}$

2. $\dfrac{12}{18}$

3. $\dfrac{25}{30}$

4. $\dfrac{12}{20}$

5. $\dfrac{3}{18}$

6. $\dfrac{24}{27}$

7. $\dfrac{30}{68}$

8. $\dfrac{30}{66}$

PAGES 61-62

1. 15
2. 20
3. 60
4. 60
5. 12
6. 42
7. 12
8. 200
9. 36
10. 30
11. 20
12. 24
13. 16
14. 36
15. 42

PAGE 64

1. $\dfrac{7}{10}$

2. $1\dfrac{1}{4}$

3. $1\dfrac{7}{22}$

4. $\dfrac{13}{14}$

5. $1\dfrac{19}{55}$

6. $\dfrac{9}{10}$

7. $7\dfrac{1}{12}$

8. $10\dfrac{29}{35}$

9. $13\dfrac{7}{8}$

10. 7

11. $10\dfrac{31}{40}$

12. $\dfrac{7}{9}$

13. $10\dfrac{1}{4}$

14. $9\dfrac{1}{8}$

15. $4\dfrac{11}{14}$

16. $2\dfrac{37}{60}$

17. $17\dfrac{4}{9}$

18. $1\dfrac{1}{4}$

19. $1\dfrac{11}{12}$

20. $3\dfrac{33}{72}$

PAGE 66

1. $2\frac{3}{4}$

2. $2\frac{3}{8}$

3. $\frac{33}{35}$

4. $4\frac{19}{20}$

5. $\frac{11}{12}$

6. $1\frac{5}{6}$

7. $4\frac{97}{99}$

8. $1\frac{19}{20}$

9. $1\frac{39}{40}$

10. $1\frac{4}{5}$

PAGE 67

1. $1\frac{5}{8}$

2. $9\frac{2}{9}$

3. $5\frac{3}{14}$

4. $5\frac{1}{3}$

5. $8\frac{1}{8}$

6. $17\frac{2}{5}$

7. $14\frac{1}{10}$

8. $16\frac{2}{3}$

9. $24\frac{2}{25}$

10. $15\frac{3}{7}$

PAGE 68

1. $4\frac{2}{5}$

2. $4\frac{1}{3}$

3. $3\frac{2}{7}$

4. $26\frac{1}{3}$

5. $19\frac{1}{3}$

6. $14\frac{3}{4}$

7. $\frac{1}{2}$

8. $3\frac{1}{3}$

9. $12\frac{1}{4}$

10. $10\frac{1}{2}$

PAGE 69: PART A

1. $1\frac{3}{4}$
2. $3\frac{2}{7}$
3. $2\frac{3}{5}$
4. $5\frac{2}{3}$
5. $4\frac{1}{2}$
6. $4\frac{1}{4}$
7. $3\frac{4}{7}$
8. $3\frac{1}{5}$
9. $3\frac{1}{2}$
10. $9\frac{2}{3}$

PAGE 70: PART B

1. $\frac{17}{7}$
2. $\frac{37}{9}$
3. $\frac{31}{5}$
4. $\frac{79}{5}$
5. $\frac{97}{9}$
6. $\frac{44}{7}$
7. $\frac{29}{9}$
8. $\frac{64}{5}$
9. $\frac{39}{5}$
10. $\frac{20}{3}$

PAGES 71- 72

1. $\frac{21}{49}$
2. $\frac{49}{63}$
3. $\frac{24}{40}$
4. $\frac{35}{42}$
5. $\frac{18}{48}$
6. $\frac{90}{150}$
7. $\frac{25}{60}$
8. $\frac{36}{81}$
9. $\frac{10}{25}$
10. $\frac{6}{27}$

PAGE 73

1. $14 = 7 \times 2$
2. $48 = 3 \times 2 \times 2 \times 2 \times 2$
3. $18 = 3 \times 3 \times 2$
4. $144 = 3 \times 3 \times 2 \times 2 \times 2 \times 2$
5. $260 = 5 \times 3 \times 3 \times 2 \times 2 \times 2$
6. $81 = 3 \times 3 \times 3 \times 3$
7. $56 = 7 \times 2 \times 2 \times 2$
8. $64 = 2 \times 2 \times 2 \times 2 \times 2 \times 2$

PAGE 74

1. 3
2. 6
3. 9
4. 28
5. 80
6. 25
7. 16
8. 8

PAGE 75

1. $\frac{1}{3}$
2. $1\frac{1}{4}$
3. $\frac{3}{4}$
4. $1\frac{1}{3}$
5. $4\frac{1}{2}$
6. $\frac{2}{9}$
7. $\frac{2}{3}$
8. $1\frac{1}{2}$
9. $4\frac{1}{4}$
10. $3\frac{1}{2}$
11. $\frac{2}{3}$
12. $\frac{3}{14}$

PAGE 77

1. $\frac{1}{21}$
2. $\frac{1}{12}$
3. $\frac{6}{7}$
4. 6
5. 2
6. $12\frac{1}{7}$
7. $3\frac{1}{2}$
8. $\frac{3}{35}$
9. $\frac{2}{3}$
10. $\frac{1}{14}$
11. $\frac{1}{4}$
12. 15
13. 14
14. $11\frac{2}{3}$
15. 1
16. $\frac{2}{15}$

PAGE 79

1. $\frac{1}{2}$
2. $\frac{7}{8}$
3. 48
4. $1\frac{1}{4}$
5. $1\frac{1}{5}$
6. $\frac{1}{3}$
7. $\frac{2}{3}$
8. 4
9. 3
10. 2
11. 21
12. $\frac{1}{18}$
13. $1\frac{1}{3}$
14. 34
15. $4\frac{2}{9}$
16. $\frac{2}{3}$

PAGE 81

1. $\dfrac{19}{42}$

2. $\dfrac{7}{8}$

3. $7\dfrac{1}{9}$

4. $1\dfrac{5}{12}$

5. 5

6. $5\dfrac{7}{8}$

7. $1\dfrac{2}{35}$

8. $\dfrac{19}{45}$

9. $\dfrac{11}{12}$

10. $8\dfrac{1}{4}$

11. $\dfrac{46}{63}$

12. 8

13. $4\dfrac{9}{40}$

14. $8\dfrac{19}{28}$

PAGE 83

1. $\dfrac{1}{4}$

2. $\dfrac{5}{8}$

3. $2\dfrac{5}{42}$

4. $3\dfrac{7}{36}$

5. $5\dfrac{1}{8}$

6. $\dfrac{2}{9}$

7. $2\dfrac{4}{5}$

8. $\dfrac{3}{20}$

9. $\dfrac{1}{2}$

10. $\dfrac{1}{21}$

11. $1\dfrac{7}{9}$

12. $2\dfrac{47}{56}$

13. $8\dfrac{1}{3}$

14. $\dfrac{7}{15}$

15. $1\dfrac{27}{28}$

16. $1\dfrac{23}{56}$

PAGE 86: PART A

1. E
2. A
3. C
4. D
5. E

PAGE 87: PART B

1. C
2. E
3. A
4. E
5. A
6. C
7. B
8. A
9. E

PAGE 89

1. $4\dfrac{1}{12}$

2. $200

3. $\dfrac{1}{6}$

4. 135

5. $\dfrac{1}{9}$

6. $406,000

7. $4.00

8. $\dfrac{1}{4}$

9. $18\dfrac{1}{12}$

10. 8 Tons

PAGE 91

1. a) 0.000001
    b) 0.00001
    c) 0.00001
    d) 0.01
    e) 0.003
2. a) 10^{-4}, 0.0001
    b) 10^{-5}, 0.00001
    c) 10^{-3}, 0.001
    d) 10^{-6}, 0.0000001
3. a) 1/100,000, 10^{-5}
    b) 1/1,000, 10^{-3}
    c) 1/10,000,000, 10^{-7}
    d) 1/1,000,000, 10^{-6}

PAGE 92

1. 2,654
2. 1,270
3. 34,750
4. 167.5
5. 4.3
6. .00675
7. .0003956
8. .00000675

PAGE 93

1. 6.5
2. .00173
3. .00069
4. .000079
5. .73
6. 18,000
7. 36,900
8. 4,598,000,000

PAGE 94

1. a) 243,000
    b) 1,570
    c) 79,000
    d) 67,890
    e) .000057
    f) .0029
    g) .0000000000592
    h) .000000000000067
2. a) 3.57×10^{3}
    b) 6.79×10^{2}
    c) 1.8×10
    d) 8.1×10^{-3}
    e) 7.1×10^{-2}
    f) 2.345678×10^{6}
    g) 3.0×10^{-7}
    h) 1.8×10^{-7}

PAGE 96: Exercise 1

a) 600 cm.
b) 400 cg.
c) 1,210 cl.
d) 2,500 cm.
e) 50 cg.
f) 6 cl.
g) .3 mm.
h) 630 mg.

PAGE 96: Exercise 2

a) .3 m.
b) .2 g
c) 5.4 L
d) 2.4 g
e) .4 g
f) 4.8 L
g) 4 g

PAGES 97-98

1. 1760 feet
2. 3,520 feet
3. 190,080 inches
4. 196 cups
5. 2 quarts
6. 3 gallon containers
7. 9 boxes
8. 2.5 pounds

PAGES 99-100

1. 3619.9 lb.
2. 180.34 cm.
3. 152.4 cm.
4. 2 in.
5. 2.838 L
6. 3.784 L
7. .95 cm.
8. 198.9 lb
9. 91.44 cm., 86.36 cm
10. 36,960 ft.

PAGE 116- I

Number	Real	Integer	Rational	Irrational	None of these
Example: 5.2	✓		✓		
1. $\frac{3}{5}$	✓		✓		
2. 6.285	✓		✓		
4. $\sqrt{18}$	✓			✓	
5. 2π				✓	
6. $2\sqrt{25}$	✓	✓	✓		
7. 8%	✓		✓		
8. 200%	✓	✓	✓		
9. 5/0					✓
10. $-\sqrt{49}$	✓	✓	✓		
11. $\sqrt{-4}$					✓

PAGE 117- II

1. Commutative
2. Associative
3. Distributive
4. Commutative
5. Commutative
6. Commutative
7. Commutative
8. Identity
9. Identity
10. Inverse
11. Inverse
12. Commutative

PAGE 119: PART A

1. -7
2. 5
3. 3
4. 3
5. -11
6. -1
7. 0
8. -3

PAGE 119: PART B

1. 4
2. 4
3. 5
4. -3
5. 9
6. -4
7. 14
8. -2
9. -11
10. 1
11. 5
12. 11

PAGES 123-124

(Problem set #2)

1. -9
2. 9
3. 48
4. 16
5. 8
6. -24
7. -7
8. 30
9. 31
10. 7
11. 144
12. -243
13. 78
14. -169
15. -48
16. 42
17. 165
18. -11
19. 81
20. -32
21. -14
22. -363
23. 239
24. -47
25. -281
26. -32
27. 25
28. 367
29. -160
30. 245
31. -12
32. -228

PAGE 121

1. -12
2. -35
3. 12
4. 15
5. -56
6. 60
7. 9
8. -3
9. -4
10. 3
11. -7
12. -9

PAGE 126

1. $5 + x$
2. $x - 7$
3. $x - 6$
4. $x + 5$
5. $7x$
6. $x - 4$
7. $x + 14$
8. $4 + x/2$
9. $3 + 4x$
10. $3x - 6$

PAGE 127

1. $5n + 2q$
2. $10d + 25q$
3. $10d + 5n$
4. $5n + 10d + 25q$

PAGES 130-131

1. $9x + 15y$
2. $7a - 9b$
3. $8x^3 + 6x^2 - 2x$
4. $10b + 5$
5. $4x^2 - 10x + 8$
6. $10y^2 + 10y - 8$
7. $-4a^2 - 3a - 2$
8. $4x - 14$
9. $8x^2 - 16x$
10. $3x^2 + 8x - 7$
11. $-14y$
12. $8x^2 - 11x + 16$
13. $-2x - 3$
14. $-6x^2 + 14x - 12$
15. $8x^2 + 3x - 12$
16. $-3x^2 + 3x - 3$
17. $2x^2 - 10x - 6$
18. $-6x^2$
19. $11x + 17y$
20. $9a - 11b$
21. $9x^3 + 7x^2 - 12x - 11$
22. $13a^2 - 10a$
23. $-6x^2 - 3x + 20$
24. $4b^2 + 3a$
25. $-16y$
26. $-3x - 3$
27. 20
28. $-14x^2 - 14x - 20$

PAGE 132
1. x^5
2. x^2y^3
3. a^3
4. a^9
5. 2^{11}
6. a^4
7. y^9
8. y^8x
9. y^3x
10. y^9

PAGE 133
1. $12x^3y^3$
2. $-14x^5y^8$
3. $-14r^2s^2t^2$
4. $-12x^5y^{11}$
5. $-12a^2b^3c^2$
6. $32x^5$
7. $-14x^2y^3z^2$
8. $-12a^3b^3c^3$
9. $-14r^3s^2t^3$
10. $12x^4y^4z^3$

PAGE 134
1. $3x - 6$
2. $-2y + 8$
3. $a^2 + 4a$
4. $-b^2 + 7b$
5. $-3x^2 + 18x$
6. $-4y^2 + 28y$
7. $-10z^3 + 35z^2$
8. $-56x^3 + 64x^2$
9. $-10s^3 + 35s^2$
10. $8a^3b^2 - 28ab^2$
11. $21x^3y^3 - 7xy^2$
12. $-12a^3b^3 - 12a^2b^4$
13. $-28a^3b^3 + 21a^4b^2$
14. $-6x^4y^6 + x^3y^5$
15. $-21x^4y^2 + 63x^2y^2$
16. $12x^3y^2 + 15x^2y^3$
17. $-4x^2 + 28x$
18. $18x^3 - 21x^2$

PAGE 136
1. $x^2 + 2x - 3$
2. $x^2 + x - 20$
3. $4x^2 + 2x - 12$
4. $6x^2 - x - 2$
5. $y^2 - 4$
6. $y^2 - 25$
7. $x^2 - 4x - 21$
8. $x^2 + x - 30$
9. $9x^2 - 36$
10. $6x^2 + 4x - 32$
11. $x^2 - 4x + 4$
12. $x^2 + 10x + 25$

PAGE 137
1. $x^2 + 2x - 3$
2. $x^2 + x - 20$
3. $4x^2 + 2x - 12$
4. $6x^2 - x - 2$
5. $y^2 - 4$
6. $y^2 - 25$
7. $x^2 - 4x - 21$
8. $x^2 + x - 30$
9. $9x^2 - 36$
10. $6x^2 + 4x - 32$

PAGE 139
1. -10
2. -12
3. -25
4. 14
5. -53
6. -7
7. 166
8. 33
9. -60
10. 48
11. -48
12. -8
13. 46
14. -100

PAGES 140-141
1. $y^2 + 10y$
2. $x^2 + 6x$
3. $x^3 - 7x^2 + 3x$
4. $-4y^3 + 36y^2 + 4y$
5. $-x^2 + 28x$
6. $-y^2 + 4y$
7. $-2x^3 - x^2$
8. $-4y^3 - 25y^2$
9. $a^2b + 14a$
10. $-7x^3 - 20x^2y$
11. $52x^2y^2 - 7x^2y$
12. $6x^2y + 15xy^2 - 6xy$
13. $-15a^2b + 6ab^2$
14. $10x^2y + 15xy^2$
15. $y^2 + 14y$
16. $x^2 - 4x$
17. $-4x^3 - 21x^2$
18. $5y^3 + 28y^2$
19. $x^2 - 8x$
20. $6y^3 + 40y^2$

PAGE 141
(Problem set #3)
1. $x + 6$
2. $x - 8$
3. $x - 6$
4. $x + 7$
5. $8x$
6. $x - 5$
7. $x + 14$
8. $x/3 = 4$
9. $6x + 5$
10. $4x - 7$
11. $10d + 25g$
12. $5n + 25g$

PAGE 141 Bottom
(Problem set #4)
1. 10
2. $8x + 6y$
3. $8x^3 + 3x^2 + 7y^2 - 18z$
4. $-y^2 + 2y - 4$
5. $2x^3 + 9x - 8$
6. $2a^2b + 5ab^2 + 10a - 7$

PAGE 142 Top
(Problem set #5)
1. $x - 4y + 9$
2. $x^2 - 5x + 2$
3. $5x^2 + 2c^2 - 3$
4. $5xy - 4x$
5. $3x^3 - 6x^2 + 8x - 6$
6. $-14xy^2 + 8x^2y$

PAGE 142 Bottom
(Problem set #6)
1. $6a - 6b$
2. $2x^2 - 2y - 6z$
3. $x^2y - 2y^2x$
4. $7x^4 - 21x^3 - 35x^2$
5. $-2x^3y^3 + 6x^3y^2$
6. $10x^2y^2z + 15x^2yz^2 + 20xy^3z$
7. $2x^2 - 2x - 12$
8. $-6x^2 + 21x - 9$
9. $12x^2 + 17x - 5$
10. $x^2 - 6x + 9$
11. $9x^2 - 6xy + y^2$
12. $x^2 - xy - 6y^2$
13. $x^2 - 2xy + y^2$
14. $x^3 + 7x^2 + 17x + 15$
15. $x^3 - 2x^2 - 22x + 35$
16. 16. $x^3 - 5x^2 + 16$

PAGE 143 Top
(Problem set #7)
1. -14
2. 65
3. -36
4. -59
5. 156
6. 3
7. -48
8. 216
9. 61
10. -180

PAGE 143 Middle
(Problem set #8)
1. -1
2. 26
3. -30
4. 31
5. 28
6. 1

PAGE 143 Bottom
(Problem set #9)
1. $y^2 + 12y$
2. $x^2 - 2x$
3. $x^3 - 7x^2 + 4x$
4. $-5y^3 + 50y^2 + 5y$
5. $-x^2 + 40x$
6. $-5x^3 - 36x^2$
7. $x^2 - 7x$
8. $9x^2 - 42x$

PAGES 144-145
1. C
2. B
3. A
4. E
5. E
6. A
7. E
8. B
9. A

PAGE 146
1. x^2
2. a^5
3. b^6
4. x^7/y
4. x^{-4}
6. a^5
7. b^4
8. x^8/y^2

PAGE 147
1. $3x$
2. 4
3. $-2a + 4$
4. $-2y + 4$
5. $-2a + 1$
6. $-2y^2 + 3/2y$

PAGE 148
(Problem set #10)
1. x^{15}
2. y^{102}
3. x^4y^{12}
4. a^8b^4
5. $c^{30}d^{30}$
6. $216x^6$
7. $-243x^{10}y^{20}$
8. $9x^6y^4$
9. $64x^{12}y^{42}$
10. $a^{15}b^{20}$
11. $8x^3y^{12}$
12. $81x^4y^{16}$

PAGES 148-149
(Problem set #11)
1. $4x^2$
2. 7
3. $-2 + 4/b$
4. $-4y + 8$
5. $-3y^2 + 6$
6. $2x^2 - 1$
7. $-8x^5 + 2x^3$
8. $-2xy^7$
9. $-9x^6y^7$
10. $-8y^2 + 3y$
11. $6x^5 - 1$
12. $-2xy^6 + x^2$
13. $7/2 + 4z/y$
14. $x^{-7} y^{-2}$
15. $x^{-2} y^2$
16. $2/5z^4$
17. $5x^{-2}y^{-6}$
18. $-7 + 6/x$ or $-7 + 6x^{-1}$
19. $ax + b$
20. $-14x^2 - 8x + 3$
21. $7y/2 - 4z$
22. $-3z/2 - 3$
23. $(-7/2)x^3 - 3x^2$
24. $5 - 6/x$ or $5 - 6x^{-1}$
25. $2x^2 - 3x + 1$

PAGE 150
1. $3(x^2 + 2)$
2. $12(a - 2)$
3. $2(3x^2 - 8)$
4. $x(x + 6)$
5. $a^3(a + 7)$
6. $6x(x + 2)$
7. $3x(x - 2)$
8. $9(x^2 - 2)$
9. $3x(xy + 2)$
10. $10y(x^2 + 2y)$
11. $9x^6y(2x - y^5)$
12. $6x^2y^6(xy - 2)$
13. $x(x - 4)$
14. $3(2a^2 + b^2)$
15. $6ab(1 - 2ab)$
16. $7x^2y^3(y - 2x^{12})$
17. $9(x^2 + 2y^2)$
18. $7x(x + 2y)$

PAGE 152
1. $(x + 5) (x - 5)$
2. $(y + 8) (y - 8)$
3. $4(x^2 + 4)$
4. $(x + 7) (x - 7)$
5. $(3x + 4y) (3x - 4y)$
6. $(7y + 5x) (7y - 5x)$
7. $3(x + 4) (x - 4)$
8. $2(x + 3) (x - 3)$
9. $(3 + x) (3 - x)$
10. $(4 + y) (4 - y)$
11. $(x + 4) (x - 4)$
12. $(x^3 + 6) (x^3 - 6)$
13. $(x^4 + 9) (x^2 + 3)(x^2 - 3)$
14. $9(x^2 + 3) (x^2 - 3)$

PAGE 154
1. $(x + 4) (x + 1)$
2. $(x + 4) (x + 3)$
3. $(x - 2) (x - 1)$
4. $(x - 5) (x + 1)$
5. $(y + 4) (y - 3)$
6. $(y - 5) (y - 4)$
7. $(x + 6) (x + 1)$
8. $(x + 7) (x + 6)$
9. $(y + 6) (y - 3)$
10. $(x + 8) (x + 7)$
11. $2(x + 2) (x + 1)$
12. $2y(y^2 + 2y + 15)$
13. $2(y + 7) (y + 2)$
14. $5x(x + 5) (x + 4)$

1. $y(y + 7)$
2. $(x + 6)(x - 6)$
3. $4x(x - 2)$
4. $(x + 5)(x + 1)$
5. $(y + 3)(y - 2)$
6. $3(A + 4)(A - 4)$
7. $(x + 12)(x - 12)$
8. Cannot be Factored
9. $6x(1 + 2x)(1 - 2x)$
10. $(x - 3)(x - 2)$
11. $6x(x + 3)(x - 3)$
12. $(x - 4)(x - 5)$
13. $(x - 4)(x - 3)$
14. $5B(B + 5)(B + 4)$
15. $10x(2xy - 3)$
16. $(7A - 8B)(7A +8B)$
17. $(x - 4)(x - 1)$
18. $(x + 5)(x + 4)$
19. $2(x + 7)(x + 2)$
20. $9(2x - 3y)(2x + 3y)$
21. $9x^5y^2(2x - y^3)$
22. $4(x + 2y)(x - 2y)$
23. $(x + 2)(x + 1)$
24. $(x - 9)(x - 6)$
25. $(x^3 + 9)(x^3 - 9)$
26. $(x^4 + 6)(x^4 - 6)$
27. $(2x^2 + 9)(2x^2 - 9)$
28. $7x^3y^2(1 - 2x^2)$
29. $(x + 5)(x - 1)$
30. $(4 - x)(4 + 4)$
31. $4(7x + y)(7x - y)$
32. $7x(x + 3)$
33. $b(x^2 + 4)$
34. $(x - 5)(x + 2)$
35. $(x - 4)(x + 2)$
36. $(x - 8)(x + 4)$
37. $(x + 9)(x - 6)$
38. $(x + 10)(x + 3)$
39. $(x + 15)(x - 2)$
40. $(x - 10)(x + 4)$

PAGE 157

(Problem set #13)

1. $(3x - 1)(x - 12)$
2. Cannot be factored
3. $(4x - 3)(2x + 1)$
4. $(5x - 1)(3x - 4)$
5. $(3x - 5)(2x + 7)$
6. $(8x + 3)(x + 1)$
7. $(3x - 1)(x - 3)$
8. $(6x - 1)(x + 7)$
9. $(77 + 2)(y - 6)$
10. $(11x - 3)(2x + 1)$
11. $(4x - 1)(3x - 2)$
12. Cannot be factored
13. Cannot be factored
14. $(10x + 9)(x - 1)$
15. $(2x + 5)(x + 3)$
16. $(2x + 5)(x - 3)$
17. $(2x - 3)(x + 4)$
18. Cannot be factored
19. $(2x + 1)(x - 5)$
20. $(3x + 5)(x - 1)$
21. $(3x + 2)(x + 1)$
22. $(3x + 4)(x - 2)$
23. Cannot be factored
24. $(6x - 5)(x + 2)$
25. $(8x - 3)(x + 2)$

PAGE 159

1. 7
2. −3
3. 3
4. −3
5. 8
6. −5
7. −2
8. 4
9. 2
10. 8
11. −3

PAGE 160

1. −4
2. −23
3. 4
4. 9
5. 60
6. −12
7. 20
8. −28
9. 6

1. $x = 10$
2. $x = -2$
3. $x = -4$
4. $y = 4$
5. $y = 12$
6. $x = 2$
7. $y = 5$
8. $y = -2$
9. $x = 21$
10. $x = 5$
11. $x = 5$
12. $x = 2$
13. $y = 7$
14. $x = -12$
15. $x = 0$
16. $x = 4$
17. $x = 5$
18. $x = 6$
19. $x = 2$
20. $y = -3$
21. $x = 12$
22. $x = 4$
23. $x = \dfrac{22}{3}$
24. $x = 10$
25. $y = -6$
26. $x = \dfrac{2}{3}$
27. $x = -3$
28. $x = 0$
29. $y = 2$
30. $x = \dfrac{12}{7}$
31. $x = 1$
32. $y = 6$
33. $x = 1$
34. $x = \dfrac{1}{3}$

35. $x = 27$
36. $y = 6$
37. $x = 2$
38. $x = \dfrac{31}{4}$
39. $x = 9$
40. $x = 24$
41. $x = \dfrac{-120}{19}$
42. $x = \dfrac{7}{3}$
43. $x = -\dfrac{7}{2}$
44. $x = 9$
45. $y = -12$
46. $x = 12$
47. $x = -40$
48. $y = 5$
49. $y = 240$
50. $x = -30$
51. $y = \dfrac{11}{5}$
52. $x = \dfrac{19}{5}$
53. $x = 144/7$
54. $x = -\dfrac{49}{2}$
55. $x = 84$

PAGE 163

1. $x = 7 + y$
2. $y = x - 3$
3. $a = 7b$
4. $b = \dfrac{a}{b}$
5. $x = \dfrac{y+2}{3}$
6. $y = \dfrac{4x-6}{5}$
7. $x = 2y - 8$
8. $x = 3y + 21$
9. $z = 6 - x - y$
10. $y = \dfrac{3x+7y-9)}{4}$
11. $a = 4c + b$
12. $x = 2 - y$
13. $x = y - z - 6$

PAGES 163-164

(Problem set #15)

1. $x = 9 + y$
2. $a = -8b$
3. $x = \dfrac{y + 5}{4}$
4. $y = \dfrac{5x - 7}{6}$
5. $x = 3y - 12$
6. $x = 4y + 32$
7. $y = \dfrac{x}{2}$
8. $B = -A - C$
9. $x = \dfrac{5y - 8z + 3}{4}$
10. $y = -x + \dfrac{3}{2}$
11. $x = 3c + y$
12. $A = 2D + B$
13. $x = 4y + 32$
14. $a = \dfrac{3b + 4c}{2}$
15. $M = F/A$
16. $Y = \sqrt{r^2 - x^2}$
17. $x = M + sz$
18. $b = y - mx$
19. $p = \dfrac{A}{1 + r}$
20. $h = \dfrac{\sqrt{}}{\Pi r^2}$
21. $a = \dfrac{b}{c - d}$
22. $L = \dfrac{P - 2w}{2}$
23. $h = \dfrac{2A}{b}$

PAGES 165-166

1. $x = 3$
2. $x = 1/2$
3. $x = 6, x - 4 = 2$
4. $x = -2$
5. $x = 7$
6. $x = 9$
7. $x = 2$
8. $x = 3$

PAGES 167-168

(Problem set #16)

1. $x = 15$
2. $x = 9$
3. $x - 6 = 3$
4. $x = 6$
5. $x = 16$
6. $x = 300$
7. $x = 7$
8. $x - 10 = 20$
9. 500
10. 3,000
11. $x = 12$
12. $x = 30$
13. $x = 22$
14. $x = 32$
15. $x = 20$
16. $x = 12$
17. $x = 42$
18. Tie = $4.00, Shirt = $12.00
19. $x = 22, x + 1 = 23, x + 2 = 24$
20. Tom = $60, Sam = $180, Mike = $70
21. $x = 2, 3x + 2 = 8$
22. 4lbs. at 40 cents / pound, 6lbs. at 70 cents / pound
23. Jim = 3, Perry = 6
24. 200 tickets / student; 300 tickets / non-students

PAGE 169
1. x = 2
2. x = 6
3. x = 240
4. x = 4
5. x = –4/5
6. x = –1/9

PAGE 170 (Problem set #17)
1. 91 grams
2. 5 inches
3. 2,275 miles
4. 756 miles
5. 200 grams
6. 10 baskets
7. 119 grams
8. 990 miles
9. 11 inches
10. 180 grams
11. 100 hits

PAGE 172
1. x = 3, y = 1
2. a = 4, b = –1
3. x = 4, y = –1/2
4. x = –1, y = 4
5. a = b, y = –2

PAGE 173
1. x = 4, y = 0
2. x = 2 $^3/_5$, y = 1/5
3. x = 3, y = 6
4. a = 0, b = 1
5. x = -2, y = 1

PAGES 174-175
1. x = $\frac{10}{7}$, y = $\frac{3}{7}$
2. x = 1, y = 1
3. x = -1, y = 3
4. x = 3, y = 0
5. x = 4, y = -1
6. x = -2, y = 4
7. x = 2, y = 2

PAGE 175 (Problem set #18)
1. x = 4, y = 3
2. x = 4, y = 0
3. x = 3, y = 0
4. x = 0, y = 3
5. A = 4, B = 1
6. A = 4, B = 3
7. A = 3, B = 1
8. A = 1, B = 3
9. x = 3, y = 1
10. A = 1, B = -4
11. x = 1, y = 3
12. x = 2, y = –2
13. A = 3, B = –1
14. x = 2, y = 2
15. x = 2, y = 1
16. x = 8, y = –1
17. A = 6, B = 12
18. x = 1, y = 1
19. x = –1, y = 4
20. A = –1, B = 3
21. x = 5, y = –1

PAGE 176
1. (–5, –2)
2. (–11, –1)
3. (–4, –1)
4. (5, 4)
5. (1, –3)
6. (4, –4)
7. (3, –2)
8. (5, –5)
9. (4, 3)
10. (–3, –1)
11. (–3, –2)
12. (–5, –3)

PAGE 177 (Problem set #19
1. (–4, –5)
2. (1, 3)
3. (–1, –8)   )
4. (–6, 6)
5. (3, 5)
6. (–4, –5)
7. (1, –4)
8. (–1, –7)
9. (–2, –4)
10. (–2, –3)
11. (1, –10)
12. (–2, 9)
13. (1, 2)
14. (–2, 8)
15. (2, 7)
16. (–5, 5)
17. (–2, 2)
18. (0, 7)
19. (0, –5/4)
20. (–3, 7)
21. (2, 5/2)
22. ($\sqrt{7}, \sqrt{-7}$)
23. (0, –8)
24. (–3, –5)

PAGES 179-180
1. D
2. B
3. C
4. B
5. C
6. B
7. B

PAGE 182
1. x = 3
2. x = 3
3. x = –2
4. x = 4
5. x = 3
6. y = –2
7. x = $\frac{1}{3}$
8. y = ½

PAGE 184

1. a) $x - y = 2$
   b) $-4x + 3y = 12$
2. a) $-2x + y = 2$
   b) $x + y = 2$

PAGE 185

1. $\frac{3}{2}$
2. $\frac{4}{3}$
3. $\frac{-1}{4}$
4. 1
5. $\frac{5}{3}$
6. 3
7. 1
8. $\frac{5}{4}$
9. 3
10. $-\frac{2}{3}$

PAGE 186

1. $y = 4x + 1$
2. $y = 3x - 6$
3. $y = -2x + 4$
4. $y = -5x - 6$
5. $y = -x - 1$
6. $y = 2x + 2$
7. $y = (\frac{2}{3})x + 6$
8. $y = (\frac{-2}{5})x + \frac{3}{4}$

PAGE 187

1. $m = -4, b = 6$
2. $m = -3, b = 4$
3. $m = 2, b = -5$
4. $m = 5, b = -6$
5. $m = -2, b = 3$
6. $m = -1/2, b = 3/2$
7. $m = 1, b = -2$
8. $m = -\frac{2}{3}, b = 2$

PAGE 188

1. $y = 3x - 5$
2. $y = -2x$
3. $y = 5x + 2$
4. $y = -x + 3$
5. $y = -6x + 14$

PAGE 189 Top

Problem set #20

1. $x = 0$
2. $y = 2$
3. $x = 4$
4. $y = -2$
5. $x = -5$
6. $y = 2$
7. $x = 8$
8. $y = -2$

PAGE 189 Middle

Problem set #21

1. $m = 2$
2. $m = 4$
3. $m = -7/2$
4. $m = 1/3$
5. $m = -1$
6. $m = \frac{6}{31}$
7. $m = \frac{4}{5}$
8. $m = -3$
9. $m = \frac{-7}{2}$
10. $m = -6$
11. $m = \frac{-16}{7}$
12. $m = \frac{-16}{7}$
13. $m = -1$
14. $m = -1$
15. $m = 3$

PAGE 189 Bottom

Problem set #22

1. $y = 5x + 2$
2. $y = 3x - 7$
3. $y = -2x + 5$
4. $y = -5x - 7$
5. $y = -2x - 1$
6. $y = 2x + 3$
7. $y = -\frac{2}{3}x + 9$
8. $y = -\frac{3}{5}x + \frac{1}{4}$
9. $y = \frac{7}{9}x + \frac{4}{5}$

PAGE 190 Top

Problem set #23

1. B
2. C
3. D
4. B
5. A
6. D
7. C

PAGE 190 Bottom

Problem set #24

1. $m = \frac{1}{4}, b = 2$
2. $m = -3, b = 12$
3. $m = -3, b = 6$
4. $m = -1, b = 6$
5. $m = -\frac{2}{3}, b = 4$
6. $m = -2, b = 4$
7. $m = 1, b = -4$
8. $m = -3, b = 9$
9. $m = \frac{3}{7}, b = -3$
10. $m = 1, b = 0$
11. $m = -3, b = 6$
12. $m = -1, b = -7$

PAGE 191
(Problem set #25)
1. $y = 5x + 4$
2. $y = -2x - 3$
3. $y = 4x - 5$
4. $y = -x + 6$
5. $y = \dfrac{x - 9}{2}$
6. $y = \dfrac{-2x - 8}{3}$
7. $y = -x - 10$
8. $y = \dfrac{3}{4}x - 10$

PAGE 194
1. 61°
2. 121°
3. 150°
4. 18°, 72°
5. 60°, 120°
6. 39°
7. 120°
8. 60°, 120°

PAGE 195
1. 55°
2. 90°
3. 50°
4. 90°

PAGE 197
1. 88 cm.
2. 1.75 cm.
3. 154 sq. cm.
4. 44 cm.
5. 3.5 cm.
6. 201 cm.

PAGE 199
1. 52 cm.
2. 12 cm.
3. 4 cm.
4. 8 cm.
5. 36 sq. cm.
6. 4 cm.

PAGE 201
1. $\sqrt{56}$
2. 10
3. 3
4. 5
5. $\sqrt{29}$
6. $\sqrt{60}$

PAGE 201
(Problem set #26)
1. 29°
2. 59°
3. $x = 20°$
4. $x = 75°$
5. $x = 50°$, $x + 80 = 130°$
6. $x = 33°$
7. $x = 150°$
8. $x = 60°$

PAGE 202 Top
(Problem set #27)
1. $x = 65°$
2. $4x = 80°$
3. $x = 70°$
4. $3x = 108°$

PAGE 202 Middle
(Problem set #28)
1. 138.16 cm.
2. 4.46 cm.
3. 615.44 cm.
4. 87.92 cm.
5. 7.01 cm.
6. 615.44 cm.

PAGE 202 Bottom
(Problem set #29)
1. 52 cm.
2. 15 cm.
3. 10 cm.
4. 12 ft.
5. 4 cm.
6. 200 sq. ft.
7. 254.8 ft.
8. 360 sq. cm.

PAGE 203
(Problem set #30)
1. 52 cm.
2. 15 cm.
3. 10 cm.
4. 12 ft.
5. 4 cm.
6. 200 ft^2
7. 504.8
8. 360 cm^2

88. HOMEWORK SECTION

Exercise 1
Book pages 1 – 4

I. Answer the following questions:

1.	The counting numbers larger than six.	Answer_____
2.	The counting numbers four through nine.	Answer_____
3.	The first six whole numbers.	Answer_____
4.	The first four odd numbers.	Answer_____

II. Find the value of the digit "8" in the following numbers:

1.	865	Answer_____
2.	8	Answer_____
3.	81	Answer_____
4.	8,954	Answer_____

III. Translate the following using mathematics symbols:

1.	Eight hundred fifty-seven	Answer_____
2.	Five thousand sixty-one	Answer_____
3.	Four hundred fifty	Answer_____
4.	Nine thousand six hundred	Answer_____

IV. Write the following in words using the place value chart:

1.	7,459	Answer_____
2.	9,317	Answer_____
3.	493	Answer_____
4.	643,275	Answer_____

Exercise 2
Book Pages 5 - 6

On a separate sheet of paper

I.   List all the possible factors for each example below:

     1.   50   4.   52
     2.   42   5.   125
     3.   46   6.   68

II.   Write all the prime numbers between 50 and 60.

III.   Write all the composite numbers larger than 40 but smaller than 50.

Exercise 3
Book pages 7 - 9

Name the property illustrated in the following examples:

1. $8 + 3 = 3 + 8$ Answer_____
2. $7 + 0 = 7$ Answer_____
3. $8 (1) = 8$ Answer_____
4. $6 \cdot 7 \cdot 8 = 7 \cdot 6 \cdot 8$ Answer_____
5. $(4 + 5) + 6 = 6 + (4 + 5)$ Answer_____
6. $4 (7) = 7(4)$ Answer_____
7. $5(4 + 9) = 5 \cdot 4 + 5 \cdot 9$ Answer_____

Exercise 4
Book page 12

1. $37 + 150 + 6$ Answer_____
2. $179 + 18 + 505$ Answer_____
3. $2{,}459 + 39 + 279 + 6{,}179$ Answer_____
4. $8 + 439 + 449 + 69$ Answer_____
5. $23, 459, 7{,}945 + 6{,}259$ Answer_____
6. $79 + 2{,}170 + 88{,}888$ Answer_____
7. $49 + 2{,}107 + 9{,}456 + 67$ Answer_____
8. $7{,}171 + 2{,}170 + 8 + 88{,}888$ Answer_____
9. $617 + 39 + 8 + 71{,}498$ Answer_____
10. $3 + 33 + 333 + 3{,}333 + 33{,}333$ Answer_____

Exercise 5
Book pages 12-17

Answer the following questions:

1. 849 – 67   Answer_____
2. 748 – 689   Answer_____
3. 5,009 – 3,998   Answer_____
4. 709 – 598   Answer_____
5. 3,461 – 3,001   Answer_____
6. 5,000 – 2,139   Answer_____
7. Subtract 69 from 349.   Answer_____
8. Subtract 122 from 621.   Answer_____
9. 749 – 398   Answer_____
10. 6,349 – 5,991   Answer_____
11. Subtract 74 from 241.   Answer_____
12. Subtract 167 from 170.   Answer_____

Exercise 6
Book pages 12-17

Answer the following questions:

1. 12 x 17   Answer_____
2. 101 x 20   Answer_____
3. 439 x 27   Answer_____
4. 1,234 x 5,678   Answer_____
5. 29 x 307   Answer_____
6. 407 x 207   Answer_____
7. 469 x 32   Answer_____
8. 7,429 x 9,247   Answer_____
9. 789 x 65   Answer_____
10. 69 x 74   Answer_____
11. 134 x 12   Answer_____
12. 111 x 111   Answer_____

Exercise 7
Book pages 12-17

Answer the following questions:
1. $96 \div 2$ Answer_____
2. $0 \div 12$ Answer_____
3. $12 \div 0$ Answer_____
4. $750 \div 25$ Answer_____
5. 16 into 64   Answer_____
6. 12 into 144   Answer_____
7. $6090 \div 30$ Answer_____
8. $8,008 \div 8$ Answer_____
9. $1,414 \div 7$ Answer_____
10. $1,818 \div 18$ Answer_____
11. $12,006 \div 6$ Answer_____
12. $403 \div 13$ Answer_____

Exercise 8
Book pages 12-17

1. $2,049 + 35 + 6,849$ Answer_____
2. $34,591 + 67 + 1,201$ Answer_____
3. $367 + 129 + 1,750$ Answer_____
4. $804 - 309$ Answer_____
5. $4,001 - 3,999$ Answer_____
6. 429×202 Answer_____
7. 205×310 Answer_____
8. $2,424 \div 12$ Answer_____
9. $3,075 \div 25$ Answer_____
10. $405 + 78 + 3,619$ Answer_____
11. $604 - 409$ Answer_____
12. 341×209 Answer_____
13. $3,090 \div 41$ Answer_____
14. $607 - 39$ Answer_____
15. $307 + 27 + 1,707$ Answer_____
16. 200×300 Answer_____
17. $1,290 - 748$ Answer_____
18. $4,000 \times 3,000$ Answer_____
19. $2,037 + 145 + 89$ Answer_____
20. 307×125 Answer_____
21. $607 - 309$ Answer_____
22. $4,107 \div 34$ Answer_____
23. $741 - 59$ Answer_____
24. 210×16 Answer_____
25. $3,070 \div 45$ Answer_____

Write in numerals:

1. Three hundred forty-nine   Answer_____

2. Four hundred seven   Answer_____

3. Two thousand three hundred forty-seven   Answer_____

4. Eight thousand fifty-five   Answer_____

5. Twenty-five thousand three hundred   Answer_____

6. Four-thousand one hundred five   Answer_____

7. Sixty-seven thousand fifty-nine   Answer_____

8. Thirty thousand one   Answer_____

9. One hundred eighty-nine thousand three hundred   Answer_____

10. Seven hundred five thousand one hundred forty-nine   Answer_____

11. Eight million seventy-nine thousand   Answer_____

12. Six hundred nine   Answer_____

13. Seven million eighty-six thousand seven   Answer_____

14. Three hundred thousand four hundred fifty-six   Answer_____

15. Nine million eight hundred seven thousand four   Answer_____

Adding and subtracting units:

1. 5 hours 36 minutes
    + 4 hours 39 minutes   Answer_____

2. 3 hours 4 minutes
    +7 hours 12 minutes   Answer_____

3. 7 hours 6 minutes
    –3 hours 10 minutes   Answer_____

4. 3 hours 24 minutes
        – 1 hour 39 minutes   Answer_____

5. 6 pounds 15 ounces
    + 5 pounds 12 ounces   Answer_____

6. 12 pounds 13 ounces
    +6 pounds 13 ounces   Answer_____

7. 15 pounds 5 ounces
    –12 pounds 13 ounces   Answer_____

8. 7 pounds 5 ounces
    –4 pounds 15 ounces   Answer_____

9. A movie began at 5:04 p.m. and ended at 7:00 p.m.
    How long did it last?   Answer_____

10. Richard leaves his father's house at 4:45 p.m. and arrives
    home at 6:07 p.m. How long did he travel?   Answer_____

11. Seth buys a piece of wood 12 feet six inches long. He cuts
    a piece 3 feet 9 inches long. How much wood is left?   Answer_____

12. Philip buys three pounds seven ounces of sweet potatoes
    and two pounds twelve ounces baking potatoes. How many
    pounds of potatoes did he buy?   Answer_____

Exercise 11
Book pages 21 - 22

Average Problems:

1. 12, 14, 16   Answer_____
2. 39, 43, 44   Answer_____
3. 93, 106, 113   Answer_____
4. 70, 78, 83, 97   Answer_____
5. 47, 52, 54, 61, 71   Answer_____
6. 38, 50, 61, 62, 69   Answer_____
7. Zelma scores 97, 91, 94 on her Chemistry exams.
    Find her average.   Answer_____
8. Elliot has grades of 97, 100, 91, and 92 on his math
    quizzes. What is the average of these grades?   Answer_____
9. A salesman spends $48, $54, $49, and $57 per night
    for his hotel room. What is the average cost per night
    for the hotel room?   Answer_____
10. The average monthly snow for Buffalo is as follows:
    December: 2 feet 6 inches; January: 3 feet 4 inches;
    February: 1 foot 5 inches. What is the average monthly
    snow in Buffalo during this period?   Answer_____
11. A student scored 60, 0, and 90 on her physics tests.
    What is the average?   Answer_____
12. The costs to produce four coats are $75, $85, $90, and
    $70. What is the average?   Answer_____

Exercise 12
Book pages 22 - 23

Answer the following questions:

1. $35 - 3(8 - 2)$ Answer_____
2. $7 + 5 \times 9 - 3$ Answer_____
3. $18 - 6 \div 2$ Answer_____
4. $56 \div 7 \div 4$ Answer_____
5. $8 \div 2 \times 3$ Answer_____
6. $3 + 4(5 + 6)^2$ Answer_____
7. $2(8) + 3(7)$ Answer_____
8. $4 + (3 + 5)^2$ Answer_____
9. $3 + 2(4 + 5)$ Answer_____
10. $6 + (7 + 1)^2$ Answer_____
11. $18 \div 6 \div 3$ Answer_____
12. $3(9) + 2(7)$ Answer_____

Exercise 13
Book pages 24 - 26

Round the number to the indicated place.

1. 286 tens   Answer_____
2. 284 tens   Answer_____
3. 6,495 hundreds   Answer_____
4. 6,401 hundreds   Answer_____
5. 5,423 thousands   Answer_____
6. 5,723 thousands   Answer_____
7. 5,731,259 millions   Answer_____
8. 2,345,678 millions   Answer_____
9. 249 tens   Answer_____
10. 241 tens   Answer_____
11. 17,495 thousands   Answer_____
12. 8,765,432 millions   Answer_____

Exercise 14
Book pages 26 - 27

1. In which place is the digit 7?
   a) 7.056   Answer_____
   b) 54.079   Answer_____
   c) 13.721   Answer_____
   d) 2.5796   Answer_____
   e) 18.157   Answer_____
   f) 70.0593   Answer_____

2. Write out the number as you would read it.
   a) 53.64   Answer_____
   b) 79.8   Answer_____
   c) 14.235   Answer_____
   d) 17.0387   Answer_____
   e) 200.4   Answer_____
   f) 400.35   Answer_____

3. Write in decimal notation
   a) Eight and four thousandths   Answer_____
   b) Twenty-three and fourteen hundredths   Answer_____
   c) Three hundred and eight thousandths   Answer_____
   d) Two hundred and fifty-four ten thousandths   Answer_____
   e) Nine hundred fifty-one and seven tenths   Answer_____
   f) Seventy-two ten thousandths   Answer_____

Exercise 15
Book pages 28 - 29

A.   Which number is the smallest?

1.   a) .41   b) .44   c) .46   d) .49   e) .40   Answer_____
2.   a) .52   b) .5   c) .55   d) .59   e) .50   Answer_____
3.   a) .256   b) .251   c) .252   d) .257   e) .258   Answer_____
4.   a) 2.85   b) 2.75   c) 2.764 d) 2.759 e) 2.77   Answer_____
5.   a) .09   b) .009   c) .0009 d) .9   e) .00009   Answer_____
6.   a) 7.45   b) 7.451   c) 7.5   d) 7.407 e) 7.42   Answer_____

B.   Which number is the largest?

1.   a) .94   b) .99   c) .92   d) .97   e) .96   Answer_____
2.   a) .41   b) .44   c) .4   d) .49   e) .47   Answer_____
3.   a) 7.1   b) 7.07   c) 7.21   d) 7.04   e) 7.39   Answer_____
4.   a) 4.7   b) 4.07   c) 4.75   d) 4.72   e) 4.79   Answer_____
5.   a) 6.09   b) .069   c) 6.9   d) 6.009 e) 6.097   Answer_____
6.   a) .98   b) .0991   c) 0.999 d) .099   e) .0909   Answer_____

Exercise 16
Book pages 30-31

A.   Change each fraction to a decimal rounded to nearest tenth.

     1. $\dfrac{3}{8}$ Answer_____

     2. $\dfrac{2}{7}$ Answer_____

     3. $\dfrac{4}{9}$ Answer_____

     4. $\dfrac{2}{5}$ Answer_____

     5. $\dfrac{1}{8}$ Answer_____

     6. $\dfrac{4}{7}$ Answer_____

B.   Change each fraction to a decimal rounded to nearest hundredth.

     1. $\dfrac{5}{7}$ Answer_____

     2. $\dfrac{7}{9}$ Answer_____

     3. $\dfrac{11}{17}$ Answer_____

     4. $\dfrac{15}{19}$ Answer_____

     5. $\dfrac{6}{7}$ Answer_____

     6. $\dfrac{2}{9}$ Answer_____

C.   Verbal problems:

   1. Multiply 3.7 x 4.6 and round off answer to nearest tenth.

                                                   Answer_____

   2. Multiply 6.7 x 2.5 and round off answer to nearest tenth.

                                                 Answer_____

   3. Multiply 6.75 x 2.9 and round off answer to nearest hundredth.

                                                 Answer_____

   4. Multiply 1.27 x 83.1 and round off answer to nearest hundredth

                                                 Answer_____

Exercise 17
Book pages 31 - 32

A. Add each of the following:

1. 8.2 + 3.9 + 7.6   Answer_____
2. 5.3 + 2.5 + 7.3   Answer_____
3. 6.85 + 12.9 + 17   Answer_____
4. 6.82 + 3.89 + 2.74   Answer_____
5. 19 + 12.1 + .08   Answer_____
6. 7.09 + 70.9 + 709   Answer_____
7. 13.49 + 134.9 + 134   Answer_____
8. 7.6 + 2.1 + 3.89   Answer_____
9. 6.74 + 12.9 + 7.2   Answer_____
10. 12.9 + 1.29 + 129   Answer_____
11. 1.2 + 2.3 + 3.4   Answer_____
12. 7.619 + 12 + 1.89   Answer_____
13. 7.2 + 12.8 + 139.7   Answer_____
14. 61.2 + 12.7 + 139.84   Answer_____
15. 17 + 1.7 + .17   Answer_____

B. Subtract each of the following:

1. 12.9 – 3.2   Answer_____
2. 14.8 – 6.9   Answer_____
3. 13.1 – 7.07   Answer_____
4. 11.04 – 7.09   Answer_____
5. 6 – .078   Answer_____
6. 12 – .12   Answer_____
7. 55.7 – 10.84   Answer_____
8. 202.8 – 2.028   Answer_____
9. 7.2 – 6.9   Answer_____
10. 13.75 – 12.79   Answer_____
11. 6.2 – 3.89   Answer_____
12. 6 – .078   Answer_____
13. 12.2 – 3.98   Answer_____
14. 7.2 – 5.87   Answer_____
15. 8.3 – 6.91   Answer_____

Exercise 18
Book pages 33 - 34

A.   Multiply each of the following:

1. .4 x .6   Answer_____
2. .5 x 3   Answer_____
3. 6.7 x 2.9   Answer_____
4. 2.5 x 3.7   Answer_____
5. 48 x .06   Answer_____
6. 37 x 2.4   Answer_____
7. .01 x .01   Answer_____
8. .001 x .4   Answer_____
9. .069 x .7   Answer_____
10. 290 x .51   Answer_____
11. 3.71 x 2.09   Answer_____
12. .075 x .029   Answer_____
13. 5.04 x 2.16   Answer_____
14. 17.1 x .025   Answer_____
15. .035 x .01   Answer_____

B.   Verbal Problems:

1. Find the cost of 15 candy bars at $.55 per candy bar.   Answer_____
2. A book salesman sells 12 copies of a book at $8.95 per copy. What is the total cost?   Answer_____
3. How much do 8 quarts of juice cost at $1.39 per quart?   Answer_____
4. A roll of wallpaper costs $10.95. If a bedroom requires 38 rolls of paper, what is the cost to wallpaper the bedroom?   Answer_____
5. A salesman earns $7.95 per hour he works. If he works 29 hours, how much does the salesman earn?   Answer_____
6. Pears sell for $.99 per pound. What is the cost of 7 pounds of pears?   Answer_____

Exercise 19
Book pages 34 - 35

A.   Divide each of the following:

1. $36 \div .6$ Answer_____

2. $150 \div .5$ Answer_____

3. $48 \div .04$ Answer_____

4. $.01 \div 10$ Answer_____

5. $10 \div .01$ Answer_____

6. $6,000 \div .60$ Answer_____

7. $840 \div .42$ Answer_____

8. $5.2 \div .13$ Answer_____

9. $2.6 \div .13$ Answer_____

10. $242 \div 22$ Answer_____

11. $3.6 \div .6$ Answer_____

12. $.84 \div 12$ Answer_____

13. $.4949 \div 7$ Answer_____

14. $4.949 \div .7$ Answer_____

15. $1.68 \div .8$ Answer_____

B.   Verbal Problems:

1. If notebooks cost $1.70 a piece, how many can
you purchase for $32.30?   Answer_____

2. Pens cost $1.50 each. How many pens can you purchase
for $60.00?   Answer_____

3. Chocolate candy sells for $7.20 per pound. How many
pounds can be purchased for $144.00?   Answer_____

4. Zelma pays $11.60 for a tank of gasoline. If gasoline
sell for $1.16 a gallon, how many gallons does she buy?   Answer_____

Multiply or divide in your head.

1. 0.05 x 10   Answer_____

2. 0.495 x 100   Answer_____

3. 9,815 ÷ 1000   Answer_____

4. 638 ÷ 100   Answer_____

5. 0.0953 x 100   Answer_____

6. 0.067 x 1000   Answer_____

7. 0.07 x 1,000   Answer_____

8. 81.9 ÷ 100   Answer_____

9. 937 ÷ 10,000   Answer_____

10. 0.072 x 100   Answer_____

11. 7.5 x 1000   Answer_____

12. 7.5 ÷ 1,000   Answer_____

Exercise 21
Book pages 42 - 44

A.   Change each fraction to a decimal.

1. $\dfrac{7}{40}$ Answer_____

2. $\dfrac{5}{4}$ Answer_____

3. $\dfrac{7}{100}$ Answer_____

4. $\dfrac{1}{20}$ Answer_____

5. $\dfrac{4}{5}$ Answer_____

6. $\dfrac{3}{10}$ Answer_____

7. $\dfrac{1}{50}$ Answer_____

8. $\dfrac{7}{8}$ Answer_____

9. $\dfrac{4}{9}$ Answer_____

10. $\dfrac{2}{7}$ Answer_____

B.	Change each decimal to a fraction (reduce answer to lowest terms).

1. .45							Answer_____

2. .04							Answer_____

3. .035						Answer_____

4. 1.4							Answer_____

5. 9.85						Answer_____

6. 7.8							Answer_____

7. .019						Answer_____

8. .055						Answer_____

9. .85							Answer_____

10. 7.69						Answer_____

C.	Change each percentage to a fraction (reduce answer to lowest terms).

1. 95%						Answer_____

2. 4%							Answer_____

3. 21%						Answer_____

4. 26%						Answer_____

5. 250%						Answer_____

6. 80%						Answer_____

7. 89%						Answer_____

8. 765%						Answer_____

9. 72%						Answer_____

10. 8%							Answer_____

D. Change each percent to a decimal.

1. 49%   Answer_____

2. 8%   Answer_____

3. 245%   Answer_____

4. .9%   Answer_____

5. 7%   Answer_____

6. 65%   Answer_____

7. 539%   Answer_____

8. .09%   Answer_____

9. 3.7%   Answer_____

10. .79%   Answer_____

Cost and profit problems:

1. What is the total cost of 45 pens at $.75 each?

   Answer_____

2. Find the total cost of 4 pounds of peaches at $.79 per pound and 6 pounds of plums at $.89 per pound.

   Answer_____

3. A mathematics teacher charges $25.00 for the first lesson and $19.00 for each additional lesson. What is the cost of 21 lessons?

   Answer_____

4. The Santiago Moving Company charges $45.00 for the first hour of work and $39.00 for each additional hour. What is the cost of a moving job that takes nine hours?

   Answer_____

5. A theatre group sells 425 tickets to a play written by Shakespeare. Each ticket sells for $6.00. The group spends $575.00 on rent and $179.00 in additional expenses. What is the profit?

   Answer_____

6. A department store buys 175 coats for $6,000.00. All the coats are sold at $79.00 each. What is the profit?

   Answer_____

7. Abraham Lincoln High School sells 745 tickets to a basketball game at $8.00 per ticket. It costs $2,100 a month to rent the stadium. Other expenses add up to $789.00 What is the profit?

   Answer_____

8. Hector's Superette buys 27 dozen rolls at $0.89 per dozen. Only 21 dozen are sold at $1.89 per dozen. What is the profit?

   Answer_____

9. Elliot spends $14.37 in the Superette. How much change does he receive from a $100.00 bill?

   Answer_____

Exercise 23
Book pages 45 - 48

Percent problems.

1. What is 15% of 75?

   Answer_____

2. What is 17% of 90?

   Answer_____

3. If 40% of a number is 80, what is the number?

   Answer_____

4. If 25% of a number is 480, find the number.

   Answer_____

5. What is 15% of 60?

   Answer_____

6. What is 60% of 70?

   Answer_____

7. If 40% of a number is 120, what is the number?

   Answer_____

8. If 75% of a number is 375, find the number.

   Answer_____

9. What is 70% of 30?

   Answer_____

10. What is 16% of 90?

    Answer_____

Sales tax and percent increase.

1. A coat sells for $70.00. There is a 7% sales tax. What is the total price?

   Answer_____

2. A dress sells for $29.00. There is a 6% sales tax. What is the sales tax?

   Answer_____

3. Eddie buys Zelma a Movado watch for $2,500.00; there is an 8% sales tax. What is the total price?

   Answer_____

4. Seth earns $79,000 a year. He receives a 9% increase in salary. What is his new salary?

   Answer_____

5. Philip's variety store gross sales were $7,000,000 last year. The sales this year increased by 21%. What is the increase in sales?

   Answer_____

6. Box seat tickets to Yankee games was increased by 18%. Last year the tickets sold from $30.00 each. What do they sell for this season?

   Answer_____

Exercise 25
Book pages 49 - 50

Discount and percent decrease:

1. John's weekly salary is $525.00. It is reduced by
    7%. What is his new weekly salary?   Answer_____

2. There is a 30% decrease on all luggage. Zelma
    bought an attaché case that originally sold for
    $189.00. What is the sale price?   Answer_____

3. New York City has 9,000,000 people. It loses 8%
    of its population. What is the new population?   Answer_____

4. Sally earns $35,000 a year. She has 14% of her pay
    deducted for taxes. What is her yearly take-home
    pay?   Answer_____

5. A dress that sold for $47.95 is reduced by 7%.
    What is the sale price?   Answer_____

6. Seth buys a sweater that originally sells for $95.00.
    It is reduced by 45%. What is the sale price?   Answer_____

Exercise 26
Book pages 51 - 53

Area, perimeter and cost:

1. Find the area of a room 9 yards by 6 yards.

   Answer_____

2. Find the area of a sheet that is 75 inches long and 40 inches wide.

   Answer_____

3. How much does it cost to carpet a room 12 yards by 11 yards at $9.00 per square yard?

   Answer_____

4. Find the perimeter of a rectangle whose length is 10 feet and whose width is 7 feet.

   Answer_____

5. How much fencing is needed to fence in a swimming pool 45 feet long and 30 feet wide.

   Answer_____

6. How much does it cost to fence in a rectangular garden 28 feet by 18 feet at $14.00 per foot of fencing?

   Answer_____

7. Carpeting costs $24.00 per square yard. How much does it cost to carpet a room 12 yards by 11 yards?

   Answer_____

8. Find the perimeter of a triangle whose sides are 6, 8 and 10 inches.

   Answer_____

Change the improper fraction to a mixed number:

1. $\dfrac{9}{4}$ Answer_____

2. $\dfrac{29}{7}$ Answer_____

3. $\dfrac{19}{5}$ Answer_____

4. $\dfrac{7}{3}$ Answer_____

5. $\dfrac{17}{5}$ Answer_____

6. $\dfrac{39}{4}$ Answer_____

7. $\dfrac{17}{8}$ Answer_____

8. $\dfrac{18}{4}$ Answer_____

9. $\dfrac{27}{2}$ Answer_____

10. $\dfrac{27}{4}$ Answer_____

Change the mixed number to an improper fraction:

1. $4\dfrac{3}{7}$ Answer_____

2. $6\dfrac{1}{9}$ Answer_____

3. $7\dfrac{2}{5}$ Answer_____

4. $6\dfrac{11}{14}$ Answer_____

5. $3\dfrac{2}{11}$ Answer_____

6. $12\dfrac{4}{9}$ Answer_____

7. $3\dfrac{4}{5}$ Answer_____

8. $1\dfrac{2}{3}$ Answer_____

9. $6\dfrac{7}{8}$ Answer_____

Exercise 28
Book pages 59-60

Write the equivalent fractions.

1. $\dfrac{4}{7} = \dfrac{x}{49}$

   Answer_____

2. $\dfrac{5}{9} = \dfrac{x}{63}$

   Answer_____

3. $\dfrac{2}{3} = \dfrac{x}{9}$

   Answer_____

4. $\dfrac{2}{5} = \dfrac{24}{x}$

   Answer_____

5. $\dfrac{1}{6} = \dfrac{35}{x}$

   Answer_____

6. $\dfrac{7}{8} = \dfrac{x}{48}$

   Answer_____

7. $\dfrac{2}{5} = \dfrac{x}{150}$

   Answer_____

8. $\dfrac{2}{9} = \dfrac{x}{36}$

   Answer_____

9. $\dfrac{5}{9} = \dfrac{x}{27}$

   Answer_____

10. $\dfrac{3}{5} = \dfrac{x}{9}$

    Answer_____

Exercise 29
Book page 72

Factor each of the following into prime factors:

1. 28   Answer_____   6. 68   Answer_____

2. 96   Answer_____   7. 42   Answer_____

3. 36   Answer_____   8. 70   Answer_____

4. 180   Answer_____   9. 18   Answer_____

5. 54   Answer_____   10. 72   Answer_____

Exercise 30
Book page 73

Find the greatest common factor.

1. 50, 125   Answer_____

2. 12, 15   Answer_____

3. 18, 45   Answer_____

4. 16, 38   Answer_____

5. 68, 144   Answer_____

6. 72, 256   Answer_____

7. 28, 84   Answer_____

8. 9, 45   Answer_____

9. 68, 144   Answer_____

10. 40, 180   Answer_____

Exercise 31
Book pages 74 - 75

Reducing Fractions:

1. $\frac{6}{8}$ Answer_____   7. $\frac{3}{9}$ Answer_____

2. $\frac{8}{6}$ Answer_____   8. $\frac{12}{9}$ Answer_____

3. $\frac{6}{32}$ Answer_____   9. $\frac{12}{16}$ Answer_____

4. $\frac{32}{6}$ Answer_____   10. $\frac{16}{12}$ Answer_____

5. $\frac{12}{34}$ Answer_____   11. $\frac{12}{38}$ Answer_____

6. $\frac{34}{12}$ Answer_____   12. $\frac{38}{12}$ Answer_____

Multiplication of fractions:

1. $\frac{3}{7} \times \frac{1}{9}$ Answer_____   9. $3\frac{1}{4} \times 8$ Answer_____

2. $\frac{1}{4} \times \frac{8}{9}$ Answer_____   10. $2\frac{1}{7} \times 49$ Answer_____

3. $\frac{3}{5} \times \frac{7}{9}$ Answer_____   11. $2\frac{2}{3} \times 1\frac{4}{9}$ Answer_____

4. $\frac{6}{7} \times \frac{1}{2}$ Answer_____   12. $3\frac{1}{5} \times 4\frac{3}{7}$ Answer_____

5. $\frac{3}{4} \times 16$ Answer_____   13. $3\frac{1}{8} \times 4$ Answer_____

6. $\frac{3}{10} \times 50$ Answer_____   14. $\frac{1}{5} \times 25$ Answer_____

7. $4 \times \frac{1}{8}$ Answer_____   15. $3\frac{2}{7} \times 1\frac{5}{6}$ Answer_____

8. $12 \times \frac{1}{16}$ Answer_____   16. $6\frac{7}{8} \times 1\frac{1}{9}$ Answer_____

Exercise 33
Book pages 77 – 79

Division of fractions:

1. $\dfrac{5}{6} \div \dfrac{1}{6}$ Answer_____

2. $\dfrac{5}{9} \div \dfrac{5}{27}$ Answer_____

3. $\dfrac{3}{5} \div \dfrac{9}{25}$ Answer_____

4. $\dfrac{3}{8} \div \dfrac{5}{16}$ Answer_____

5. $3 \div \dfrac{1}{12}$ Answer_____

6. $4 \div \dfrac{1}{8}$ Answer_____

7. $\dfrac{3}{7} \div 5$ Answer_____

8. $\dfrac{4}{5} \div 12$ Answer_____

9. $1\dfrac{3}{4} \div 7$ Answer_____

10. $3\dfrac{2}{7} \div 1\dfrac{1}{14}$ Answer_____

11. $3\dfrac{1}{4} \div 4\dfrac{5}{8}$ Answer_____

12. $2\dfrac{5}{8} \div \dfrac{9}{16}$ Answer_____

13. $4\dfrac{3}{5} \div 1\dfrac{3}{10}$ Answer_____

14. $2\dfrac{1}{6} \div 3\dfrac{7}{12}$ Answer_____

15. $6 \div \dfrac{1}{12}$ Answer_____

16. $\dfrac{3}{7} \div 18$ Answer_____

Exercise 34
Book pages 80 - 81

Addition of fractions:

1. $\frac{3}{8} + \frac{1}{4}$ Answer_____

2. $\frac{1}{3} + \frac{5}{9}$ Answer_____

3. $\frac{1}{2} + \frac{3}{4}$ Answer_____

4. $\frac{3}{7} + \frac{1}{5}$ Answer_____

5. $\frac{2}{5} + \frac{7}{8}$ Answer_____

6. $\frac{3}{7} + \frac{1}{6}$ Answer_____

7. $4 + \frac{1}{5}$ Answer_____

8. $6 + \frac{7}{9}$ Answer_____

9. $2\frac{3}{4} + 3\frac{5}{8}$ Answer_____

10. $5\frac{1}{4} + 1\frac{3}{7}$ Answer_____

11. $2\frac{1}{9} + 3\frac{5}{6}$ Answer_____

12. $5\frac{3}{4} + 4\frac{1}{4}$ Answer_____

13. $6 + \frac{1}{5}$ Answer_____

14. $\frac{5}{12} + \frac{5}{6}$ Answer_____

15. $2\frac{1}{7} + 3\frac{1}{4}$ Answer_____

16. $2\frac{1}{9} + 3\frac{5}{6}$ Answer_____

Exercise 35
Book pages 82 - 83

Subtraction of fractions:

1. $\frac{3}{4} - \frac{1}{4}$ Answer_____

2. $\frac{7}{8} - \frac{1}{8}$ Answer_____

3. $\frac{3}{4} - \frac{3}{8}$ Answer_____

4. $\frac{7}{16} - \frac{1}{4}$ Answer_____

5. $\frac{3}{7} - \frac{1}{6}$ Answer_____

6. $\frac{7}{9} - \frac{3}{8}$ Answer_____

7. $\frac{3}{5} - \frac{1}{6}$ Answer_____

8. $\frac{4}{9} - \frac{3}{8}$ Answer_____

9. $3 - \frac{1}{4}$ Answer_____

10. $4 - \frac{4}{5}$ Answer_____

11. $6\frac{4}{9} - 2\frac{7}{9}$ Answer_____

12. $3\frac{2}{7} - 1\frac{4}{7}$ Answer_____

13. $5\frac{3}{4} - 2\frac{1}{8}$ Answer_____

14. $6\frac{7}{9} - 2\frac{1}{4}$ Answer_____

15. $5\frac{1}{4} - 2\frac{3}{7}$ Answer_____

16. $6\frac{3}{8} - 4\frac{6}{7}$ Answer_____

271

Exercise 36
Book pages 84 - 87

A   Which fraction is the smallest?

1.   a. $\frac{2}{7}$ b. $\frac{3}{4}$ c. $\frac{1}{5}$ d. $\frac{2}{9}$ e. $\frac{3}{11}$ Answer_____

2.   a. $\frac{3}{8}$ b. $\frac{1}{4}$ c. $\frac{2}{9}$ d. $\frac{4}{5}$ e. $\frac{2}{7}$ Answer_____

3.   a. $\frac{1}{3}$ b. $\frac{2}{7}$ c. $\frac{3}{13}$ d. $\frac{1}{11}$ e. $\frac{2}{19}$ Answer_____

4.   a. $\frac{2}{5}$ b. $\frac{2}{3}$ c. $\frac{3}{5}$ d. $\frac{7}{10}$ e. $\frac{4}{9}$ Answer_____

5.   a. $\frac{9}{11}$ b. $\frac{7}{9}$ c. $\frac{10}{11}$ d. $\frac{7}{8}$ e. $\frac{19}{21}$ Answer_____

6.   a. $\frac{1}{7}$ b. $\frac{1}{4}$ c. $\frac{3}{11}$ d. $\frac{3}{10}$ e. $\frac{2}{9}$ Answer_____

7.   a. $\frac{5}{12}$ b. $\frac{7}{17}$ c. $\frac{1}{3}$ d. $\frac{2}{7}$ e. $\frac{3}{8}$ Answer_____

8.   a. $\frac{2}{9}$ b. $\frac{1}{4}$ c. $\frac{7}{8}$ d. $\frac{2}{5}$ e. $\frac{3}{11}$ Answer_____

9.   a. $\frac{7}{20}$ b. $\frac{1}{3}$ c. $\frac{5}{12}$ d. $\frac{5}{11}$ e. $\frac{4}{15}$ Answer_____

10. a. $\frac{8}{13}$ b. $\frac{7}{11}$ c. $\frac{5}{7}$ d. $\frac{13}{20}$ e. $\frac{7}{20}$ Answer_____

B   Which fraction is the largest?

1.   a. $\dfrac{2}{5}$ b. $\dfrac{3}{4}$ c. $\dfrac{4}{11}$ d. $\dfrac{13}{16}$ e. $\dfrac{5}{12}$ Answer_____

2.   a. $\dfrac{7}{9}$ b. $\dfrac{1}{3}$ c. $\dfrac{8}{11}$ d. $\dfrac{3}{8}$ e. $\dfrac{7}{10}$ Answer_____

3.   a. $\dfrac{7}{15}$ b. $\dfrac{5}{7}$ c. $\dfrac{1}{2}$ d. $\dfrac{4}{5}$ e. $\dfrac{4}{7}$ Answer_____

4.   a. $\dfrac{1}{2}$ b. $\dfrac{2}{9}$ c. $\dfrac{1}{6}$ d. $\dfrac{2}{3}$ e. $\dfrac{13}{17}$ Answer_____

5.   a. $\dfrac{3}{5}$ b. $\dfrac{2}{3}$ c. $\dfrac{7}{12}$ d. $\dfrac{11}{15}$ e. $\dfrac{2}{7}$ Answer_____

6.   a. $\dfrac{3}{7}$ b. $\dfrac{3}{5}$ c. $\dfrac{2}{5}$ d. $\dfrac{5}{9}$ e. $\dfrac{7}{11}$ Answer_____

7.   a. $\dfrac{1}{8}$ b. $\dfrac{3}{4}$ c. $\dfrac{7}{9}$ d. $\dfrac{4}{5}$ e. $\dfrac{2}{7}$ Answer_____

8.   a. $\dfrac{1}{4}$ b. $\dfrac{3}{7}$ c. $\dfrac{4}{13}$ d. $\dfrac{2}{11}$ e. $\dfrac{4}{7}$ Answer_____

9.   a. $\dfrac{3}{4}$ b. $\dfrac{3}{7}$ c. $\dfrac{4}{13}$ d. $\dfrac{7}{9}$ e. $\dfrac{7}{8}$ Answer_____

10.   a. $\dfrac{5}{11}$ b. $\dfrac{7}{9}$ c. $\dfrac{10}{17}$ d. $\dfrac{5}{8}$ e. $\dfrac{19}{23}$ Answer_____

Exercise 37
Book pages 88 - 90

Solve each of the following verbal problems:

1. Zelma purchased 8 ¾ yards of linen to make a dress. She used 4 $^2/_3$ yards. How much linen is not used?

2. Phil bought a suit for $600. He put $\frac{2}{5}$ down as a deposit. How much does he owe?

3. Phil has a full tank of gasoline. He used $\frac{1}{5}$ of the tank driving to see his brother Elliot and $\frac{2}{5}$ of the tank driving to see his other brother Seth. How much gasoline did he use?

4. Find $\frac{3}{5}$ of $\frac{1}{8}$.

5. On her butcher bill Zelma saw an item for $34 for 4 ¼ pounds of steak. What was the cost per pound?

6. Zelma and Eddie purchased a house for $906,000. They are required to put a $\frac{1}{3}$ down payment in order to obtain a mortgage. How much is the mortgage?

7. Elliot spent $\frac{1}{8}$ of the day sleeping, $\frac{1}{6}$ of the day in school and $\frac{1}{4}$ of the day commuting. What part of the day was left over for Elliot to do as he wishes?

8. Seth owns an export import business of cellular components. He sold $3,000,000 worth of cellular parts. If all the costs and overhead was $\frac{1}{3}$ of his gross sales, what was Seth's profit?

Exercise 38
Book pages 90 - 93

1. Write as a fraction and as a decimal:
    a. 10^{-3} d. 10^{-5}
    b. 10^{-7} e. 10^{-8}
    c. 10^{-1} f. 10^{-6}

2. Write in exponential notation and as a decimal:
    a. 1/100   d. 1/10,000
    b. 1/100,000   e. 1/1000
    c. 1/10   f. 1/10,000,000

3. Write in exponential notation and as a fraction:
    a. 0.01   d. 0.0001
    b. 0.0001   e. 0.000001
    c. 0.002   f. 0.0000001

Exercise 39
Book pages 93 - 94

Multiply (do not use calculator).
1. 2.75×10^3 5. 27.85×10^3
2. 14.7×10^2 6. 7.95×10^{-4}
3. 561×10^{-2} 7. 56.87×10^5
4. 0.95×10^{-3} 8. 2.98×10^{-5}

Divide: (do not use calculator)
1. $750 \div 10^2$ 5. $8,954 \times 10^{-6}$
2. $18.6 \div 10^4$ 6. $936 \div 10^{-2}$
3. $0.079 \div 10^3$ 7. $18.9 \div 10^4$
4. $0.083 \div 10^{-1}$ 8. $54 \div 10^{-3}$

Exercise 40
Book pages 94

On a separate sheet of paper

Write your answer in standard notation:

1. 3.24×10^5
2. 7.5×10^{-5}
3. 7.15×10^2
4. 2.59×10^{-11}

5. 97×10^3
6. 9.2×10^{-3}
7. 987.6×10^4
8. 7.6×10^{-14}

Write your answer in scientific notation

1. 6,753
2. 967
3. 81
4. 0.0081

5. 0.091
6. 2,354,789
7. 0.0000003
8. 0.00375

Exercise 41
Book Pages 95 - 97

Convert each metric unit to the smaller unit.

1. 7m = _____ cm.
2. 5g = _____ cg
3. 13.1L = _____ cl
4. 35m = _____ cm

5. 1.5 g = _____ cg
6. 0.07L = _____ cl
7. 0.004m = _____ mm
8. 0.73g = _____ mg

Convert each metric unit to the larger unit.

1. 400mm = _____ M
2. 300mg = _____ g
3. 6,400ml = _____ L
4. 340hg = _____ g

5. 500mg = _____ g
6. 5,800 ml = _____ L
7. 5,000 mg = _____ g
8. 300mm = _____ L

Exercise 42
Book pages 97-98

Answer the following questions:

1. How many feet are there in ¼ of a mile?

2. Three-fourths of a mile is equivalent to how many feet?

3. How many pounds are there in 88 ounces?

4. Each sixth grade student eats five ounces of cereal for break fast. There are 34 students in Mr. Chavin's class. How many 1-pound boxes of cereal are needed to feed the entire class next Thursday?

5. Zelma drank 12 cups of water. How many quarts of water did she drink?

6. How many 1-gallon containers are needed to hold 60 cups of orange juice?

7. How many inches are there in 2.75 miles?

8. How many pounds are there in 60 ounces?

Exercise 43
Book pages 99 - 100

Answer the following questions:

1. Convert 5 tons to kilograms.

2. Eddie is 6 feet 11 inches tall. What is his height in centimeters?

3. Convert 6.08 centimeters to inches.

4. Zelma drank last month 6 quarts of orange juice. How many liters of orange juice did she drink?

5. Philip has 5/8 inch wrench. What would this be in centimeters?

6. Convert 7.08 centimeters to inches.

7. Convert 9 liters to quarts.

8. Convert 70 inches to centimeters.

Exercise 44
Book pages 112 - 117

State the property of real numbers for each of the following problems.

1. $40 + 20 = 20 + 40$ Answer_____

2. $5 + (4+2) = (5+4) + 2$ Answer_____

3. $4 (2 \times 6) = 4(2) + 4(6)$ Answer_____

4. $6 + 0 = 0 + 6$ Answer_____

5. $4A + 5B = 5B + 4A$ Answer_____

6. $6(0) = 0(6)$ Answer_____

7. $7 \cdot 1 = 1 \cdot 7$ Answer_____

8. $5 + 0 = 5$ Answer_____

9. $5 - 0 = 5$ Answer_____

10. $6 \cdot 1/6 = 1$ Answer_____

11. $5 + (-5) = 0$ Answer_____

12. $6 (5 \times 2) = (6 \times 5 + 2)$ Answer_____

Exercise 45
Book pages 118 - 119

A) Addition signed numbers:

1. $(-4) + (7)$ Answer_____

2. $(-7 + 4)$ Answer_____

3. $(-3) + (-9)$ Answer_____

4. $(-7) + (8)$ Answer_____

5. $(-3) + (-9)$ Answer_____

6. $5 + (-8)$ Answer_____

7. $(-8) + 9$ Answer_____

8. $-3 + (7)$ Answer_____

9. $-3 + 7 - 4 + 1 - 5 + 6$ Answer_____

10. $-3 + 1 + 7 - 9 + 3 - 4$ Answer_____

B) Subtraction signed numbers:

1. $-3 - (-1)$ Answer_____
2. $4 - (-7)$ Answer_____
3. $-2 - (-9)$ Answer_____
4. $3 - (7)$ Answer_____
5. $4 - (-9)$ Answer_____
6. $-4 - (-7)$ Answer_____
7. $-3 - (-1)$ Answer_____
8. $-2 - (-4)$ Answer_____
9. $-3 - (4)$ Answer_____
10. $-2 - (-9)$ Answer_____

Exercise 46
Book pages 120 - 122

A) Multiply signed numbers.

1. $6(-7)$ Answer_____
2. $-7(-6)$ Answer_____
3. $(-3)(4)$ Answer_____
4. $(7)(-2)$ Answer_____
5. $(-1)(-2)(-3)$ Answer_____
6. $(-6)(-7)(-1)(-2)$ Answer_____

B) Divide signed numbers.

1. $\dfrac{-81}{3}$ Answer_____

2. $\dfrac{6}{2}$ Answer_____

3. $\dfrac{6}{-3}$ Answer_____

4. $\dfrac{-4}{-2}$ Answer_____

5. $\dfrac{-9}{3}$ Answer_____

6. $\dfrac{-81}{-3}$ Answer_____

Order of operations

1. -4^2 Answer_____

2. $(-4)^2$ Answer_____

3. $3(4+5)$ Answer_____

4. $7(6-1)$ Answer_____

5. $5(-3-7)$ Answer_____

6. $4(3-7)$ Answer_____

7. $5(7)^2$ Answer_____

8. $-3(6+8)^2$ Answer_____

9. $-3+(6+8)^2$ Answer_____

10. $6-7(4)^2$ Answer_____

11. $-4(5+6)^2$ Answer_____

12. $-4+(5+6)^2$ Answer_____

13. $-4(-6)^2$ Answer_____

14. $-8(6-2)$ Answer_____

15. $-8(-6-2)$ Answer_____

16. $-4(-5-6)^2$ Answer_____

17. $3(-4)^2$ Answer_____

18. $5-3(-4)^2$ Answer_____

19. $(-3-7)^2$ Answer_____

20. $(-3+7)^2$ Answer_____

Exercise 48
Book pages 125-127

Express as algebraic expressions:

1. 6 more than a number   Answer_____

2. A number minus 8   Answer_____

3. A number decreased by 7   Answer_____

4. A number plus 6   Answer_____

5. 8 times a number   Answer_____

6. 5 less than a number   Answer_____

7. A number increased by 16   Answer_____

8. 5 more than half a number   Answer_____

9. 4 more than 5 times a number   Answer_____

10. 4 less than 2 times a number   Answer_____

11. Represent the value of "n" nickels and "q"   Answer_____

12. Represent the value of "d" dimes and "n" nickels   Answer_____

Exercise 49
Book pages 127 - 131

A) Perform the indicated:

1. Add: $(4x + 7y)$ and $(7x + 9y)$ Answer_____

2. Add: $(4a - 8b)$ and $(-7a + 12b)$ Answer_____

3. Sum: $(3x - 7y)$ and $(-7x + 8y)$ Answer_____

4. Sum: $(-7x^2 + 6x) + (-9x + 3)$ Answer_____

5. Sum: $(-9x^2 + 3x) + (-7x^3 + 5)$ Answer_____

6. Sum: $(-9x^2 + 3x - 6) + (-12x^2 - 18)$ Answer_____

7. Subtract: $7y - 3$ from $9y - 8$ Answer_____

8. Subtract: $-2x^2 + 6x$ from $-3x^2 - 9x$ Answer_____

9. Simplify: $(3x^2 - 9x) + (7x - 8)$ Answer_____

10. Simplify: $(-7x^2 + 9x - 7) - (-9x^2 + 9)$ Answer_____

11. Simplify: $(3x^2 + 9x) + (-18x^2 + 4)$ Answer_____

12. Simplify: $(-3x^2 - 9x) - (7x - 8)$ Answer_____

B) Exponent rule.

1. $(y^2)(y)$ Answer_____

2. $(x^3)(x^4)$ Answer_____

3. $(A^7)(A^2)$ Answer_____

4. $(A^7)(B^9)$ Answer_____

5. $(x^4)(x)$ Answer_____

6. $(x^3)(y^7)$ Answer_____

7. $(B^7)(B)$ Answer_____

8. $(B^4)(A^3)$ Answer_____

9. $(x^2)(y^4)$ Answer_____

10. $(x^{11})(x^7)$ Answer_____

Exercise 50
Book pages 132 - 133

Multiply:

1. $(-7 \, ABC) \, (-9 \, ABC)$ Answer_____

2. $(6x^2 \, y^4) \, (-2x^3 \, y^7)$ Answer_____

3. $(3x^2 y) \, (4xy^2)$ Answer_____

4. $(-2ab^2 c) \, (-9a^2 bc^2)$ Answer_____

5. $(7ABC) \, (-12 \, A^2 B^2 C^2)$ Answer_____

6. $(-4x) \, (-7x)$ Answer_____

7. $(-4x^2 y) \, (-7xy^2)$ Answer_____

8. $(-8A^2 BC^3) \, (-2AB^3 C)$ Answer_____

9. $(3RST) \, (-9RST)$ Answer_____

Exercise 51
Book pages 133-134

Multiply:

1. $4(x - 7)$ Answer_____

2. $-3(x + 4)$ Answer_____

3. $x(x - 7)$ Answer_____

4. $-a(a - 9)$ Answer_____

5. $-4x \, (x - 7)$ Answer_____

6. $5y \, (-y + 9)$ Answer_____

7. $-6z(3z^2 - 9z)$ Answer_____

8. $-5ab^2(-3a + 9)$ Answer_____

9. $9a^2 b(4a^2 b + 5ab^2)$ Answer_____

10. $9x^2 y(-4x^2 + 7y)$ Answer_____

11. $-9x(x - 7)$ Answer_____

12. $4y^2(7y - 16)$ Answer_____

Exercise 52
Book pages 135 - 136

Multiply:

1. $(x - 2)(x+4)$ Answer_____

2. $(x - 5)(x+3)$ Answer_____

3. $(6x - 7)(3x - 9)$ Answer_____

4. $(x - 5)(x+5)$ Answer_____

5. $(3x - 7)(4x +9)$ Answer_____

6. $(x + 6)(x - 6)$ Answer_____

7. $(2x - 7)(2x + 7)$ Answer_____

8. $(3x - 9)(4x - 6)$ Answer_____

9. $(x + 5)^2$ Answer_____

10. $(x - 5)^2$ Answer_____

Exercise 53
Book page 137

Multiply:

1. $(x + 3)(x^2 + 4x + 5)$ Answer_____

2. $(y - 5)(y^2 + 3y + 7)$ Answer_____

3. $(3x + 2)(x^2 - 9x + 5)$ Answer_____

4. $(y + 4)(y^2 - 7x + 8)$ Answer_____

5. $(x - 1)(x^2 + 3x + 8)$ Answer_____

6. $(y - 4)(y^2 - y + 5)$ Answer_____

7. $(3y^2 + 2y + 4)(-6y^2 + 7y - 9)$ Answer_____

8. $(2x^2 - x - 1)(x^2 + 4x - 3)$ Answer_____

9. $(y - 6)(y^2 + 7y + 3)$ Answer_____

10. $(4x - 7)(2x^2 - 5x + 8)$ Answer_____

Exercise 54
Book pages 138 - 139

Evaluate:

1. Find the value of $3x - 5$, when $x = 4$.   Answer_____

2. Find value $a^2 - 8a$, when $a = -6$.   Answer_____

3. Evaluate $-x^2$, when $x = -6$.   Answer_____

4. Evaluate $2t^2 - 8t + 2$, when $t = 8$.   Answer_____

5. Find the value of $3a + 6b$, when $a = -6$ and $b = -9$.   Answer_____

6. Evaluate $-6x^2$, when $x = -7$.   Answer_____

7. Evaluate $8x^2 - 5y^2$, when $x = 8$, $y = -5$.   Answer_____

8. If $a = 4bc$, find "a," when $b = -5$ and $c = -6$.   Answer_____

9. Find the value of x; when $x = 3y^2$ and $y = -2$.   Answer_____

10. Evaluate $8x^2 - 7y^2$, when $x = -8$ and $y = -7$.   Answer_____

Exercise 55
Book pages 139 - 140

Perform the indicated:

1. $4y + y(y + 8)$ Answer_____

2. $3x + x(x + 5)$ Answer_____

3. $5y + 5y^2(-2y - 7)$ Answer_____

4. $7x^2 - 8x(x - 6)$ Answer_____

5. $4a^2b - 3a(ab - 9)$ Answer_____

6. $4y^2 + 7y^2(-2y - 9)$ Answer_____

7. $3x^2y - 8x(x^2 + 4xy)$ Answer_____

8. $7a^3b - 4ab(8a - 3b)$ Answer_____

9. $-7xy + 3x(y + 7)$ Answer_____

10. $5y^2 + 7y^2(y+9)$ Answer_____

Exercise 56
Book page 141

Interpret each of the following algebraic expressions:

1. Seven more than a number   Answer_____

2. A number minus nine   Answer_____

3. A number decreased by seven   Answer_____

4. A number plus 8   Answer_____

5. 6 less than a number   Answer_____

6. A number increased by 21   Answer_____

7. 6 more than 7 times a number   Answer_____

8. 8 less than 5 times a number   Answer_____

9. A number increased by 18   Answer_____

10. 6 more than 18 times a number.   Answer_____

Exercise 57
Book pages 144-145

Perform indicated:

1. $(x^6)^4$ Answer_____

2. $(y^{24})^2$ Answer_____

3. $(y^3)^2$ Answer_____

4. $(xy^3)^6$ Answer_____

5. $(c^6d^9)^3$ Answer_____

6. $(5x^2)^3$ Answer_____

7. $(3x^5y^6)^4$ Answer_____

8. $(x^6y^7)^2$ Answer_____

9. $(-3x^7y^4)^5$ Answer_____

10. $(-2x^6y^9)^6$ Answer_____

Exercise 58
Book pages 145-146

Perform indicated:

1. $\dfrac{x^9}{x^3}$ Answer_____

2. $\dfrac{a^7}{a}$ Answer_____

3. $\dfrac{b^4}{b^3}$ Answer_____

4. $\dfrac{x^6}{x^2}$ Answer_____

5. $\dfrac{x^3}{x}$ Answer_____

6. $\dfrac{x^6}{x^2}$ Answer_____

7. $\dfrac{x^{12}}{x^2}$ Answer_____

8. $\dfrac{y^7}{y^3}$ Answer_____

9. $\dfrac{x^4}{x}$ Answer_____

10. $\dfrac{c^9}{c^2}$ Answer_____

Exercise 59
Book pages 146 - 148

Divide:

1. $\dfrac{8x^2}{-2x}$ 　　　　　　　　　　　Answer_____

2. $\dfrac{-6y^2}{y^2}$ 　　　　　　　　　　　Answer_____

3. $\dfrac{8a-16}{4}$ 　　　　　　　　　　　Answer_____

4. $\dfrac{16a-8}{4}$ 　　　　　　　　　　　Answer_____

5. $\dfrac{3y-6}{3}$ 　　　　　　　　　　　Answer_____

6. $\dfrac{30y^2-15y}{5y}$ 　　　　　　　　　Answer_____

7. $\dfrac{12a^7-4a^6}{4a^6}$ 　　　　　　　　Answer_____

8. $\dfrac{9x^{11}-3x}{3x}$ 　　　　　　　　　Answer_____

9. $\dfrac{6x^2y^7-3xy}{3xy}$ 　　　　　　　Answer_____

10. $\dfrac{18x^9y^7-12x^4y^{18}}{6x^2y^7}$ 　　　　Answer_____

Exercise 60
Book pages 149 – 150

Factor each of the following:

1. $4x^2 + 16$ Answer_____

2. $8x^3 + 4x^2$ Answer_____

3. $y^2 + 8y$ Answer_____

4. $6x^3 + 12x^2$ Answer_____

5. $18x^2 - 9$ Answer_____

6. $18^7y^4 + 6x^3y^7$ Answer_____

7. $10yx^2 + 20x^2$ Answer_____

8. $6x^2y + 9x$ Answer_____

9. $12x^9y^{12} - 8x^2y^4$ Answer_____

10. $7x^4y^2 - 14x^3y^{14}$ Answer_____

11. $14x^2 + 7xy$ Answer_____

12. $12a^2b^4 - 9ab^3$ Answer_____

Exercise 61
Book pages 151 - 152

Factor completely:

1. $A^2 - 81$ Answer_____

2. $y^2 - 9$ Answer_____

3. $4x^2 - 36$ Answer_____

4. $3x^2 - 27$ Answer_____

5. $64y^2 - 25x^2$ Answer_____

6. $3B^2 - 12$ Answer_____

7. $2x^2 - 72$ Answer_____

8. $16 - y^2$ Answer_____

9. $x^6 - 81$ Answer_____

10. $36 - A^2$ Answer_____

11. $x^4 - 36$ Answer_____

12. $16x^4 - 64$ Answer_____

Exercise 62
Book pages 152 - 157

Factor completely:

1. $x^2 + 6x + 5$ Answer_____

2. $A^2 + 7A + 10$ Answer_____

3. $x^2 + 10x + 9$ Answer_____

4. $B^2 - 7B + 12$ Answer_____

5. $C^2 - 9C + 20$ Answer_____

6. $X^2 - 5x - 6$ Answer_____

7. $X^2 - 13x + 42$ Answer_____

8. $Y^2 - 3y - 18$ Answer_____

9. $A^2 - 15x + 56$ Answer_____

10. $2A^2 - 14A + 20$ Answer_____

11. $3B + 21B^2 + 36B$ Answer_____

12. $y^3 + 3y^2 - 18y$ Answer_____

Exercise 63
Book pages 157-159

Solve the following equations:

1. $x - 3 = 4$ Answer_____
2. $x + 9 = 2$ Answer_____
3. $3x = 12$ Answer_____
4. $-4x = 24$ Answer_____
5. $2y - 7 = 3$ Answer_____
6. $-2x - 4 = -8$ Answer_____
7. $6 - y = 0$ Answer_____
8. $x - 18 = 19$ Answer_____
9. $3x + 4y + 7 = 42$ Answer_____
10. $6x - 7 = x + 28$ Answer_____
11. $-7(x + 7) = -49$ Answer_____
12. $A + 3A + 7 = -21$ Answer_____
13. $-4(x + 4) = 16$ Answer_____
14. $A - 7 = 14$ Answer_____
15. $2A - 9 = 15$ Answer_____
16. $-6x - 3 = -2x - 19$ Answer_____

Exercise 64
Book pages 159 - 160

Solve each of the following equations:

1. $\dfrac{x+3}{7} = \dfrac{x+4}{6}$ Answer_____

2. $\dfrac{x}{3} + 4 = \dfrac{1}{2}$ Answer_____

3. $\dfrac{x}{2} \times \dfrac{x}{5} = 7$ Answer_____

4. $\dfrac{x}{3} + \dfrac{x}{5} = 80$ Answer_____

5. $\dfrac{x+1}{3} = \dfrac{x+9}{4}$ Answer_____

6. $\dfrac{x}{7} + 6 = \dfrac{3}{4}$ Answer_____

Exercise 65
Book pages 162 - 163

Solve for the following equations for the indicated variable:

1. $y - x = 6$. Solve for y.   Answer_____

2. $x - y = 9$. Solve for x.   Answer_____

3. $a - 8b = 0$. Solve for "a."   Answer_____

4. $4x - 2 = y$. Solve for x.   Answer_____

5. $5x - 6y = 9$. Solve for x.   Answer_____

6. $A + B + C = 9$. Solve for B.   Answer_____

7. $\dfrac{c - d}{4} = e$ Solve for c.   Answer_____

8. $4x - 5y + 6z = 7$. Solve for z.   Answer_____

9. $4(x + y) = 8$. Solve for y.   Answer_____

10. $\dfrac{c - d}{6} = e$. Solve for c.   Answer_____

Exercise 66
Book pages 164 - 166

Solve the following verbal problems. Algebraic solutions only.

1. The sum of twice a number and eight is twenty.
   Find the number.   Answer_____

2. Six times the sum of a number and eight is sixty.
   Find the number.   Answer_____

3. One number is six less than another.
   Their sum is thirty-six. Find both numbers.   Answer_____

4. The sum of twice a number and six is thirty.
   Find the number.   Answer_____

5. One number is eight less than another.
   Their sum is fifty-six. Find the larger number.   Answer_____

6. Five times the sum of a number and six is sixty.
   Find the number.   Answer_____

Exercise 67
Book pages 168 - 170

Solve each of the following. (Verbal problems—algebraic solution only.)

1. $\dfrac{x}{12} = \dfrac{1}{2}$ Answer_____

2. $\dfrac{6}{x} = \dfrac{3}{2}$ Answer_____

3. $\dfrac{x}{9} = \dfrac{1}{18}$ Answer_____

4. $\dfrac{x}{7} = \dfrac{6}{7}$ Answer_____

5. $\dfrac{3}{x} = \dfrac{1}{2}$ Answer_____

6. $\dfrac{x}{9} = \dfrac{2}{3}$ Answer_____

7. If 400 grams of ice cream contain 60 grams of fat. How many grams of fat are there in 1,400 grams of ice cream?   Answer_____

8. A map is drawn so that 3 inches represents 930 miles. If the distance between 2 cities is 1,550 miles, how far apart are they on the map?   Answer_____

9. An airplane flies 2,400 miles in 8 hours. At this rate, how far does it travel in 17 hours?   Answer_____

10. A man drives his car 930 miles in 10 hours. At this rate, how far will he travel in 18 hours?   Answer_____

Exercise 68
Book pages 171 - 175

A) Solve each of the following simultaneous equations:

1. $x - y = 6$
   $\underline{x + y = 2}$

   Answer_____

2. $a - b = 6$
   $\underline{a + b = 8}$

   Answer_____

3. $x - 3b = 10$
   $\underline{x + 3b = 6}$

   Answer_____

4. $a - b = 12$
   $\underline{a + b = 4}$

   Answer_____

5. $-3x + y = 12$
   $\underline{3x + 2y = 9}$

   Answer_____

B) Solve each of the following simultaneous equation:

1. $2x - y = 16$
   $\underline{x + 3y = 1}$

   Answer_____

2. $x + 4y = 8$
   $\underline{2x - 3y = -3}$

   Answer_____

3. $2x - 6y = 12$
   $\underline{x + y = 2}$

   Answer_____

4. $4A - B = 6$
   $\underline{A + 2B = 15}$

   Answer_____

5. $6x - 2y = 12$
   $\underline{x + y = 6}$

   Answer_____

C) Solve each of the following simultaneous equation:

1. $2A + 3B = 7$

    $\underline{\quad A = B + 4}$

    Answer_____

2. $6x + 4y = 18$

    $\underline{\quad y = x - 3}$

    Answer_____

3. $3x - 7y = 9$

    $\underline{\quad x = y - 1}$

    Answer_____

4. $3C + 6D = 12$

    $\underline{\quad\quad C = 20}$

    Answer_____

Exercise 69
Book page 176

D) Solve each of the following quadratic equations:

1. $x^2 - 7x + 10 = 0$ Answer_____
2. $x^2 + 12x + 11 = 0$ Answer_____
3. $y^2 + 3y = 0$ Answer_____
4. $x^2 = 36$ Answer_____
5. $x^2 - 8x = -15$ Answer_____
6. $x^2 + 6x = 7$ Answer_____
7. $y^2 + 3y = -2$ Answer_____
8. $A^2 - 6A = 16$ Answer_____
9. $x^2 - 36 = 0$ Answer_____
10. $2x^2 + 14x = -20$ Answer_____

Exercise 70
Book pages 178 - 180

Answer the following questions:

1. Which one of the following points lies on the graph $2x + 2y = 8$?

    a) $(1, 3)$ b) $(2, 2)$ c) $(7, 2)$ d) $(2, 9)$

    Answer_____

2. Which one of the following points lies on the graph $3x - y = 9$?

    a) $(2, 7)$ b) $(1, 1)$ c) $(4, 3)$ d) $(2, 7)$

    Answer_____

3. Which one of the following points lies on the graph $2x + y = 9$?

    a) $(1, 1)$ b) $(7, 2)$ c) $(3, 9)$ d) $(2, 5)$

    Answer_____

4. Which one of the following points lies on the graph $3x + 2y = 5$?

    a) $(1, 1)$ b) $(2, 9)$ c) $(3, 8)$ d) $(4, 7)$

    Answer_____

Exercise 71
Book page 182

Answer the following questions:

1. Find the "x" intercept $3x - y = 9$ Answer_____
2. Find the "y" intercept $3x - y = 9$ Answer_____
3. Find the "x" intercept $-9x + 9y = 18$ Answer_____
4. Find the "y" intercept $-9x + 9y = 18$ Answer_____
5. Find the "x" intercept $-x - y = -18$ Answer_____
6. Find the 'y" intercept $-x - y = -18$ Answer_____
7. Find the "x" intercept $-3x - 7y = -21$ Answer_____
8. Find the "y" intercept $-3x - 7y = -21$ Answer_____

Exercise 72
Book page 185

Find the slope for each of the following sets of points:

1. $(3,7)$ $(2,9)$ Answer_____

2. $(-3, 9)$ $(7, -4)$ Answer_____

3. $(2, -8)$ $(-6, 3)$ Answer_____

4. $(-1, -4)$ $(-2, -5)$ Answer_____

5. $(6, 7)$ $(2, 3)$ Answer_____

6. $(5, 4)$ $(8, 9)$ Answer_____

7. $(2, 5)$ $(-6, -9)$ Answer_____

8. $(-3, -1)$ $(4, 9)$ Answer_____

9. $(3, 1)$ $(-4, -9)$ Answer_____

10. $(-2, -5)$ $(6, 9)$ Answer_____

Exercise 73
Book page 186

For each of the following questions, write an equation of a straight line:

1. $M = -4$ $b = -1$ Answer_____

2. $M = 2$ $b = -4$ Answer_____

3. $M = -3$ $b = 6$ Answer_____

4. $M = 5$ $b = 6$ Answer_____

5. $M = -3$ $b = 5$ Answer_____

6. $M = -4$ $b = 4$ Answer_____

7. $M = -2$ $b = -5$ Answer_____

8. $M = -1$ $b = -6$ Answer_____

Exercise 74
Book page 187

Find the slope and the y–intercept for each of the following equations:

1. $x + 4y = 6$ Answer_____

2. $x + 3y = 4$ Answer_____

3. $y - 2x = 5$ Answer_____

4. $2x + 3y = 6$ Answer_____

5. $-y -2x = -9$ Answer_____

6. $-3y - 7y = -21$ Answer_____

7. $x - y = 6$ Answer_____

8. $3x + 2y = -9$ Answer_____

Exercise 75
Book page 188

Write an equation of a straight line given the following information:

1. $M = 6$ Point $(6, 8)$ Answer_____

2. $M = -4$ Point $(-1, -1)$ Answer_____

3. $M = 7$ Point $(-1, -3)$ Answer_____

4. $M = 6$ Point $(-2, -2)$ Answer_____

5. $M = -1$ Point $(-4, -3)$ Answer_____

Exercise 76
Book pages 193 - 194

Answer the following questions:

1. Find the complement of 59°.

   Answer_____

2. Find the supplement of 29°.

   Answer_____

   An angle is five times its complement.

   Find the smaller angle.

   Answer_____

3. An angle is four times its supplement.

   Find the larger angle.

   Answer_____

4. An angle is 60° more than its complement. Find

   both angles.

   Answer_____

5. An angle is 12° less than its supplement. Find

   the larger angle.

   Answer_____

6. An angle exceeds its complement by 20°.

   Answer_____

7. An angle is four times its supplement.

   Find both angles.

   Answer_____

Exercise 77:
Book pages 194 - 195

Answer all of the following questions:

1. The vertex angle of an isosceles triangle is 40^0.

   Find the value of each base angle.

   Answer_____

2. The three angles of a triangle are in the ratio of 1:2:7.

   Find the value of the larger angle.

   Answer_____

3. The base angle of an isosceles triangle is 40^0.

   Find the value of the vertex angle.

   Answer_____

4. The values of the angles of a scalene triangle are

   x^0, $x + 10^0$ and $x + 20^0$. Find the value of all three angles.

   Answer_____

Exercise 78
Book page 196

Answer all of the following questions:

1. Find the circumference of a circle whose radius is 7 cm. Answer_____

2. Find the area of a circle whose radius is 16 cm. Answer_____

3. Find the radius of a circle whose circumference is 68 cm. Answer_____

4. Find the radius of a circle whose area is 314 sq. cm. Answer_____

Exercise 79
Book pages 197-199

Answer each of the following questions:

1. Find the perimeter of a rectangle whose dimensions are 16 cm. and 14 cm. Answer_____

2. Find the side of a square whose area is 144 sq. cm. Answer_____

3. The area of a triangle is 96 sq. cm. If the base is 48 cm, find the value of the altitude. Answer_____

4. If the perimeter of a square is 100 meters, what is the value of the side of a square? Answer_____

5. Find the area of a square whose perimeter is 48 cm. Answer_____

6. Find the area of a rectangle whose perimeter is 200cm. and length is 60 cm. Answer_____

7. The area of a trapezoid is 144 sq. cm. and the sum of the basis is 72 cm. Find the altitude. Answer_____

Exercise 80
Book pages 200 - 201

Write the length of the missing side:

1.

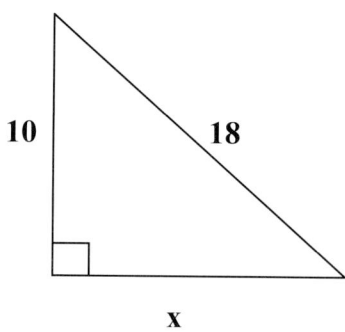

10   18

x

4.

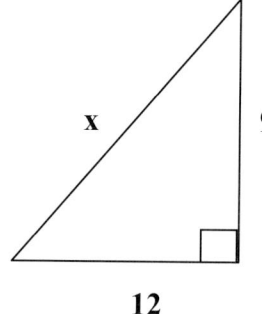

x   9

12

2.

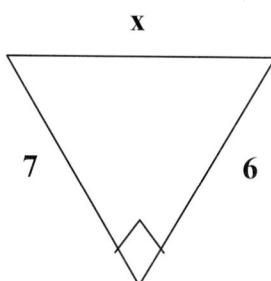

x

7   6

5.

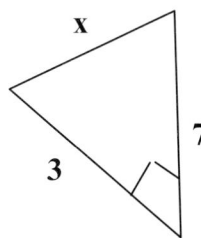

x

3   7

3.

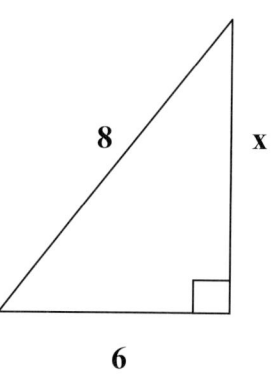

8   x

6

6.

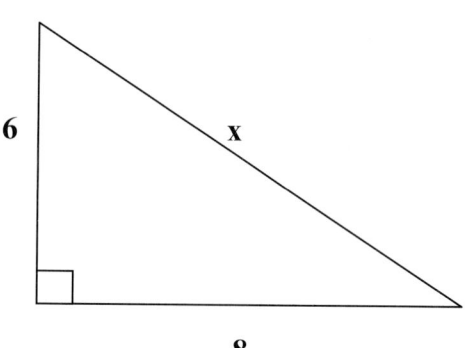

6   x

8

89. Introduction—Tests

The arithmetic and algebra exams were developed to help measure individual student progress. They can be used in the following ways:

1. Students can test themselves. Those questions answered incorrectly will inform the students of the topics they need to master. They can take the extra to the academic resource center in their school and receive the necessary tutoring.

2. Also, the exams can be used by the teachers to develop individual student profiles. A cooperative learning atmosphere that is student-centered can be developed. The teacher becomes the facilitator. Instruction can be designed to meet individual student needs. Teachers can use the additional exams to update academic progress, for individual students. The profiles can be updated.

ARITHMETIC EXAMINATION # 1

Directions: Answer each of the following questions by choosing the appropriate letter. Reduce all fractional answer to lowest terms. **Show all written work in the space provided for each question.** You have 45 minutes.

1. The number Fifty Six million, Six Hundred Sixty Five Thousand, Seven, may be written in standard form as:

   a) 56,665,070   b) 66,656,700   c) 56,665,007   d) 65,506,007

2. Find the sum: $105 + 1.55 + 15.065 =$

   a) 1261.15   b) 121.615   c) 12.1615   d) 216.112

3. Sam drove 88 miles on Monday, 115 miles on Tuesday, 67 miles on Wednesday and 26 miles on Thursday. What is the average distance Sam drove each day?

   a) 84   b) 74   c) 76   d) 64

4. What is 8 pounds, 7 ounces, minus 6 pounds 10 ounces?

   a) 1 lb. 13 oz   b) 2 lbs. 3 oz   c). 2lbs. 13 oz   d). 14 lbs. 17 oz

Reminder: Change improper fractions to mixed numbers and reduce all fractional units to lowest terms.

5.   Add: $\frac{5}{6} + \frac{4}{5} =$

     a) $1\frac{15}{30}$ b) $1\frac{1}{2}$ c) $\frac{45}{30}$ d) $1\frac{19}{30}$

6.   Subtract: $8 - 2\frac{7}{8} =$

     a) $5\frac{1}{8}$ b) $6\frac{7}{8}$ c) $6\frac{1}{16}$ d) $5\frac{7}{8}$

]

7.   Find the quotient: $3\frac{3}{5}$ divided by $\frac{1}{2}$

     a) $1\frac{10}{18}$ b) $7\frac{2}{5}$ c) $3\frac{3}{10}$ d) $7\frac{1}{5}$

8.   Which of the following fractional units has the largest value?

     a) $\frac{3}{10}$ b) $\frac{1}{9}$ c) $\frac{2}{7}$ d) $\frac{4}{5}$

9.   What is the quotient of 86,496 divided by 24?

   a) 3406   b) 4360   c) 3064   d) 3604

10.   Find the difference: 109 – 89.8 =

   a) 18.2   b) 19.2   c) 20.2   d) 19.8

11.   Multiply 6.46 x 0.7 (Round your answer to the nearest hundredth).

   a) 4.52   b) 4.252   c) 4.522   d) 4.50

12.   Divide: 0.514 ÷ 0.4 =

   a) 0.1825   b) 1.285   c) 12.75   d) 2.185

13.   Which of the following is the smallest number?

   a) 0.3042   b) 0.3202   c) 0.3024   d) 0.3124

14. A maintenance engineer earns $960 for a forty-hour job. This week he worked 6 hours of overtime at a rate of $36 per hour. How much was his total income for this week?

    a.) $1761   b) $1176   c) $1261   d) $1067

15. Express 0.09 to percent.

    a) 90%   b) 900%   c) 0.9%   d) 9%

16. What is 16% of 45?

    a) 7.2   b) .27   c) 7.3   d) 6.7

17. 15% of what number is 600?

    a) 250   b) 400   c) 4000   d) 500

18. A freshman student took a Math qualifying exam and answered 16 questions correctly and 4 questions incorrectly. Approximately what percent of the total number of questions did he answer incorrectly?

a) 15%   b) 20%   c) 80%   d) 25%

19. Find the cost to carpet an office that measures 16 feet wide and 14 feet long, at $9.50 per square foot.

a) $2282   b) $1822   c) $2128   d) $281

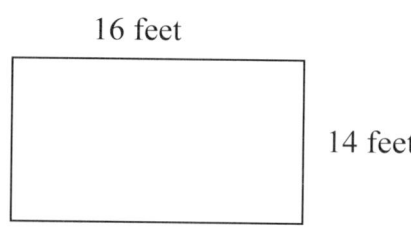

16 feet

14 feet

20. The graph below shows the annual profit of Ron's company for a five-year period.

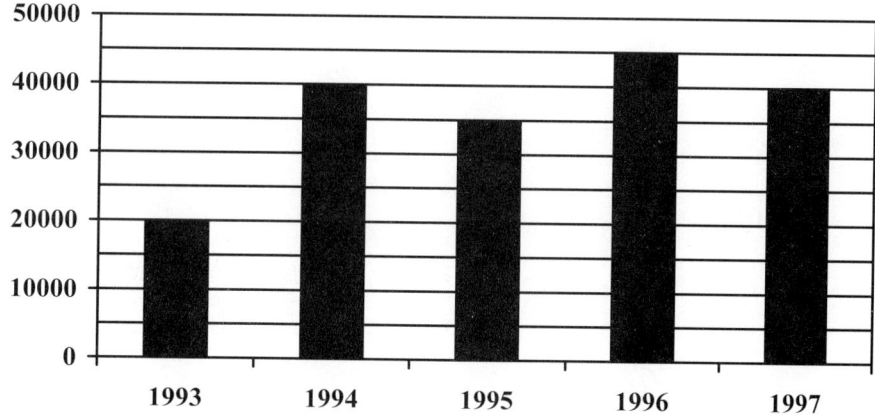

What was the total profit for the years 1995 and 1996?

a) 65,000   b) 85,000   c) 80,000   d) 90,000

Answers

Arithmetic Examination #1

1.	C	11.	A
2.	B	12.	B
3.	B	13.	C
4.	A	14.	B
5.	D	15.	D
6.	A	16.	A
7.	D	17.	C
8.	D	18.	B
9.	D	19.	C
10.	B	20.	C

ARITHMETIC EXAMINATION #2

Directions: Answer each of the following questions by choosing the appropriate letter. Reduce all fractional answers to lowest terms. **Show all written work in the space provided for each question.** You have 45 minutes.

1.   Write two hundred thirty million, three hundred thousand, eighty-nine in standard form.

   a) 23,300,089   b) 23,003,089   c) 230,300,089   d) 23,003,890

2.   Find the quotient: $12\overline{)28871}$

   a) 24436   b) 2406   c) 2360   d) 802

3.   A student received grades of 83, 90, and 91 on three mathematics tests. What is the student's test score average on the mathematics tests?

   a) 270   b) 90   c) 91   d) 88

4.   Find the sum: $8\,{}^{2}/_{3} + 6\,{}^{4}/_{5} =$

   a) 15   b) $14{}^{6}/_{8}$ c) $15{}^{7}/_{15}$ d) $15{}^{8}/_{15}$

5. Find the difference: $7\dfrac{3}{5} - 3\dfrac{5}{7} =$

    a) $3\dfrac{31}{35}$ b) $4\dfrac{2}{12}$ c) $3\dfrac{8}{12}$ d) $4\dfrac{1}{35}$

6. Find the quotient: $7\dfrac{3}{5} \div 2 =$

    a) $3\dfrac{4}{5}$ b) $5\dfrac{1}{5}$ c) $6\dfrac{3}{5}$ d) $\dfrac{9}{10}$

7. Which number has the smallest value?

    a) $\dfrac{1}{8}$ b) $\dfrac{2}{5}$ c) $\dfrac{2}{7}$ d) $\dfrac{2}{11}$

8. A plumber used 4ft. 5 in., 8 ft. 6 in., and 11 in. of copper tubing to install a sink. Find the total length of copper tubing he used to install the sink.

    a) 12 ft. 21 in.   b) 13 ft. 11in.   c) 13 ft. 10 in.   d) 32 ft.

9. Find the difference: 64 – 6.4 =
    a) 0   b) 49.6   c) 48.6   d) 57.6

10. Calculate 72.3 x 0.08 rounded to the nearest *hundredth.*

    a) 6.52   b) 0.578   c) 5.51   d) 5.78

11. Find the quotient: 11.2 ÷ 44.8 =
    a) 80   b) 8   c) 0.25   d) 0.125

12. Which number has the largest value?

    a) 9.73   b) 9.701   c) 9.079   d) 9.9

13. An office manager paid $15.50 for desk pad set, $35.95 for a lamp, and $4.95 for a desk calendar. She also paid $3.58 in sales tax for the items. She took $60 from petty cash to make the purchases at a local office supply outlet. How much should she return to petty cash after the purchases?

    a) 10¢   b) 5¢   c) 2¢   d) 8¢

14.   Express 35% as a decimal.

    a) 35   b) 0.35   c) 0.053   d) 0.0035

15.   What is 10% of 360?

    a) 36   b) 3600   c) 90   d) 9

16.   60% of what number is 360?

    a) 0.0006   b) 60   c) 6   d) 600

17.   A student driver answered 21 questions correctly and 4 questions incorrectly on the written portion of his driver's test. What percent of the questions did he answer correctly?

    a) 2.1%   b) 84%   c) 8%   d) 21%

18.   Jones' Cadillac Dealership bought a used Cadillac Seville for $ 20,000 and sold the Cadillac for $25,000. What is the percent increase in the selling price of this car?

    a) 80%   b) 25%   c) 5,000%   d) 50%

19. If carpeting cost $12.45 per square yard, how much will it cost to carpet the floor represented by the diagram below?

15 yards

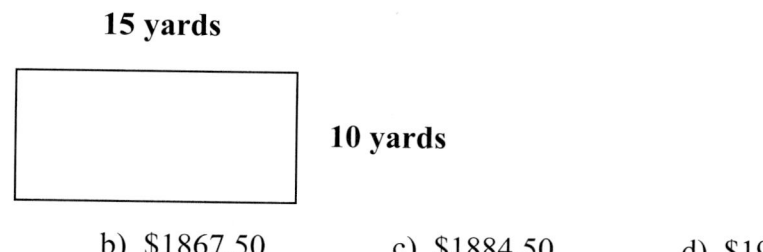

10 yards

a) $1280.50

b) $1867.50

c) $1884.50

d) $1927.50

20. The graph below shows the number of students at a school who could do at least 30 pushups. How many more students could do at least 30 pushups in 1996 than in 1994?

YEAR	NUMBER OF STUDENTS
1993	☺ ☺ ☺
1994	☺ ☺ ☺ ☺
1995	☺ ☺ ☺ ☺ ☺ ☺ ☺ ☺
1996	☺ ☺ ☺ ☺ ☺ ☺ ☺ ☺ ☺
Each ☺ stands for 50 students	

a) 400

b) 250

c) 200

d) 1150

Answers

ARITHMETIC EXAMINATION ON #2

1.	C	11.	C
2.	B	12.	D
3.	D	13.	C
4.	C	14.	B
5.	A	15.	A
6.	A	16.	D
7.	A	17.	B
8.	C	18.	B
9.	D	19.	B
10.	D	20.	B

ARITHMETIC EXAMINATION # 3

Directions: Answer each of the following questions by circling the appropriate letter. Reduce all fractional answers to lowest terms. **Show all written work in the space provided for each question.** You have 45 minutes.

1.   The number seventy-nine billion, two hundred fifty million, two hundred fifty-six thousand, one hundred forty-eight, may be written in standard form as:

a) 97,025,206,184   b) 79,205,256,148

c) 79,250,256,148   d) 79,250,256,108

2.   Find the sum: 5.20 + 2.87 + 0.109 + 234.6 =

a) 224.779   b) 242.779   c) 242.797   d) 232.779

3.   Find the average of the following daily sales: $190.75, $270.45, $340.45, $400.25, and 450.00.

a) 338.80   b) 330.38   c) 230.86   d) 330.83

4.   What the sum of 9 pounds, 14 ounces and 5 pounds, 10 ounces?

a) 14 lbs. 4 oz.   b) 4 lbs. 23 oz.   c) 15 lbs. 8 oz.   d) 13 lbs. 24 oz.

Reminder: Change improper fractions to mixed and reduce all fractional units to lowest terms.

5.   Add: $17\frac{11}{12}$ and $9\frac{3}{4}$

a) $27\frac{2}{3}$ b) $26\frac{2}{3}$ c) $27\frac{8}{12}$ d) $26\frac{20}{12}$

6.   Subtract: $4\frac{2}{5}$ and $9\frac{1}{10}$

a) $4^8/_{10}$ b) $4^7/_{20}$ c) $5^1/_{10}$ d) $4^7/_{10}$

7.   Find the quotient: $2\frac{5}{6}$ divided by $\frac{2}{3}$.

a) $4\frac{1}{4}$ b) $\frac{17}{4}$ c) $4\frac{3}{12}$ d) $5\frac{1}{5}$

8.   Which of the following fractional units has the largest value?

a) $\frac{5}{10}$ b) $\frac{1}{9}$ c) $\frac{2}{7}$ d) $\frac{2}{5}$

9.   What is the quotient of 141,288 divided by 28?

   a) 5406   b) 5360   c) 5046   d) 5604

10.   Find the difference: 238 – 9.87 =

   a) 218.12   b) 228.13   c) 282.13   d) 229.87

11.   Multiply 8.75 x 0.06. (Round your answer to the nearest hundredth.)

   a) 0.63   b) 0.54   c) 0.525   d) 0.53

12.   Divide: $0.4\overline{).514}$

   a) 0.1825   b) 1.2845   c) 12.75   d) 2.185

13.   Which of the following is the smallest number?

   a) 2.3042   b) 2.3202   c) 2.3024   d) 2.3124

14. The teacher has 24 boxes of pencils with 25 pencils in each box. If these pencils were divided evenly among 50 students, how many pencils would each student receive?

    a) 12   b) 120   c) 60   d) 62

15. Convert $\frac{1}{8}$ to a decimal.

    a) .108   b) 125   c) 0.125   d) 12.5

16. What is 15% of 950?

    a) 1.425   b) 1425   c) 14.25   d) 142.5

17. 12% of what number is 360?

    a) 300   b) 3,000   c) 30,000   d) 4,000

18. An Algebra student took a final exam and answered 19 questions correctly and one question incorrectly. Approximately what percent of the total number of questions did he answer correctly?
    a) 95%   b) 97.5%   c) 90%   d) 100%

320

19. A rectangular vegetable garden measures 16 feet long and 12 feet wide. At $5.50 per foot, how much does it cost to put a fence around the garden?

a) $ 1056   b) $ 475   c) $ 308   d) $ 281

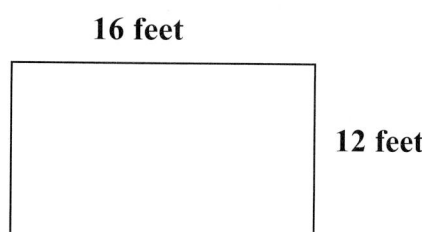

16 feet

12 feet

20. The graph below shows annual car sales from 1996 to 2000. How many more cars were sold in 1998 than in 2000?

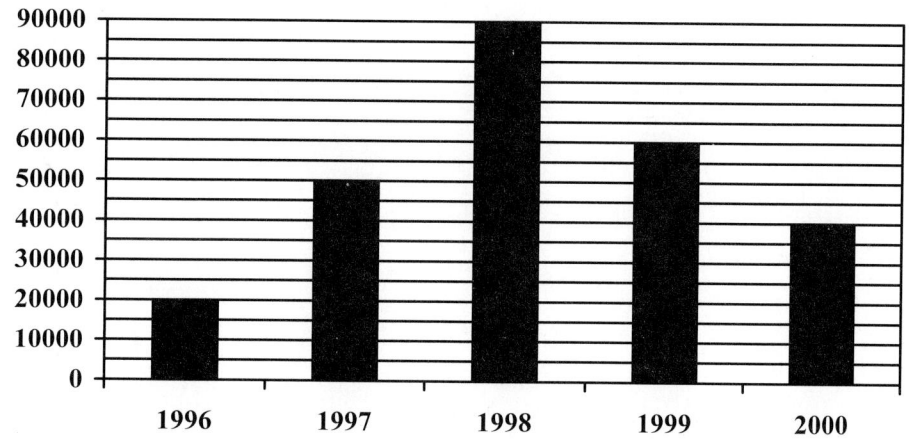

a) 30,000   b) 40,000   c) 50,000   d) 70,000

Answers

ARITHMETIC EXAMINATION # 3

1.	C	11.	D
2.	B	12.	B
3.	B	13.	C
4.	C	14.	A
5.	A	15.	C
6.	D	16.	D
7.	A	17.	B
8.	A	18.	A
9.	C	19.	C
10.	B	20.	C

ARITHMETIC EXAM # 4

Directions: Answer each of the following questions by choosing the appropriate letter. Reduce all fractional answers to lowest terms. **Show written work in the space provided**. You have 45 minutes.

1. In the following number 98,567,421, which digit is in the HUNDRED THOUSAND place?

    a) 7   b) 4   c) 6   d) 5

2. Find the difference: $2,089.7 - 195.68 =$

    a) 1984.20   b) 1894.02   c) 1784.22   d) 1687.2

3. Susan typed 55wpm on Monday, 58 wpm on Tuesday, 60 wpm on Wednesday, 62 wpm on Thursday, and 65 wpm on Friday. Find the average wpm that she typed each day?

    a) 60   b) 70   c) 65   d) 59

4. What is 5 ft., 2 inches *minus* 3 ft., 8 inches?

    a) 1 ft., 4 inches b) 1 ft., 6 inches   c) 1 ft., 4 inches   d) 2 ft., 7 inches

Reminder: Change improper fractions to mixed numbers and reduce all fractional units to lowest terms.

5.   Find the sum: $6\,^4/_5 + 3\,^5/_6$.

   a) $10\,^{15}/_{30}$ b) $10\,\frac{1}{2}$ c) $9\,^{45}/_{30}$ d) $10\,^{19}/_{30}$

6.   Subtract $2\,^7/_8$ from $11\,^3/_4$.

   a) $5\,^1/_8$ b) $8\,^7/_8$ c) $7\,^1/_8$ d) $9\,^7/_8$

7.   Find the quotient: $3\,^3/_5$ divided by 4.

   a) $9/10$ b) 15 c) $1\,^5/_{16}$ d) $7\,^1/_5$

8.   Which of the following fractional units has the largest value?

   a) $3/4$ b) $1/9$ c) $2/7$ d) $6/5$

9.   What is 190,872 divided by 36?

   a) 5032   b) 5,302   c) 3,052   d) 5,230

10. Take away 105.72 from 139.8.

   a) 34.18   b) 24.90   c) 34.08   d) 33.08

11. Multiply 8.47 x .05 (Round your answer to the nearest thousandth.)

   a) 0.4235   b) 4.252   c) 4.223   d) 0.424

12. Divide: $59.64 \div 0.4$

   a) 149.1   b) 14.91   c) 158.1   d) 1.491

13. Which of the following has the smallest value?

   a) 0.90142   b) 0.92002   c) 0.91024   d) 0.90124

14. An insurance broker earned $535.25 commission last month. This month he earned only $245.58. He deposited all the money in his checking account. Then he wrote a check for $405.65. How much is left in his account?

   a) $365.28   b) $475.18   c) $375.18   d) $374.38

15.   Express 0.05 to fraction.

    a) 5/100   b) 1/20   c) 1/10   d) 5/10

16.   What is 70% of 450?

    a) .315   b) 31.5   c) 315   d) 3.15

17.   25% of what number is 500?

    a) 2000   b) 200   c) 2500   d) 1500

18.   A statistics student answers 46 questions correctly and 4 questions incorrectly in the mid-term exam. What **percent** of the **total number** of questions did he **answer correctly?**

    a) 85%   b) 92%   c) 88%   d) 95%

19.　An office space that measures 17 feet long and 15 wide needs to be carpeted at $12.50 per square foot. Calculate the carpeting cost.

a) $ 800　　　　b) $1822　　　　c) $3188　　　　d) $3187.50

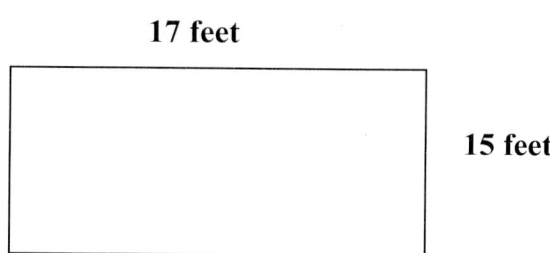

17 feet

15 feet

20.　The graph below shows annual car sales from 1996 to 2000. How many more cars were sold in 1999 than in 2000?

a) 30,000　　　　b) 40,000　　　　c) 20,000　　　　d)　　70,000

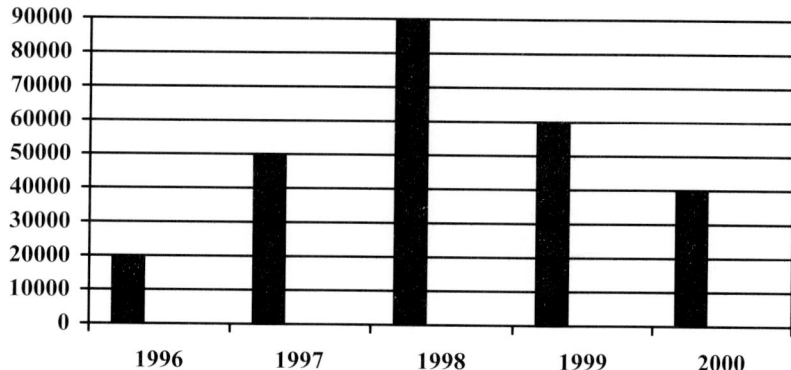

Answers

ARITHMETIC EXAMINATION #4

1. D
2. B
3. A
4. B
5. D
6. B
7. A
8. D
9. B
10. C

11. D
12. A
13. D
14. C
15. B
16. C
17. A
18. B
19. D
20. C

ARITHMETIC EXAM #5

Directions: Answer each of the following questions by circling the appropriate letter. Reduce all fractional answers to lowest terms. **Show all written work in the space provided.** You have 45 minutes.

1. The number nine billion, two hundred fifty million, two hundred fifty-six thousand, one hundred forty-eight and twelve thousandths may be written in standard form as:

    a) 90,025,206,184.12

    b) 9,205,256,148.0012

    b) 9,250,256,148.012

    c) 79,250,256,108.0120

2. Find the sum: $5.20 + 2.87 + 0.109 + 234.6 =$

    a) 224.779   b) 242.779   c) 242.797   d) 232.779

3. Find the average of the following daily sales:
    $190.75, $270.45, $340.45, $400.25, and $450.00.

    a) 338.80   b) 330.38   c) 230.86   d) 330.83

4. What is the sum of 8 pounds, 15 ounces and 10 pounds, 11 ounces?

    a) 18 lbs.   26 oz.

    b) 19 lbs.   10 oz.

    c) 19 lbs.   8 oz.

    d) 13 lbs   24 oz.

Reminder: Change improper fractions to mixed numbers and reduce all fractional units to lowest terms.

5.　Add: $17\dfrac{11}{12}$ and $9\dfrac{3}{4}$

　　a) $27\,^2/_3$ 　　　　b) $26\,^2/_3$ 　　　　c) $27\,^8/_{12}$ 　　　　d) $26\,^{20}/_{12}$

6.　Subtract: $16\,^3/_{10} - 4\,^2/_5 =$

　　a) $12\,^8/_{10}$ 　　　　b) $12\,^7/_{20}$ 　　　　c) $5\quad 12\,^1/_{10}$ 　　　　d) $11\,^9/_{10}$

7.　If you divide $2\dfrac{5}{6}$ by $\dfrac{1}{4}$ what is the quotient?

　　a) $11\dfrac{1}{6}$ 　　　　b) $\dfrac{68}{6}$ 　　　　c) $11\dfrac{1}{3}$ 　　　　d) $10\dfrac{1}{5}$

8.　Which of the following fractional unit has the largest value?

　　a) $\dfrac{9}{10}$ 　　　　b) $\dfrac{1}{9}$ 　　　　c) $\dfrac{2}{5}$ 　　　　d) $\dfrac{4}{5}$

330

9.   What is 141,288 divided by 28?

    a) 5406   b) 5360   c) 5046   d) 5604

10.   Find the difference: 240 – 9.87.

    a) 218.12   b) 230.13   c) 282.13   d) 229.87

11.   Multiply 8.75 x 0.6 (Round your answer to the nearest tenth.)

    a) .52   b) .53   c) 5.2   d) 5.3

12.   Divide: $.04\overline{)514}$

    a) 12,850   b) 1,285   c) 12.75   d) 2.185

13. Which of the following is largest number?

   a) 2.3042   b) 2.3202   c) 2.3024   d) 2.3124

14. A teacher bought 48 boxes of pencils with 25 pencils in each box. If these pencils were divided evenly among 50 students, how many pencils would each student receive?

   a) 24   b) 120   c) 16   d) 60

15. Convert $\frac{3}{8}$ to decimals.

   a) 3.75   b) 375   c) .375   d) 37.5

16) What is 4.5% of 350?

   a) 15.75   b) 152.5   c) 1,575   d) 1.575

17) 12% of what number is 480?

    a) 400   b) 4,000   c). 40,000   d). 40

18) A Biology student took a final exam and answered 23 questions correctly and 27 questions incorrectly. Approximately what percent of the total number of questions did he answer correctly?

    a) 90%   b) 54%   c) 46%   d) 85%

19) Find the carpeting cost of an office space that measures 18 ft. long and 14 ft. wide at $18.50 per square foot.

    a) $4562   b) $4662   c) $1308   d) 4062

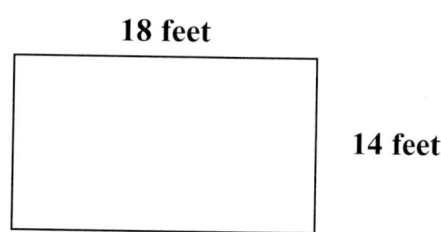

18 feet

14 feet

20) Multiply $3\frac{1}{4}$ by 8.

    a) $\frac{13}{32}$ b) $3\frac{1}{2}$ c) 26   d) $3\frac{1}{32}$

Answers

ARITHMETIC TEST #5

1. B
2. B
3. B
4. B
5. A
6. D
7. C
8. A
9. C
10. B
11. D
12. B
13. B
14. A
15. C
16. A
17. B
18. C
19. B
20. C

ARITHMETIC EXAM # 6

Directions: Answer each of the following questions by circling the appropriate letter. Reduce all the fractional answers to lowest terms. **Show all written work in the space provided for each question.** You have 45 minutes.

1.   In the number 96,065,874, 0 is in the:

   a) hundred millions place   b) millions place

   c) ten thousands place   d) hundred thousands place

2.   Find the sum: $207 + 25.982 + 450.5 =$

   a) 603.472   b) 683.482   c) 578.582   d) 727.482

3.   Sam scored 88 in a Psychology test on Monday, 85 on Tuesday, 89 on Wednesday, and 90 on Thursday. What is the average score that Sam obtained each day?

   a) 84   b) 85   c) 88   d) 86

4.   A movie starts 7:48 pm and ends at 10:27 pm. How long is the movie?

   a) 2 hrs and 39 min.   b) 3 hrs. and 29 min.

   c) 2 hrs. and 49 min.   d) 3 hrs and 19 min.

Reminder: Change improper fractions to mixed numbers and reduce all fractional units to lowest terms.

5. Add: $5/18 + 4\,2/3 =$

   a) $4\,17/18$ b) $4\,7/18$ c) $4\,2/6$ d) $3\,5/18$

6. Subtract $2\,3/9$ from 11.

   a) $8\,6/9$ b) $9\,3/9$ c) $9\,2/3$ d) $8\,2/3$

7. Find the quotient: $2\,3/4$ divided by $2/10$.

   a) $5\,4/5$ b) $55/4$ c) $13\,3/4$ d) $12\,3/4$

8. Which of the following fractional unit is the smallest?

   a) $\dfrac{1}{9}$ b) $\dfrac{2}{4}$ c) $\dfrac{5}{7}$ d) $\dfrac{4}{5}$

9.   What is 237,315 divided by 39?

    a) 8063   b) 6805   c) 6085   d) 8650

10. How much will Bob spend to install some decorative lights in his rectangular roof that measures 50 ft. long and 35 ft. wide, at $8.00 per foot.

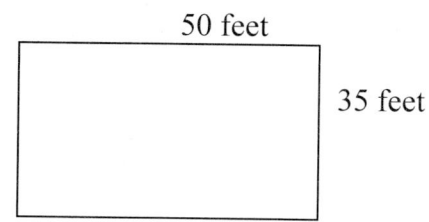

50 feet

35 feet

    a) $1,360   b) $14,000   c) $1,342   d) $1,765

11. When you subtract 54.07 from 60, what's the difference?

    a) 5.93   b) 6.03   c) 59.3   d) 6.07

12. Multiply 8.465 x 0.4 (Round your answer to the nearest *tenths*).

    a) 3.4   b) 33.86
    c) 3.39   d) 3.386

13. Divide: $0.06\overline{)8.52}$

    a) 0.142   b) 1.42   c) 122   d) 142

14. Which is the largest number?

    a) 0.03542   b) 0.30024   c) 0.06402   d) 0.03202

15. An adjunct professor earns $600 weekly at CUNY. He also teaches at SUNY where he earns $150 *less* for the same period of time. What is his gross income for the month?

    a) $4,500   b) 2,600   c) $50,000   d) $4,200

16. If the professor in question 15 is single and pays 32% tax, what is his monthly take-home pay?

    a) $3500   b) $2,656   c) $3,200   d) $2,856

17. Convert $\frac{2}{3}$ to a decimal, and round your answer to the nearest hundredths.

    a) 0.67   b) 60   c) 0.66   d) .06

18. 5% of what number is 95?

    a) 190   b) 2,000   c) 1,900   d) 4.75

19. What are the factors of 96?

    a) (1, 2, 3, 4, 5, 7, 12, 16, 24, 32, 48, 96)

    b) (1, 2, 3, 4, 6, 8, 12, 16, 24, 32, 48, 96)

    c) (1, 2, 3, 4, 5, 12, 13, 14, 24, 32, 48, 96)

    d) (1, 2, 3, 4, 9, 10, 11, 13, 14, 16, 18)

20. A freshman student took an MA098 final exam and answered 3 questions correctly and 22 questions incorrectly. Approximately what percent of the total number of questions did he answer incorrectly?

    a) 40%   b) 15%   c) 12%
    d) 88%

Answers

ARITHMETIC TEST #6

1.	D	11.	A
2.	B	12.	A
3.	C	13.	D
4.	A	14.	B
5.	A	15.	D
6.	D	16.	D
7.	C	17.	A
8.	A	18.	C
9.	C	19.	B
10.	A	20.	D

ARITHMETIC EXAM #7

Directions: Answer each of the following questions by choosing the appropriate letter. **Show all written work in the space provided for each question.** You have 45 minutes.

1. In the following number 5,738,167,420, which digit is in the hundred million place?

   a) 3   b) 6   c) 7   d) 5

2. Find the sum: $30.797 + 167.35 + 0.003 =$

   a) 198.15   b) 188.13   c) 131.15   d) 198.05

3. Bob drove 451 miles on Monday, 369.5 miles on Tuesday, and 160.5 miles on Wednesday. What was the average distance that Bob drove each day?

   a) 337   b) 327   c) 345.5   d) 317.5

4. Subtract 21 ounces from 6 lbs. and 14 ounces.

   a) 5 lbs. & 5 oz.   b) 5 lbs. & 9 oz.
   c) 5 lbs. & 7 oz.   d) 6 lbs & 9 oz.

Reminder: Change improper fractions to mixed numbers and reduce all fractional units to lowest terms.

5. Find the sum: $12 \frac{4}{5}$ and $10 \frac{1}{2}$.

   a) $22 \frac{15}{30}$ b) $23 \frac{3}{10}$ c) $23 \frac{5}{10}$ d) $22 \frac{39}{30}$

6. What is $12 \frac{7}{8}$ minus $11 \frac{3}{4}$?

   a) $1 \frac{1}{8}$ b) $1 \frac{2}{8}$ c) $\frac{3}{8}$ d) $\frac{7}{8}$

7. Find the quotient: $1 \frac{3}{5}$ divided by $1 \frac{2}{3}$.

   a) $\frac{23}{25}$ b) $\frac{24}{20}$ c) $2 \frac{2}{3}$ d) $\frac{24}{25}$

8. Which of the following fractional units has the smallest value?

   a) $\frac{1}{8}$ b) $\frac{4}{5}$ c) $\frac{2}{7}$ d) $\frac{2}{13}$

9.   What is 162,864 divided by 27?

        a) 6,032   b) 6,302   c) 6,052   d) 5,030

10.   Take away 305.72 from 538.7.

        a) 232.78   b) 224.88   c) 232.98   d) 233.08

11.   Multiply 5.604 x .35 (Round your answer to the nearest hundredth).

        a) 1.97140   b) 1.86
        c) 1.97   d) 1.96

12.   An electronics industry made an annual profit of $250,415.75. If this amount has
        to be shared by five shareholders, how much will each shareholder receive?

        a) $50,083.15   b) $58,083.15   c) $50,003.17   d) 53,038.25

13.   Which of the following has the largest value?

        a) 3.0204   b) 3.0014   c) 2.9999   d) 3.0024

14. A bank teller has $875.00 in her checking account. Last month she made a deposit of $305.75, and then wrote two checks amounting to $118.95 and $98.17, respectively, to pay the car insurance and cell phone bills. What is the new balance?

a) $903.36 b) $693.36 c) $963.63 d) $936.63

15. Convert $\frac{1}{9}$ to decimals rounded to the nearest hundredth.

a) 0.011 b) 0.22 c) 0.11
d) 0.222

16. A pair of sneakers originally sold for $59 was reduced by 25%. What is the discount?

a) $14.05 b) $1.47 c) $44.25 d) 14.75

17. If 27% of a number is 54, what is the number?

a) 200 b) 2 c) 2000 d) 20

18. An accounting student answered 16 questions correctly and 4 questions incorrectly in the mid-term exam. Approximately what percent of the total number of questions did he answer correctly?

a) 45% b) 20% c) 85%
d) 80%

19. How much will the chief security spend to change the tiles of his office that measures 18 feet long and 12 feet wide, at $6.50 per square foot.

a) $4104 b) $1044 c) $1404 d) $390

18 feet

112 feet

20.   The graph below shows the number of freshmen in a certain school during each year from 1998 to 2003. The change from 2002 to 2003 was closest to:

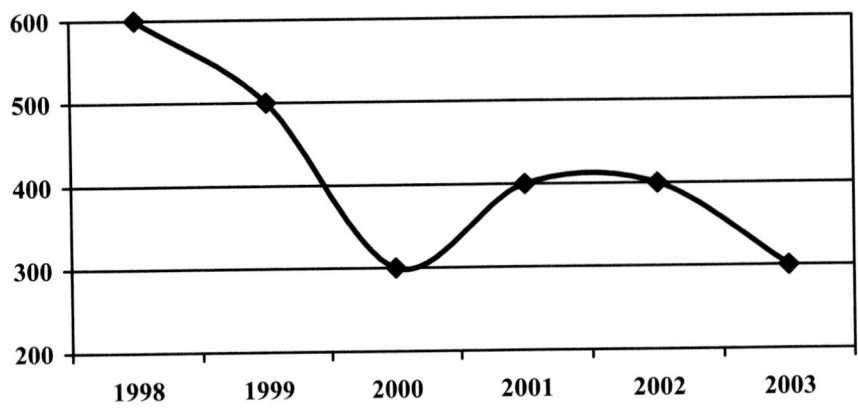

a) A decrease of 50

b) A decrease 100

c) An increase of 100

d) An increase of 50

Answers

ARITHMETICTEST #7

1.	C	11.	D
2.	A	12.	A
3.	B	13.	A
4.	B	14.	C
5.	B	15.	C
6.	A	16.	D
7.	D	17.	A
8.	A	18.	D
9.	A	19.	C
10.	C	20.	B

ARITHMETIC EXAM # 8

Directions: Answer each of the following questions by choosing the appropriate letter. Reduce all fractional answers to lowest terms. **Show all written work in the space provided for each question.** You have 45 minutes.

1. In the following number, 1,398,567,420, which digit is in the *Hundred–Million* place?

   a) 7   b) 3   c) 6   d) 4

2. Subtract 195.76 from 4,069.

   a) 3894.24   b) 3984.26   c) 3873.24   d) 2873.24

3. A cosmetics company earned $35, 100 in two years operation. What is the company's average monthly profit?

   a) $1462.50   b) $ 1426.50   c) $1362.50   d) $ 1642.50

4. What is 9 lbs. 12 ounces *minus* 4 lbs. 15 ounces?

   a) 5 lbs. 13 oz.   b) 4lbs.   c) 13 lbs. 27 oz.   d) 4 lbs. 13 oz.

Reminder: Change improper fractions to mixed numbers and reduce all fractional units lowest terms.

5.   Find the sum: $3\dfrac{4}{5} + 6\dfrac{5}{7}$

a) $10\dfrac{18}{35}$ b) $10\dfrac{1}{4}$ c) $9\dfrac{45}{30}$ d) $10\dfrac{19}{35}$

6.   Find the difference $11\dfrac{3}{4} - 2\dfrac{7}{8}$

a) $5\dfrac{1}{8}$ b) $9\dfrac{7}{8}$ c) $7\dfrac{1}{8}$ d) $8\dfrac{7}{8}$

7.   If you divide $4\dfrac{3}{4}$ by 4, what is the quotient?

a) $2\,{}^{9}/_{10}$ b) 3 c) $1\,{}^{3}/_{20}$ d) $2\,{}^{5}/_{20}$

8.   Of the following fractional units, which one has the smallest value?

a) $\dfrac{3}{4}$ b) $\dfrac{4}{5}$ c) $\dfrac{2}{7}$ d) $\dfrac{6}{9}$

9. What is 120,345 divided by 15?

   a) 8,302   b) 8,023   c) 8,003   d) 8,230

10. Take away 85.72 from 170.8.

    a) 75.08   b) 94.18   c) 84.18   d) 85.08

11. Multiply 7.48 x 0.09 (Round your answer to the nearest tenths).

    a) 0.7   b) 0.6732   c) 0.7623   d) 0.6

12. 20 % of what number is 500?

    a) 200   b) 2,000   c) 2,500   d) 1,500

13. Divide: 2.415 by 0.7.

    a) 24.5   b) 34.06   c) 34.5   d) 35.4

14. Which of the following has the largest value?
    a) 0.81204   b) 0.81024   c) 0.80004   d) 0.80142

15. A telephone company has a promotional offer of $1.45 for the first five minutes long distance call, and then charges $0.32 per minute for extra minutes used. If you call your friend for 20 minutes, how much will you pay?

    a) $5.95   b) $6.15   c) $5.75   d) $6.25

16. Convert .025 to a fraction in lowest terms.
    a) ¼   b) $^1/_{40}$ c) 2 ½   d) 2 $^1/_{20}$

17. Convert $\frac{2}{9}$ to a decimal.

    a) 0.022   b) 0.12   c) 0.012   d) 0.22

18. What is 12% of 450?

    a) 45   b) 50   c) 54   d) 540

19.   20% of what number is 300?

   a) 120   b) 1,200   c) 2,500   d) 1,500

20.   The graph below shows sales for four months for a certain company. About how
       many more sales were there in September than October.

   a) $ 10,000   b) $20,000   c) $20,000   d) $50,000

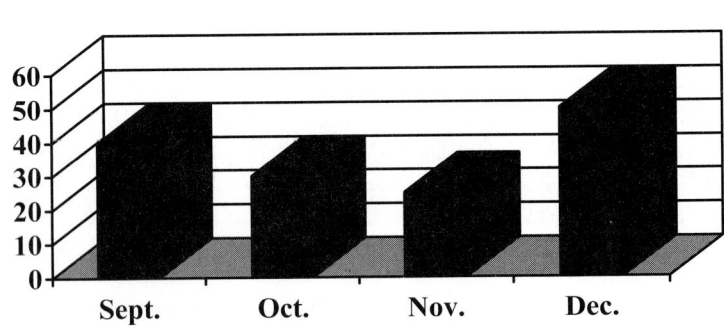

Answers

ARITHMETIC TEST # 8

1.	B	11.	A
2.	C	12.	C
3.	B	13.	C
4.	D	14.	A
5.	A	15.	D
6.	D	16.	B
7.	C	17.	D
8.	C	18.	C
9.	B	19.	D
10.	D	20.	A

90. Algebra Exams

Directions: Answer each of the following questions by circling the appropriate letter.
   Show all written work in the space provided for each question.
   You have 60 minutes.

1.   Add: $(2x^2 + 4x + 12) + (3x^2 + x - 8)$.

   a) $-5x^2 + 5x - 4$ b) $5x^2 + 5x + 4$

   c) $5x^2 - 7x + 20$ d) $6x^2 + 4x - 20$

2.   Subtract: $(2y^2 - 10xy + 7) - (y^2 + 3xy - 4)$.

   a) $-y^2 + 13xy + 3$ b) $-y^2 + 3xy + 3$

   c) $-y^2 - 7xy + 11$ d) $y^2 - 13xy + 11$

3.   The product of $(-3a^3b)\,(2a^2b^4)$.

   a) $6a^5b^4$ b) $-5ab$ c) $-6a^5b^5$ d) $-5a^2b^3$

4. Evaluate $(-2ab + 4b)$, when $a = 2$, $b = 3$.

   a) -12 b) 0 c) -5 d) 24

5. Simplify: $(-3ab^3)^3$.

   a) $-27a^3b^9$ b) $-27a^4b^6$ c) $9a^4b^9$ d) $-9a^4b^9$

6. Find the value of: $6 - 3 + 2\,(2\text{-}\,0)^2$.

   a) 13 b) 11 c) 15 d) 12

7. Factor completely: $10x^4 - 12x^2$.

   a) $2x^2(-5x^2 - 6)$ b) $2x^2(5x^2 - 6)$ c) $2x^2(5x^2 + 6)$

   d) $-2x^2(-5x^2 + 6)$

8. Solve for x: $20 - 4 = 8x$.

a) –2   b) 3   c) 2   d) –3

9. If $x = -2$, and $y = 3$, what is the value of $x^3 - 2y$?.

a) –2   b) –14   c) 14   d) 48

10. Solve for x: $8x + 1 = 49 + 2x$.

a) –5   b) 5   c) 8   d) –8

11. If $2x + 3y = 22$, and $3x - 3y = 3$, solve for x and y.

a) x = 4, y = 5   b) x = 5, y = 4   c) x = 5, y = –3

d) x = 3, y = 6

12. Each box of pencils contains 24 pieces. If you have B boxes and an additional P pieces which are not in boxes, how many pencils do you have?

   a) $24 + B + P$

   b) $24(B + P)$

   c) $24\ BP$

   d) $24B + P$

13. Simply: $\dfrac{5x^2 + 10x}{5x}$

   a) $x^2 + 2x$

   b) $x + 2x$

   c) $x - 2x$

   d) $x + 2$

14. The sum of two numbers is 32. One of the numbers is 5 more than twice the other. What is the smallest number?

   a) 9

   b) 18

   c) 23

   d) 6

15. Simplify: $4ab - 5b(2a - 6b)$.

   a) $-6ab + 30b^2$

   b) $6ab - 30b$

   c) $6ab^2 + 11b^2$

   d) $-6ab - 30ab^2$

16. The perimeter of a square is 80 feet. Find its area.

   a) 400 feet   b) 400 square feet   c) 220 square feet   d) 200 feet

17. Which pair of coordinates solves the equation: $y = 5x - 4$?

   a) (3, 11)   b) (2, 10)   c) (2, 11)   d) (3, 9)

18. What are the coordinates of point p?

   a) (–2, 3)

   b) (–1, 4)

   b) (1, 5)

   d) (1, -4)

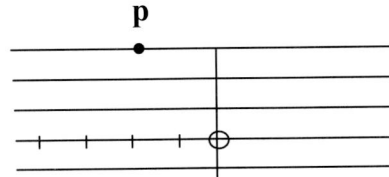

19. Simplify: $2xy(-4x^2y^2 + 3xy)$

   a) $-8x^3y^3 + 6xy$ b) $-8x^3y^3 + 6x^2y^2$ c) $8x^3y^3 + 5x^2y^3$ d) $6x^3y^3 + 8xy$

20. Roberto is three years older than his brother. The sum of their ages is 49. How old is Roberto?

   a) 23   b) 33   c) 16   d) 26

Answers

ALGEBRA EXAM # 1

1.	B	11.	B
2.	D	12.	D
3.	C	13.	D
4.	B	14.	A
5.	A	15.	A
6.	B	16.	B
7.	B	17.	A
8.	C	18.	A
9.	B	19.	B
10.	C	20.	D

ALGEBRA EXAM # 2

Directions: Answer each of the following questions by circling the appropriate letter. **Show all written work in the space provided for each question.** You have 60 minutes.

1. Find the sum: $(-10x^2 + 4x) + (5x^2 - 3x - 8)$.

    a) $-5x^2 + 7x + 4$ b) $-5x^2 + x - 8$ c) $5x^2 - 7x - 8$ d) $5x^2 + x + 8$

2. Find the difference: $(-y2 - 10xy + 7) - (-y2 + 3xy - 4)$.

    a) $- 13xy + 11$ b) $-2y2 + 13xy+3$ c) $- y2-7xy + 11$ d) $-y^2 -13xy - 3$

3. The product of $(-6a^3b)(-7a^2b^4)$.

    a) $-13a^5b^5$ b) $-42ab$ c) $42a^5b^5$ d) $13a^2b^3$

4. Find the value of $(-4a^2b + 4bc)$, when $a = 2, b = 3, c = -3$.

    a) $- 17$ b) $- 64$ c) $- 84$ d) 84

5.   Simplify: $(-7a^2b^3)^3$.

    a) $-343a^6b^9$ b) $21a^5b^6$ c) $-49a^6b^9$ d) $343a^5b^9$

6.   Find the value of: $8 - 3 + 2\,(2 - 6)^2 - 5$.

    a) 32   b) 107   c) 43   d) 51

7.   Factor completely: $56x^4y^2 - 64x^2y^3z$.

    a) $-8x^2\,y^2(7x^2 - 8yz)$ b) $7x^2y^2(x^2 - 2y)$

    c) $8x^2y^2\,(7x^2 - 8yz)$ d) $-8x^2y^2(-6x^2 - 8)$

8.   Solve for x: $-24 - 6x = 2x + 8$

    a) 4   b) 3   c) -4 d) 5

9. If $x = 2$, and $y = 3$, what is the value of $x^3 - 4xy - 7$?

a) -9 b) -23 c) 19 d) 48

10. Find the product: $(-3xy + 4)(-2xy - 5)$.

a) $-12x^2y^2 - 23xy + 10$ b) $-12x^2 + 7x - 10$

c) $-6x^2y^2 + 23xy - 20$ d) $6x^2y^2 + 7xy - 20$

11. Solve algebraically for a and b: $4a + 3b = 15$, and $3a - 3b = 6$.

a) $a = 3, \quad b = 1$ b) $a = 4, \quad b = 2$

c) $a = 0, \quad b = 3$ d) $d = -2, b = -3$

12. Interpret the following expressions algebraically and solve:
Seven times a number increased by eighteen equals two times the number decreased by two.

a) $x = 10$ b) $x = -3$ c) $x = -4$ d) $x = -2$

13. Find the quotient: $\dfrac{55x^4y^5 - 40x^3y^4 + 35x^2y}{5x^2y}$

    a) $-11x^2y^4 + 8xy^3 - 7$ b) $11x^2 y^4 - 8xy^3 + 7$

    c) $-10x^2y^4 + 8xy^3 - 7$ d) $11x^6y^6 - 8xy^3 + 7$

14. The sum of two numbers is 70. The larger number is five less than twice the smaller number. What is the larger number?

    a) 45   b) 35   c) 25   d) 30

15. Simplify: $-4a^2b - 5b(2a^2 - 6a)$.

    a) $14a^2b - 30ab$ b) $-14a^2b - 30ab$

    c) $-6ab^2 + 30ab$ d) $-14a^2b + 30ab$

16. The perimeter of a square is 100 feet. Find its area.

    a) 625 sq.ft.   b) 400 sq.ft.   c) 625 feet   d) 225 feet

17. Which pair of coordinates fit the equation: $y = -8x - 4$?

a) $(3, 9)$ b) $(2, -10)$ c) $(-2, 11)$ d) $(3, -28)$

18. What are the coordinates of point A?

a) $(-3, -3)$ b) $(1, -1)$ c) $(1, 3)$ d) $(-2, 2)$

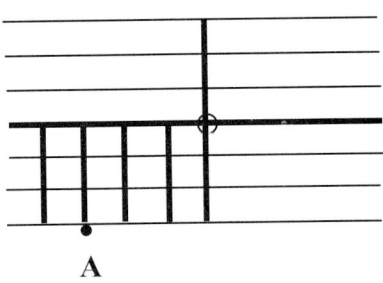

A

19. Simplify: $2xy(-4x^2y^2 - 3xy)$

a) $-8x^3y^3 + 6xy$ b) $8x^3y^3 - 6x^2y^2$ c) $-8x^3y^3 - 6x^2y^2$ d) $6x^3y^3 + 8xy$

20. Mel is six times as old as his brother. The sum of their ages is 42. How old is his brother?

a) 36   b) 6   c) 8   d) 5

Answers

ALGEBRA EXAM #2

1. B
2. A
3. C
4. C
5. A
6. A
7. C
8. C
9. B
10. D

11. A
12. C
13. B
14. A
15. D
16. A
17. D
18. A
19. C
20. B

ALGEBRA EXAM # 3

Directions: Answer each of the following questions by circling the appropriate letter. **Show all written work in the space provided for each question.** You have 60 minutes.

1.　　Subtract: $(-5x^2 - 6x + 12) - (4x^2 - 2x - 8)$.

　　a) $9x^2 - 2x + 20$　　　b) $-x^2 - 8x - 20$　　　c) $x^2 - 2x + 20$　　　d) $-9x^2 - 4x + 20$

2.　　Find the value of: $7 - 5(-3)^3$.

　　a) 52　　　　　b) -38　　　　　c) 18　　　　　d) -28

3.　　Simplify: $(-2a^2b^2)(-3ab^4)^2$.

　　a) $-18a^4b^{10}$　　　b) $-126a^4b^8$　　　c) $27a^4b^{10}$　　　d) $-6a^4b^{10}$

4.　　Sum $8a^2 + 4a - 2$ and $-14a + 3a^2 + 22$.

　　a) $5a^2 - 10a + 22$　　　　　b) $-11a^2 + 18a - 20$

　　c) $11a^2 - 10a + 20$　　　　　d) $-5a^2 - 18a + 10$

5.   Evaluate: If $x = 5$ and $y = -2$, then $2xy + 3x - y^2 =$

a) -6 b) -9 c) 31 d) -5

6.   Solve for x: $-4x + 7 = x - 18$.

a) -10 b) 8 c) -5 d) 5

7.   Factor completely: $54y^2 - 18y$.

a) $9y(6y - 2)$ b) $-6y(9y - 3y)$ c) $18y(3y-1)$ d) $9y(6y + 2)$

8.   Simplify: $-5x^2(x^2 - 2x + 4y)$.

a) $5x^4 + 10x^2 + 10x^2y$ b) $5x^2 - 10x^3 - 20x^2y$

c) $5x^4 + 10x^3 - 20x^2y$ d) $-5x^4 + 10x^3 - 20x^2y$

9. Each box of candy contains 36 pieces. If you have B boxes and an additional P pieces, which are not in boxes, how many pieces of candy do you have?

    a) $36(B+P)$ b) $36 + B + P$ c) $36B + P$ d) $36BP$

10. Simplify: $4pt - 5t(p - 7t)$

    a) $35t^2 - pt$ b) $-pt + 35t^2$ c) $-9pt^2 + 5pr$ d) $-35t^2 - 1$

11. One number is five more than twice another number. The sum of the numbers is 38. Find the product of the numbers.

    a) 297   b) 128   c) 256   d) 380

12. Which of the following points lie on the graph of the equation: $y = -2x + 9$?

    a) $(-2, 9)$ b) $(-1, -5)$ c) $(5, -1)$ d) $(-2, 5)$

13.   Simplify: $\dfrac{15a^6 + 18a^{12}}{3a^2}$

   a) $5a^6 + 18a^{12}$ b) $5a^4 + 6a^{10}$ c) $5a^4 + 6a^6$ d) $5a^3 + 6a^6$

14.   If you have n nickels, d dimes and q quarters, then the value of your coins (in cents) is:

   a) 40 ndq   b) (5n) (10d) (25q)

   c) 5n + 10d + 25q   d) (5 + n) (10 + d) (25 + q)

15.   What are the coordinates of point P?

   a) $(-1, 4)$ b) $(1, -4)$ c) $(-2, 3)$ d) $(0, 5)$

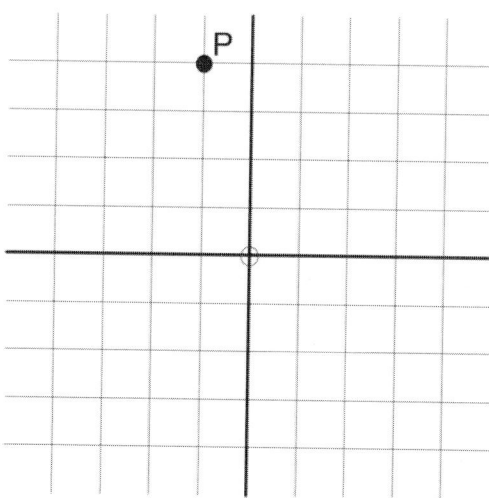

16. What is the value of: $-2ab - b^2$, when $a = 3$ and $b = -2$?

   a) -12 b) -8 c) 16 d) 8

17. If $2x + y = 6$, and $5x - y = 22$, then:

   a) $x = 4$, $y = -2$ b) $x = 4$, $y = -7$

   c) $x = 7$, $y = 4$ d) $x = 4$, $y = 2$

18. Find the perimeter of a square whose area is 225 sq. ft.

   a) 72 ft.   b) 60 sq. ft.   c) 60 feet   d) 120 feet

19. Randy weighs 90 lbs. less than his brother Carlo. Together they weigh 320 lbs. How much does Randy weigh?

   a) 110   b) 205   c) 210   d) 115

20. A father intends to leave all his money to his two sons. He has $60,000. The older son receives $6,000 more than twice as much as the younger son. Find the share the oldest son receives.

   a) $52,000   b) $42,000   c) $18,000   d) $23,000

Answers

ALGEBRA EXAM #3

1. D
2. B
3. A
4. C
5. B
6. D
7. C
8. D
9. C
10. B

11. A
12. C
13. B
14. C
15. A
16. D
17. A
18. C
19. D
20. B

ALGEBRA EXAM #4

Directions: Answer each of the following questions. Circle the appropriate letter.
 Show all written work in the space provided for each question.
 You have 60 minutes.

1. Sum: $(-8x^2 + 4x + 12) + (3x^2 + x - 8)$.

    a) $-5x^2 + 5x + 4$

    b) $-5x^2 + 5x - 4$

    c) $5x^2 - 7x + 20$

    d) $6x^2 + 4x - 20$

2. Difference: $(-2y^2 - 10xy + 7) - (-y^2 + 3xy - 4)$.

    a) $-y^2 - 13xy + 11$

    b) $-y^2 + 3xy + 3$

    c) $-y^2 - 7xy + 11$

    d) $-y^2 - 13xy \mid 4$

3. The product of $(-3a^3b)(12a^2b^3)$.

    a) $-36a^5b^5$

    b) $-25ab$

    c) $-36a^5b^4$

    d) $-35a^2b^3$

4. Solve: $(-2a^2b^2 + -4b^3)$, when $a = 2$, $b = -3$.

    a) -212

    b) 122

    c) 36

    d) 204

5.　Simplify: $(-4a^3b^3)^3$.

a) $64a^9b^9$　　　b) $-64a^6b^6$　　　c) $-64a^9b^9$　　　d) $64a^6b^6$

6.　Find the value of: $-6 - 3 + 2(2 - 0)^2 + 4$.

a) 3　　　b) 11　　　c) 13　　　d) -12

7.　Factor completely: $32x^4y^2 - 64x^2y^3$.

a) $32x^2y^2(x^2 - 2)$　　　b) $32x^2y^2(x^2 - 2y)$

c) $8x^2y^2(8x^2 + 8y)$　　　d) $-8x^2y^2(-4x^2 - 8)$

8.　Solve for x: $20 - 3x = 8x - 2$:

a) -2　　　b) 3　　　c) -4　　　d) 2

9. If $x = -2$, and $y = 3$, what is the value of $x^3 - 2xy + 5$?

a) -9 b) -14 c) 9 d) 48

10. Find the product: $(3x + 2)(4x - 5)$.

a) $-12x^2 - 23x + 10$ b) $12x^2 + 7x - 10$

c) $7x^2 + 23x - 10$ d) $12x^2 - 7x - 10$

11. Solve algebraically for a and b: $5a + 3b = 15$, and $2a - 3b = 6$.

a) $a = 3, \ b = 0$ b) $a = 5, \ b = 2$

c) $a = 0, \ b = 3$ d) $a = -2, \ b = -3$

12. Interpret the following expressions algebraically and solve:
Five times a number decreased by eighteen equals three times the number increased by six.

a) $x = 10$ b) $x = 3$ c) $x = 8$ d) $x = 12$

13. Find the quotient: $\dfrac{-55x^4y^5 - 40x^3y^4 + 35x^2y}{5x^2y}$.

    a) $-11x^2y^4 + 8xy^3 - 7$ b) $-11x^2\,y^4 - 8xy^3 + 7$

    c) $-10x^2y^4 + 8xy^3 - 7$ d) $11x^6y^6 - 8xy^3 + 7$

14. The sum of two numbers is 43. The larger number is four more than twice the smaller number. What is the greater number?

    a) 26   b) 30   c) 13   d) 43

15. Simplify: $-4a^2b - 5b(2a^2 - 6a)$.

    a) $14a^2b - 30ab$ b) $-14a^2b - 30ab$

    c) $-6ab^2 + 30ab$ d) $-14a^2b + 30ab$

16.   The perimeter of a square is 80 feet. Find its area.

     a) 400 ft.   b) 400 sq. ft.   c) 220 sq. ft.   d) 200 feet

17.   Which pair of coordinates fit the equation: $y = 7x - 4$?

     a) (3, 9)   b) (2, –10)   c) (–2, 11)   d) (2, 10)

18.   What are the coordinates of point A:

     a) (–2, 3)   b) (1, –4)   c) (1, 5)   d) (–1, –4)

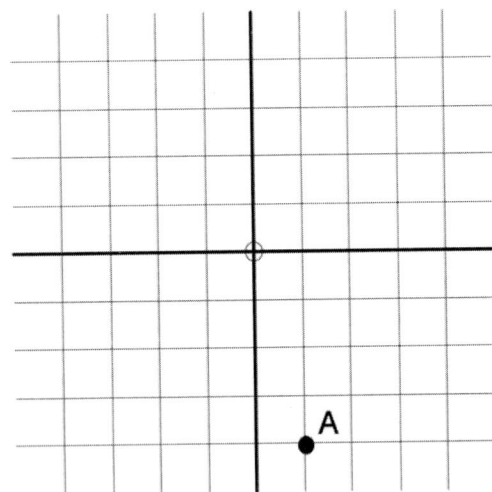

19. Simplify: $2xy(-4x^2y^2 + 3xy)$.

a) $-8x^3y^3 + 6xy$

b) $8x^3y^3 + 5x^2y^2$

c) $-8x^3y^3 + 6x^2y^2$

d) $6x^3y^3 + 8xy$

20. John is six years younger than his brother. The sum of their ages is 36. How old is John? (Algebraic solution only).

a) 15

b) 21

c) 28

d) 27

Answers

ALGEBRA EXAM # 4

1.	A	11.	A
2.	A	12.	D
3.	C	13.	B
4.	C	14.	B
5.	C	15.	D
6.	A	16.	B
7.	B	17.	D
8.	D	18.	B
9.	C	19.	C
10.	D	20.	A

ALGEBRA EXAM # 5

Directions: Circle the appropriate letter in each of the following questions.
Show all written work in the space provided for each question.
You have 60 minutes.

1. If $a = 3$ and $y = 5$, what is the value of $a^2 - 4ay + 10$?

   a) -31 b) -41 c) -44 d) 34

2. Solve the system equation $8a + 2b = 20$ and $4a - 2b = 16$.

   a) $(a = -2, \; b = 4)$ b) $(a = -4, \; b = 3)$

   c) $(a = 3, \; b = -2)$ d) $(a = 5, \; b = -3)$

3. Simplify: $(9x^2 + 4x + 12) + (-3x^2 - 8)$.

   a) $6x^2 + 5x - 4$ b) $-6x^2 + 4x + 4$

   c) $12x^2 - 4x + 20$ d) $6x^2 + 4x + 4$

4. Subtract $(2y^2 - 10xy + 7)$ from $(-10y^2 + 3xy - 4)$.

   a) $-12y^2 + 13xy - 11$ b) $-8y^2 + 7xy + 3$

   c) $12y^2 - 7xy + 11$ d) $8y^2 - 7xy - 3$

379

5. Simplify: $6 + 2(4 - 6)^3 + (-1 - 5)^2 \div 2$.

    a) 9   b) 8   c) −4   d) 15

6. Simplify: $-9m^2n + 7m(-3mn + 6n)$.

    a) $-12m^2n + 42mn$ b) $-30m^2n + 42mn$

    c) $30m^2n^2 + 42mn$ d) $12mn + 42n$

7. Find the product: $-5pt(-8p^4t^5 + 9p^3t^4)$.

    a) $-40pt - 45p^2t^3$ b) $-40p^5t^6 - 45p^4t^5$

    c) $40p^5t^6 - 45p^4t^5$ d) $13p^5t^6 + 14p^4t^5$

8. Factor completely: $14x^2y - 7x$.

    a) $7x(xy - y)$ b) $x(14xy - 7)$

    c) $7x(2xy - 1)$ d) $7xy(2x - 1)$

9.   Solve for x: -20 + 3x = x – 8.
      a) 6   b) –2   c –6   d) 5

10.   Write an equation that expresses the word sentence and solve:
      If ten times a number is increased by four, the result is twelve more than nine
      times the number. Find the number.

      a) 7   b) 5   c) 8   d) –6

11.   Find the product: $(5x + 7)(3x - 2)$.

      a) $15x^2 + 31x + 14$ b) $15x^2 + 11x - 14$

      c) $8x^2 - 11x - 14$ d) $-15x^2 - 11x + 5$

12.   The combined age of Joe and Bill is 74. If Joe is six years less than three times
      the age of Bill, how old is Joe?

      a) 15   b) 30   c) 54   d) 20

13. Two numbers have a sum of 60. If the larger number is four more than six times the smaller number, what's the smaller number?

    a) 8   b) 7   c) 9   d) 12

14. Simplify: $(-3a^3b^4c^5)^4$.

    a) $-81a^{12}b^{16}c^{20}$ b) $81a^{12}b^{16}c^{20}$

    c) $-12a^7b^8c^9$ d) $12a^7b^8c^9$

15. Which of the following points lies on the graph of $y = 4x - 5$.

    a) $(7, 23)$ b) $(3, -4)$ c) $(-1, 3)$ d) $(-2, 6)$

16. If the perimeter of a square is 48, what is its area?

    a) 60 sq. ft.   b) 144 ft.   c) 600 ft.   d) 144 sq. ft.

17. The area of a rectangle is 120 sq. ft. and the length is 12 ft. What is its perimeter?

   a) 65 sq. ft.   b) 120 ft.   c) 44 ft.   d) 40 sq.ft.

18. A commercial building has x 4-room apartments and y 6-room apartments. If there are no other apartments in the building, how many rooms does it have?

   a) $4x + 6y$ b) $4y + 6x$ c) $10xy$ d) $(4x)(6y)$

19. Find the quotient: $\dfrac{18x^4y^6 + 15x^3y^5 - 12x^2y^3}{3x^2y^2}$

   a) $6x^2y^4 + 5xy^3 - 4y$ b) $-6x^2y^3 + 5xy - 4y$

   c) $6x^3y^2 + 5xy - 4xy$ d) $6xy^2 + 5xy^3 - 4y$

20.   What are the coordinates of point Z?
       a) (5, -3)   b) (-4, -2)   c) (3, -4)   d) (1, -4)

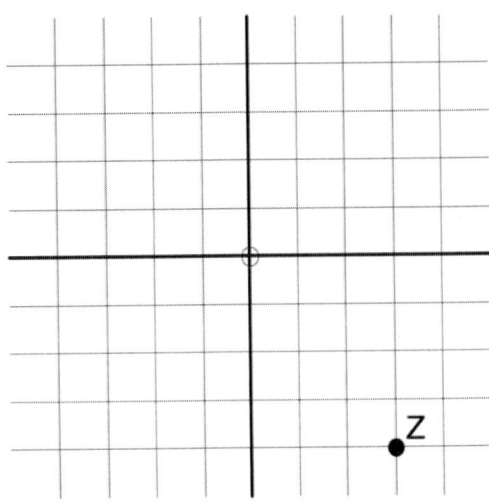

ANSWERS
Test # 5

1.	B	11.	B
2.	C	12.	C
3.	D	13.	A
4.	A	14.	B
5.	B	15.	A
6.	B	16.	D
7.	C	17.	C
8.	C	18.	A
9.	A	19.	A
10.	C	20.	C

ALGEBRA EXAM # 6

Directions: Answer each of the following questions by choosing the appropriate letter. SHOW ALL WRITTEN WORK IN THE SPACE PROVIDED FOR EACH QUESTION. You have 60 minutes.

1. What is $(8x^2 + 6x + 12)$ added to $(-3x^2 + x - 8)$?
    a) $-5x^2 + 7x + 20$ b) $5x^2 + 7x + 4$
    c) $5x^2 - 7x + 20$ d) $11x^2 + 7x - 20$

2. Subtract: $(y^2 - 10xy - 6) - (2y^2 + 3xy)$
    a) $-y^2 - 13xy - 6$ b) $y^2 + 3xy - 6$
    c) $-y^2 + 13xy + 6$ d) $-y^2 - 3xy + 6$

3. The product of $(-3a^3b)(12a^2b^4)$
    a) $-36a^5b^5$ b) $-9ab$ c) $-36a^5b^4$ d) $-15a^2b^3$

4. Evaluate: $-2a^2b - 4b^2$, when $a = -2$, $b = 3$
    a) 60   b) 12   c) -60   d) 24

5. Simplify: $(-3a^3b^4c^5)^3$
    a) $-9a^6b^{12}c^{15}$ b) $-16a^6b^7c^8$
    c) $9a^9b^{12}c^{15}$ d) $-27a^9b^{12}c^{15}$

6. Multiply and combine like terms: $(-4y + 5)(-3y - 3)$
    a) $12y^2 - 27y + 15$ b) $-12y^2 - 27y - 15$
    c) $12y^2 - 3y - 15$ d) $12y^2 + 3y + 15$

7. Factor completely: $28x^4y^5 - 12x^2y^3$
   a) $4x^2 y^3 (7x^2 y^2 - 3)$ b) $4x^2 y^3 (7x^2 - 3y)$
   c) $2x^2 (14x^2 + 6)$ d) $-2x^2 y^3 (-14x^2 y - 6)$

8. Solve for x: $9x + 10 = 50 - x$
   a) -4   b) 4   c) -5   d) 5

9. If $2x + 3y = 44$, and $3x - 3y = 6$, Solve for x and y.
   a) $x = -10, y = 8$ b) $x = 10, y = 8$
   c) $x = 5, y = 6$ d) $x = 3, y = 6$.

10. Each secretary types W words per minute and M minutes per day. If the department has S secretaries, how many words are typed each day?
    a) $W + M + S$ b) $M (W + S)$
    c) $(W) (M) (S)$ d) $M (M - S)$

11. Simplify: $\dfrac{(25x^5y^6 - 10x^4y^5)}{5x^3y^4}$
    a) $5x^2y^2 - 2xy$ b) $-5xy^2 - 2xy$
    c) $5xy - 2xy$ d) $5x^2y + 2xy$

12. The sum of two numbers is 64. One of the numbers is 4 more than twice the other number. What is the larger number?
    a) 20   b) 54   c) 10   d) 44

13. Simplify: $6 + 4(5-3)^3 \div 2$

a) 22   b) -28   c) 15   d) 34

14. What is the *perimeter* of a rectangle whose area is 54 Sq. ft. and whose length is 9 ft.?

a) 18 ft.   b) 30 ft.

c) 30 sq.ft.   d) 28 ft.

15. Find the area of a square whose perimeter is 200 ft.

a) 250 Sq. ft.   b) 625 Sq. ft

c) 2,500 Sq. ft.   d) 1000 Sq. ft.

16. What are the coordinates of point A?

a) (-5, 3)   b) (-4, -4)   c) (1, -5)   d) (0, 5)

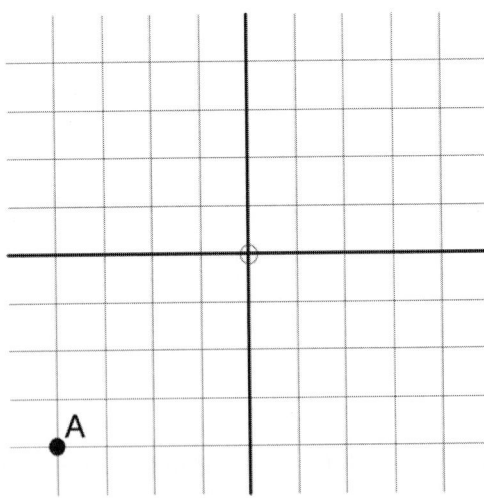

17. Simplify: $-3(-8) + 4(1-2)^2$
      a) 28   b) 32   c) -28   d) -32

18. Simplify: $6a^2 b + 2a(-3ab - 9b)$
      a) $12a^2b - 18ab$ b) $6a^2b + 18ab$
      c) $-18ab$ d) $18ab$

19. Bob and John are brothers. If Bob's age is five less than twice his brother John, and the sum of their ages is 40, what are their ages?
      a) 22 and 18   b) 16 and 24
      c) 10 and 30   d) 15 and 25

20. Which ordered pair satisfies the equation: $y = 2x - 7$
      a) (2, -3)   b) (-6, 30)
      c) (5, 25)   d) (2, 1)

ANSWERS
Test # 6

1.	B	11.	A
2.	A	12.	D
3.	A	13.	A
4.	C	14.	B
5.	D	15.	C
6.	C	16.	B
7.	A	17.	A
8.	B	18.	C
9.	B	19.	D
10.	C	20.	A

ALGEBRA EXAM # 7

Directions: Answer each of the following questions by circling the appropriate letter. SHOW ALL WRITTEN WORK IN THE SPACE PROVIDED FOR EACH QUESTION. You have 60 minutes.

1.   Sum: $(2x^2 + 6x + 12) + (3x^2 + x + 8)$
   a. $-5x^2 + 7x + 20$ b. $5x^2 + 7x + 20$
   c. $5x^2 - 7x + 20$ d. $6x^2 + 7x - 20$

2.   Difference: $(y^2 - 10xy) - (2y^2 + 3xy)$
   a. $-y^2 - 13xy$ b. $y^2 + 3xy$
   b. $-y^2 + 13xy$ d. $-y^2 - 3xy$

3.   Product: $(-3a^3)(2a^2b^4)$
   a. $6a^5b^4$ b. $-5ab$
   c. $-6a^5b^4$ d. $-5a^2b^3$

4.   Evaluate: $-2ab + 4b$, when $a = -2$, $b = 3$
   a. -12 b. 0
   c. -5 d. 24

5.   Simplify: $(-2ab^3)^4$
   a. $16a^4b^{12}$ b. $-16a^4b^{12}$
   c. $8a^4b^{12}$ d. $-8a^4b^{12}$

6.   Simplify: $(4y - 5)(3y - 3)$
   a. $12y^2 - 27y + 15$ b. $-12y^2 - 27y + 15$
   c. $-12y^2 + 27y - 15$ d. $12y^2 + 27y + 15$

7. Factor completely: $10x^4 - 12x^2$
   a. $2x^2 (-5x^2-6)$ b. $2x^2 (5x^2-6)$
   c. $2x^2 (5x^2+6)$ d. $-2x^2 (-5x^2-6)$

8. Solve for x: $6x + 2 = 51 - x$
   a. -5 b. 5
   c. 7   d. -8

9. $2x + 3y = 10$, and $3x - 3y = 15$. Solve for x and y.
   a. $x = 4$, $y = 5$ b. $x = 5$, $y = 0$
   c. $x = 5$, $y = -3$ d. $x = 3$, $y = 6$

10. Each employee in a factory produces M machine parts per hour, H hours per day. If the factory has E employees, how many parts are produced in the factory each day?
    a. $M + H + E$ b. $M (H + E)$
    c. MHE d. $H (M + E)$

11. Simplify: $\dfrac{5x^2 + 10x}{5x}$
    a. $x + 2$ b. $x + 2x$
    c. $3x$ d. $x + 10x$

12. The sum of two numbers is 32. One of the numbers is 5 more than twice the other. What is the product of the numbers?
    a. 182   b. 72
    c. 207   d. 68

13. Solve: x + 2 (x+1) = 5
   a. −1
   b. 3
   c. 1
   d. −2

14. The perimeter of a rectangle is 80 feet. If each length is 30 feet, what is the area of a rectangle?
   a. 50 square feet
   b. 120 square feet
   c. 220 square feet
   d. 300 square feet

15. If the area of a square is 100 feet long, what is its perimeter?
   a. 100 feet
   b. 140 feet
   c. 33 feet
   d. 220 feet

16. What are the coordinates of point P?
   a. (-2, 3)   b. (-1, 4)   c. (1, 5)   d. (0, 5)

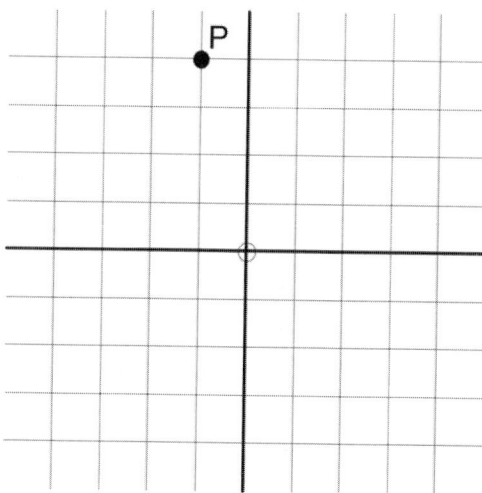

17. Simplify: $-3(-8) + 4(2-1)^3 + 7$
   a. -35
   b. -3
   c. 13
   d. 35

18. Solve: $\dfrac{x+2}{3} = \dfrac{2}{5}$

   a) $x = \dfrac{4}{5}$
   b) $x = -\dfrac{4}{5}$
   c) $x = -\dfrac{5}{4}$
   d) $x = 10$

19. Perimeter of a square is 400 cm. What is the area of the square?
   a) $10{,}000 \ cm^2$
   b) $1{,}000 \ cm^2$
   c) $10{,}000 \ cm$
   d) $1000 \ cm$

20. Claire is two years older than Dahlia. The sum of their ages is sixty-eight. How old is Claire?
   a) 20
   b) 33
   c) 35
   d) 25

ANSWERS
Test # 7

1.	B	11.	A
2.	A	12.	C
3.	C	13.	C
4.	D	14.	D
5.	A	15.	D
6.	A	16.	B
7.	B	17.	D
8.	C	18.	B
9.	B	19.	A
10.	C	20.	C

ALGEBRA EXAM 8

Directions: Answer each of the following questions by choosing the appropriate letter. SHOW ALL WRITTEN WORK IN THE SPACE PROVIDED. You have 60 minutes.

1. Find the value of $9 + 2 (5)^2$:
    a) -11 b) 275   c) 59   d) 41

2. Add $(2x^2 + 7x + 9) + (4x^2 - 6x - 10)$:
    a) $6x^2 + x - 1$ b) $4x^2 - 2x + 1$ c) $4x^2 + 2x - 1$ d) $6x^2 + x - 10$

3. Subtract $(3x^2 - 2x - 6) - (-5x^2 + 6x - 7)$:
    a) $8x^2 - 8x - 1$ b) $8x^2 - 8x + 1$ c) $-x^2 - 8x - 1$ d) $x^2 + 4x - 1$

4. Multiply: $(-6x^2y^4) (-7xy^3)$
    a) $-13xy^2$ b) $-42x^2y^7$ c) $42x^3y^7$ d) $13x^3y^7$

5. Find the value of $a^2 - b^2$ if $a = 4$ and $b = 5$
    a) 41   b) 25   c) 9   d) -9

6. Simply $(-7m^3n^2)^2$:
    a) $-49m^6n^4$ b) $49m^6n^4$ c) $-14m^5n^4$ d) $14m^5n^4$

7. Solve $3(x-4) = 12$
    a) 0   b) -8 c) 8   d) 16

8.   Solve for x: $5x - 2 = x + 2$
        a) 3   b) -1 c) 6   d) 1

9.   Factor completely $6x^9 - 3x$:
        a) $3(2x^9 - x)$ b) $3x^2(2x^7-1)$ c) $3x(2x^8 -x)$ d) $3x(2x^8-1)$

10.   What is the value in cents of d dimes and n nickels:
        a) $50(d+n)$ b) 50 dn   c) $d + n$ d) $10d + 5n$

11.   Which of these points lies on the graph of $y = 4x - 3$:
        a) (2, 1)   b) (3, 9)   c) (0, 4)   d) (6, 8)

12.   One number is eight more than twice another number. The sum of the numbers is
        38. What is the larger number?
        a) 18   b) 10   c) 28   d) 26

13.   Simplify $\dfrac{36x^7y^9}{6x^2y^3}$

        a) $6x^9y^{12}$ b) $6x^5y^6$ c) $30x^9y^{12}$ d) $30x^5y^6$

14.   What is the exact location of point z on the graph?
        a) (3,3)   b) (-2, 3)   c) (-3, -3)   d) (2, -5)

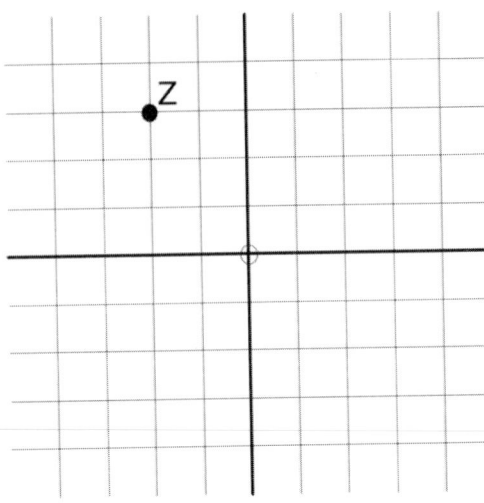

15.   Jayne is twice as old as Zelma. If the sum of their ages is 60, how old is Zelma?
        a) 15   b) 20   c) 25   d) 40

16.   The perimeter of a square is 80 feet. What is the area of the square?
        a) 40 sq.ft.   b) 400 sq.ft.   c) 64 sq.ft.   d) 225 sq.ft.

17.   Solve for x and y: x + y = 6 and x - y = 4
        a) y = 1, x = 3   b) x = 5, y = 1   c) x = 6, y = -2   d) x = 5, y =
        -1

18.   Which of the following ordered pairs solve the equation y = x - 4?:
        a) (0, -4)   b) (3, 7)
        c) (-1, 3)   d) (2, 0)

19. What is the value of $x^2 - 7xy$ when $x = 3$ and $y = 4$.
 a) 72
 b) -72
 c) -75
 d) 75

20. Steve purchased t ties at \$29 each and s shirts at \$21 each. What is the total cost of the ties and shirts?
 a) 50 ts
 b) 29 (t+s)
 c) t+s
 d) 29t + 21s

ANSWERS
Test # 8

1.	C	11.	B
2.	A	12.	C
3.	B	13.	B
4.	C	14.	B
5.	D	15.	B
6.	B	16.	B
7.	C	17.	B
8.	D	18.	A
9.	D	19.	C
10.	D	20.	D